To Pete

thanks for all
of the Effort you
put forth on our
Obehalf !

Don Miller

MILLER'S TIME

A Lifetime at Speed

by DON MILLER
with JIM DONNELLY

COASTAL 181
PUBLISHER

CREDITS

Book Design *Sandra Rigney*
Composition *Jim Rigney, Tammy Sneddon*
Cover Design *Kim Watson, Pinnacle Graphics; Joyce Cosentino Wells*
Editing *Cary Stratton*

Front Cover *Mike Mahr Photo, Competitive Motorsports Products Inc.*
Front Jacket Flap *Steven Rose Photo, © Motorsports Memories Photography, Inc.*
Back Jacket Flap *Cary Stratton Photo*

Every reasonable effort was made to locate and credit the original copyright holders and photographers of the photos included in this book. If your photo appears in this book and you are not properly credited, please contact the publisher.

ISBN 10: 0-9789261-7-X

ISBN 13: 978-0-9789261-7-5

For additional information or copies of this book, contact the publisher:

Coastal 181
29 Water Street
Newburyport, MA 01950
877 907-8181, (978) 462-2436
info@coastal181.com
www.coastal181.com

First printing April 2010

Printed in the United States of America

Contents

Foreword

I MET DON MILLER in the infield of Atlanta Motor Speedway on a brutally cold and blustery March morning sometime in the early 1980s. I wasn't dressed for it. Don didn't know me and at the time I didn't know who he was, either, but he saw me shivering. "Stay right here," he said. At the time, Don was working for Goodyear racing tires, and in a few moments he returned with a nice warm Goodyear racing jacket. "No charge," he said. "You looked cold."

A simple act of kindness, yes, but an act few would have troubled themselves with. It was typical Don Miller. I promised to do my best to see more of this warmhearted guy and I'm glad I've kept the promise. In a sport populated by people who stand out, he's one of the best I've met.

Don's fascination with cars was the foundation of a truly incredible career. He'll tell you in this book that his career was all about cars, but a lot of people are fascinated with cars yet never achieve anything important. The difference, I think, was Don's dogged determination and his winning way with people.

Our paths crossed often as I swam through many sides of auto racing. When I was trying to win races in a used Modified stock car, we met at a tiny oval track in New York where Don was on hand for no more grand purpose than to help struggling racers like me.

Any time we connected became a better day. On more than a few occasions, Don and I would meet somewhere and with a huge disarming smile, his right hand would reach forward and he'd say, "Dickie, how's it going?" I'd tell him—which usually was that it was again time for me to spill my guts about one thing or another that was going on in my personal or professional life (they were one in the same for many decades). Sometimes, he was a listener, the bartender in a big-league stock car racing garage. Sometimes, the most important times, he would make suggestions. I never knew how he could figure out when I needed Don the bartender or Don the guy who knew which way I should turn. But, he did.

There were times when, as a TV announcer, I heard conflicting stories about what was going on or was about to go on and couldn't sort out which of the versions was truth. Don was often my go-to guy at times like that. He was the ultimate insider who seemed to know everything that was important, and I knew he would give me the straight story.

Don was a most trusted source for me for years. Miller really understands racing and the people who make racing run. So, although those of us who had relied on him to help keep our own perspective on the sport in line with reality fully understood his desire to retire from running Roger Penske's stock car race teams, we all knew that when he walked out the door, the sport and those of us who remained in it would never again find anyone like him.

Over my own 40-plus-year career covering motorsports for magazines and television, I've met some pretty impressive people. Believe me, Don Miller is right up there with the most impressive of all of them. The national champion drivers, the self-made billionaires, the powerful captains of industry are in good company with Don Miller. As I look back on it, all of those people stand out in their own unique ways. Don's setting high goals and his incredible drive to reach them is in common with the others who have achieved greatness. But, Don's special asset is his way with people. Everybody who comes in contact with Don Miller leaves thinking they have just met a really nice guy. Someone they'd like to spend more time with. Someone they'd like to imagine as their father, best friend, boss at work or their brother.

I'll leave it to the pages of this book to take you through the chronology of a guy I admire enormously and who has helped me and many others achieve our own goals. Trust me when I say that his accomplishments have been many, even though through most of it, he's only had one leg to stand on, having lost the other in a pit road accident that nearly killed him and which has led to multiple surgeries and extreme pain since. Miller's life has been filled with so much adversity that he knows about succeeding against tall odds. Nobody handed Don Miller anything. He earned it all.

The book you are holding can be a path to success at almost anything. Use Miller's way of doing things as your guide and you'll do well. Take the stories, many of which have never before been told but which profoundly changed racing's landscape, as proof that people matter most in getting things done. Through these pages you'll meet a man you'll come to like and admire. You'll get to know a living example that proves good guys *can* finish first.

DICK BERGGREN
Ipswich, Massachusetts

Introduction

THIS IS A SUCCESS STORY, the life story of Don Miller, creator of drivers, teams and products that all rocked racing to its roots. Within these pages, you will learn what accomplishment in life—the real kind, the type that earns willing admiration and respect from your peers, not just a lot of money—is honestly all about. The operative term here is "honest." I like to tell people that as difficult as it is to reach the top level of motorsports, it's even harder to remain there once you arrive. Don has been there, at the top, for close to 40 years.

My own story with Don really began through Dick Berggren, who was also kind enough to contribute the Foreword to this book. It was almost certainly from either an article or Dick's monthly column in *Stock Car Racing* magazine, around the mid-1980s, in which he described Don as one of racing's most important people and Roger Penske's top lieutenant in the sport. Don became a racing newsmaker in a very big way early in the 1990s as co-founder of Penske Racing South. At the time, I worked at a daily newspaper in southern New Jersey alongside an editor named Steve Wujcik, who was an enthusiastic Rusty Wallace fan. When he asked me about Don, I said he was an extremely important guy, essentially Roger's liaison with the mega-corporations that backed the Penske race teams. I wasn't aware then of his lifelong love affair with cars and racing of all kinds, or the impact he would have on the sport during the phenomenal growth of NASCAR in the 1990s.

Fast-forward about 10 years. I joined up with Hemmings Publishing in Bennington, Vermont, where I'm now senior editor and photographer for all our monthly titles. The best known of them is *Hemmings Motor News*, the "bible." Another is *Hemmings Muscle Machines*, which covers the American high-performance car, both from the years of the original Pontiac GTO and earlier. I wrote a feature for *Muscle Machines* on a restored 1957 Chevrolet 150 with factory fuel injection, a factory-built hot rod, of which several had been raced in NASCAR, most famously by Buck Baker.

A month or two later, I received a letter from a guy in North Carolina named Don Miller, saying how much he'd enjoyed that story. I glanced over it, pleased to get it, and suddenly noticed that the bond paper it was typed on had a Penske Racing letterhead. It couldn't be *that* Don Miller, could it?

I checked, and indeed it was. Through conversations and a couple of Hemmings stories that we later worked on together, I learned that Don is not just a racing executive and world-class arbiter of driving talent. He's also an old-car guy of enormous repute, extremely well-respected in a very knowledgeable community for his background with hot rods, Ford products powered by the historic flathead V-8, and the fabled Chrysler Letter Cars, which have their own magical history from back when NASCAR raced truly stock automobiles. I was also reminded, indirectly, that Don is an amputee. He has achieved enormous success in racing, and elsewhere, despite a devastating physical injury that he received at a race track. Instead of driving him away from the sport, the injury, and its aftermath, made him an even bigger figure in its orbit.

Don doesn't talk about that, or his other accomplishments, at any sort of length. So I was surprised, and very pleasantly, when he asked me to help him compose his memoirs, following his retirement from active involvement in motorsports. I readily accepted because even before I knew its extent, I realized that when fully told, Don's life was going to make a hell of a story. Not just the issues related to his injury in 1974 at Talladega or his symbiotic relationship with Roger Penske. He's been as crazily into cars his entire life as any human being can be. That resonated loudly with me.

I think I can say with high confidence that after reading this book, you'll agree that Don and I have not wasted your time. We'll certainly not have wasted your money: All profits from *Miller's Time* will be donated toward helping abused children. If you've always aspired to get to the pinnacle of this sport, as a driver or otherwise, Don will tell you in these pages—with blunt honesty—what it takes, if you believe this demanding business is really right for you. *Miller's Time* will teach you about honesty, commitment to goals, business ethics and—vitally—about relating to others. I'm pretty certain you will learn a lot. I certainly did, just by spending time with Don and writing the text.

I feel compelled to add that despite speaking to a lot of people in the superheated, ultracompetitive Star Chamber that's big money racing today, I have never heard a derogatory word spoken about Don Miller. Not one. That says everything about this guy.

JIM DONNELLY
Bennington, Vermont

Preface

NICE PIPES! A hot cup of coffee in one hand, and a half-inch open-end wrench in my back pocket, I'm on the way out to the garage.

This is the way to start a day. No place to go and all day to get there. After spending most of my life traveling from one town to another at warp speed, this is really an adjustment. Retirement: It's what America works for and dreams about. I wonder how many people really make it work.

I often wondered if I would ever get to this point, where I could spend my time restoring vintage automobiles, building hot rods, and helping my grandsons work on their Quarter Midgets. Now it's time, and I ask myself, how did I get here?

I guess I've always had an interest in cars. I remember when I was about 10 years old and we lived in Chicago. My parents shared a two-story brick home on the South Side with my aunt and uncle. My Uncle Harry and Aunt Margaret lived on the second floor. Harry was a tool-and-die maker for Foote Brothers Machine. We lived on the first floor, and as was the case with many of the stately old brick two-stories of that era, we entered through the front door into a formal foyer, with a beautiful oaken staircase leading up to the front door of each individual, spacious living area. This was a wonderful home in a spotless old German neighborhood. Every one of the two-story brick homes was separated by a "gangway," an eight-foot-wide space containing a concrete sidewalk and a sod or flowered area. Every home had two families, most of them related; each also had a 100-foot-deep back yard with a garage that backed up to a concrete alley, which was actually two lanes wide. On weekends, everyone would pull their family cars out into the alley to wash them and perform light maintenance.

The thing that I remember most about that neighborhood was the front yards. All of the yards were about 10 feet deep and 20 feet wide, with perfectly trimmed hedges that bordered the sidewalk and the walkway to the individual front entryway of each home. Every two-story had a cement front porch with brick railings. Each morning when I went to school, the grandmas, and our mothers, would be sweeping those front porches while sending their children off to school. All of these memories are indelible, but it was the garage, and what went on in and around it, that captured both my attention and my imagination.

Our garage was a gray and white two-car framed building. The sidewalk that ran through the center of our back yard led directly to the single-man door that opened outward. The first thing I saw when I opened the door was the massive grille work of my Uncle Harry's 1936 Packard sedan, flanked by two Trippe lights that at my age then, seemed to be chest high, even though they were mounted only inches above the front bumper.

To the left of this majestic vehicle sat my father's red-and-black Chrysler 77 roadster, a vehicle that my Dad was soon to replace with a more practical 1946 Plymouth sedan, which was more to my mother's preference. Those were the formative impressions of my automotive-inclined youth.

One particular weekend from this time stands crystal-clear in my memory. It was Memorial Day in 1949. We were to have a family picnic in our yard, and several of my maternal uncles were to come over for the festivities. My sister Pat was helping my Mom and my grandmother with preparation and I was helping in the yard, setting up tables and chairs. My Dad asked me to go to the garage and bring him a stepladder. Just as I was working my way through the doorway, I heard the rumble of an engine behind our garage. As first I thought it was a fire truck, because nothing else in our neighborhood was that loud. I set the ladder against the wall and ran to the alley to have a look.

There it was: A 1947 Mercury coupe. It looked lower to the ground than most cars of this type, and the rear tires were covered by metal skirts. The driver's door swung open into the middle of the alley and out stepped my Uncle Bill. He was my mother's cousin, and like most of her brothers (there were six of them), Bill had returned from military service, and now he was all about cars and a new life without war. I quickly opened the back gate and excitedly asked Uncle Bill, "What kind of a car is that?" He smiled and answered, "Well, sport, that is a hot rod. Wanna take a ride?" I was stunned, but quickly replied yes, but I would have to ask Dad. Uncle Bill stepped past me and hollered to my father, "George, I'm gonna take the kid for a ride in my new bomb." My Dad looked surprised, but waved back with a cautionary request: "Take it easy. He's the only one I have!" I think he meant me.

I jumped in the front seat and watched Uncle Bill slide behind the wheel. He looked over at me, smiled, and reached up over the visor to pull down his aviator sunglasses. Bill Kalal was an ex-Marine fighter pilot who had served in the Pacific theater. Obviously, he was already something of a hero figure, but little did I know that he was about to reach a whole new level. Uncle Bill leaned over, turned on the ignition, and hit the starter button. The engine made less than one revolution before it burst into life. It was like a clap of thunder at first, and then it settled into a low, throaty rumble. Bill looked me straight in the eye and asked, "You ready to take off, sport?" For an instant, I could see him in the cockpit of his Corsair fighter. Then I snapped back with an excited, "YES!"

Bill slapped the column shift into first gear, and we moved off. The exhaust noise echoed off the garage doors on either side of the alley like a freight train passing through a tunnel. Bill slipped the car into second and pulled out another hundred feet, then snapped out of the throttle to let the engine slow the car to a stop at the end of the alley, resulting in a slow rap of the exhaust as the speed dissipated. Bill looked over again and said, "Nice pipes." He slipped the gear lever back into first as we headed out into the neighborhood traffic. At that point, I didn't care if we ever went back to the picnic.

When we returned from the ride, you couldn't have pried the smile off my face with a crowbar.

Uncle Bill and I helped Dad with the rest of the preparations and the other guests began to arrive. My Dad hooked our house radio to a pair of remote speakers so we could all listen to the Indianapolis 500. This was a tradition in our family.

The day wound on, and I tried hard to listen in on the adult male conversations while pacifying my younger cousins and a few of the neighborhood kids who were invited to the picnic. My uncles had all served in World War II, and their conversations ranged from the serious to the lighthearted. Jesting continued around which branch of the service had actually won the war. My Uncle Rick, who was seriously wounded in Italy, was convinced that the British were of no help whatsoever, and that "Monty"—that was Field Marshal Bernard Montgomery, the supreme British military commander—was FUBAR. Obviously, I had no idea what FUBAR meant, but later in the day, when I applied the term to my old Schwinn Roadmaster bicycle, my mother quickly corrected with a stern warning, "That term is never to be used in this house again." She also advised her brother accordingly, and just as sternly, "Richard, we don't use that kind of Army talk around here." Her little brother was amused and quickly countered with, "Alice, you just can't tell. The kid may be right. Have you tried to ride that bike lately?" His reply drew a roar of laughter from the brothers. It made me feel just a little bit better about my error in grammatical judgment. (It was years later, I should add, before I found out what FUBAR meant).

As the afternoon continued, I noticed that the adult conversations had shifted to cars. I moved closer to the table again. My Uncle Ches was carrying on about his new Plymouth convertible when Bill chimed in with a comment regarding performance. Chester countered with, "Well, I know it won't run with your Merc, but I'm not really interested in having a hot rod." There was that term again: "Hot rod." What exactly did it mean? I kept wondering about it, so I finally asked the men out loud. "Well, son, it's a car that has a modified engine that's built for speed." Bill chimed in immediately, "Yeah: Dual carbs, shaved heads, big cam and nice pipes, you know!" Well, I didn't know, but I nodded anyway. Uncle Joe, who was the youngest of the brothers and had been a B-24 navigator in Europe, said, "Let's see what you got, Bill. Pop the hood and show us all."

Everyone nodded approval, stood up and headed for the garage. My Mom and Aunt Ann, Chester's wife, followed along. Aunt Ann, always the concerned observer, cautioned, "You guys don't need to be showing off now that you have all been drinking beer."

Everyone gathered around the front of the Merc while Uncle Bill reached in the driver's door window and popped the hood latch. Joe opened the hood and everyone just oohed and aahed. I could hardly see over the top of the fender, but I still got a glimpse of two chrome pots sticking up from the top of the engine. Everyone was talking at once. I just listened. Some of our neighbors crossed the alley to get a look, and to listen as Bill filled them in on the technical details. Mom seemed unimpressed, and suggested that we all return to the yard and try some potato salad. Uncle Ches thought that was a great idea, and the spell was broken. Everybody left but me. My Dad told me not to hang on the fender, but Uncle Bill suggested that I stand up on the front bumper to get a good look. I leaned over the radiator and drank it all in. I formed a mental photograph that I can still recall to this day: A full-dress flathead V-8 with aluminum heads and chromed radiator hoses. It seemed to sparkle like a piece of fine jewelry. I just stared at it, and then Dad barked, "That's enough. Let's get back to the party before your Mom gets upset."

The rest of the day passed with a lot of laughter and good times. Bill Holland won the Indy 500. My sister Pat and I were forced to go to bed early because we had school the next day. I didn't get to see everyone leave, or hear the Mercury engine, but my dreams were filled with visions of cars and engines. No, not just cars, but *hot rods*, and the sounds of winding roads disappearing underneath my wheels. My life would never be the same again. I promised myself that I would get a second paper route, save all my money and buy a Merc like my Uncle Bill. I would build a real hot rod, maybe even a race car, with "nice pipes" and life would be a real adventure. Little did I know what adventures were around the corner.

1
Everything Counts

MY FASCINATION WITH THE AUTOMOBILE has been paramount to me as far back as I can conjure a coherent memory of my early lifetime. If I wasn't working on a car, or designing a piece for one, or dreaming about how I intended to do so, or competing in a race, I wasn't a happy guy. Everything that I wanted to do in my life centered somehow on a car—a race car—whether it was a drag car, a Bonneville car, a road racer or a stock car. Most people who know me say I'm even-tempered and usually able to communicate and socialize easily. Cars have done a lot to improve my demeanor—mostly. They've also done a lot to define my success as a racer, a business leader and as an individual. Whether it's running a race team, meeting a fan or helping Roger Penske put a deal together, it all comes back to cars for me.

It's not as if there's never been anything else in life for me. I was a normal kid from a good family. I liked baseball and played it in high school. Remarkably, even though I was a kid in Chicago, my hero in sports was Mickey Mantle—until I got my high school diploma, anyway. Once I graduated, all that fell by the wayside. Within a couple of years, I didn't even remember when the baseball season started. Instead, I just wanted to know when the engines fired up for the first practice session before the Indianapolis 500. My sister told me in high school that a lot of girls wanted to date me, but I had other priorities, usually at a drag strip or somebody's garage. That focus carried on even when I was dating Pat, who's now been my wife for more than 47 years. I'd forget to pick her up for a date, probably because I was removing the transmission from my 1957 Corvette or something like that.

Our family circa 1946. Left to right: Dad, my sister Pat, me, and my Mom in our backyard in Chicago. (Don Miller Collection)

My mind seemed to be wired directly to connecting rods, piston rings and pinion gears. I lived in an automobile, my existence defined by its dimensions. My mother, who wanted me to be a doctor, thought I was absolutely insane. My Dad was more supportive, and told me many times, "Whatever you decide to do, just be good at it." I greatly admired Dad, and I still do. I think I've lived up to his credo.

My parents instilled within me some very basic, fail-safe life instructions. Dad said: Be successful, be true to what you are. Don't be a fraud. Be honest. See the good in others. Respect them and make them your equals. Be patient—listen when people talk to you. That was what my father called being a people person, which is the advice I give to others and have tried to follow all my life.

It didn't all sink in at once. As a young man, I was not a very patient person. When somebody would say something conversationally, I'd be likely to snap back, "I don't care about that." I had to learn to be patient with people, and I made a lot of mistakes along the way. Over time, I learned to be less judgmental about others and to be able to actually help guide them, since I'd made the same stupid mistake that this person was about to make.

Pat and I at a party . . . one of the rare times I remembered to pick her up for our date. (Don Miller Collection)

My mother talked about patience. Honesty is something I learned from my father. When I was young, he caught me in a major violation of his orders that revolved around a car, and I paid a price for not being straight with him right from the start. He told me: "Look at it this way. If you tell the truth, you won't have to think about it later and hope you can remember whatever it was that you said earlier." It was an important life lesson, one of many that I've learned and hope to pass along through this book. As I got older and became involved in more and more business dealings, I learned that everyone talks to everyone else, and sooner or later, the liars always get caught.

Dad told me that I could tell people whatever I wanted to tell them, but that as time went on, I would have to deal with those same people again, and again, and they'd remember how I treated them the first time. He said it's much easier to deal with someone using a pinch of sugar than a pound of salt. That's especially true if you're in business, particularly the racing business. At the local speedway, you're going to see the same competitors week after week. Same thing at the top of NASCAR, mostly the same drivers, universe of team members, sponsors, media and officials. If you act like an idiot from the start, or if you're less than honest with them, believe me, they'll remember it. Word will get around.

My father also taught me that there are two kinds of people, givers and takers. "You can be a taker, but you're not going to be happy as you grow up." He said I would have to figure out on my own whether I wanted to be a giver or taker, and that's something I've carried with me throughout my life.

I rarely get angry but what gets me really mad? People who are full of shit, to put it in plain English. People who beat around the bush, aren't direct, or don't tell you the truth. People to whom you've given the benefit of the doubt up front, and still let you down. Most of the time, I'm pretty easygoing. Fall into one the categories I've just described, and that will change immediately. But the majority of people I've met, through business, racing or something else, aren't that way. Like my mother, I believe that people, as a whole, are decent and worthy and work hard to do what's right.

What is the bridge that gets you from being a kid in a blue-collar Chicago neighborhood to being Roger Penske's partner in owning a winning race team? Besides a lot of hard work and some luck, it's patience and the ability to listen to people. Being able to honestly admit when you've done something wrong, and recognizing that other people have dreams and goals and desires in life, just like you do.

Like a lot of bridges, before you can get across that one, you've got to pay a toll. From childhood, I wanted to be around cars, and then hot rods, and then racing. Probably before I really realized it, I was determined to make racing my life's work. I've been very successful in that field, more so than I dared to dream, in large part because I met a lot of outstanding people, among which Roger Penske, Rusty Wallace and Ryan Newman are only the most famous. I have made remarkable friendships that will last as a long as I do.

I'm comfortable financially. I was able to raise a terrific family and provide for all their needs. But that bridge collected its toll from me. I went to a race one time and when I got home from it, I was missing a leg. I very nearly bled to death right in front of Roger. I don't know how many 20-hour days I worked, seven days straight. I have no clue—a decade's worth, probably. I do know that for years, months would go by when I wouldn't come home for more than a night other

than to repack my suitcase. My family knew it. Through love, they accepted it and we stayed strong and together. I've been racked by pain from injuries for months, years, at a time. My family and I have prospered but we've also endured a lot of inconvenience, to say the least.

I am not a whiner. Like I said, I'd change nothing even if I had the opportunity. I'm telling you these things for the most important reason that I'm doing this book in the first place. If you picked this up, you're probably already a pretty serious race fan. Very possibly, you're interested in knowing how to get a job in racing, succeed at it, make connections at the very zenith of the sport, make a lot of money and become a famous person. Or perhaps, you are either operating, or would like to operate, a company that you believe would be a good fit with racing, maybe by making a performance product, and you want to know how you meet the right people. I'm confident that my story will help to answer your questions. I'm not sure it will answer them to your satisfaction, but I do believe you'll agree that when I answered them, I was telling you the truth.

If you can take to heart some of the life lessons that I learned, both from my parents and some of the most important people in rac-

Our family, at a race in Charlotte. Top: Mike Martin; bottom: my daughter Pam, grandson Jack, daughter Tricia, grandson Tom, me, Pat, and daughter Debbie. (Don Miller Collection)

ing, you'll have made a strong start at crossing that bridge. I wouldn't encourage anyone to get into racing, however, unless it gives them personal satisfaction rather than simply viewing it as a business opportunity. If you're going to get into any kind of racing venture, you've got to love it, and live it fully. If not, there's no way you can stay on the cutting edge, and the competition is going to come in and take your meter out.

I'd never try to discourage someone who wanted to put their kid in a quarter midget, maybe hoping they'll eventually make it to the big time. Ryan Newman started out in quarter midgets. Rusty Wallace grew up as the son of a racer and was winning in Late Models as a teenager. But there are many very good racers who never hit the big time and many who lost a lot of money trying. I have a very good friend, Barry Kolono, who's a stockbroker. He always talks about how much he likes the sport, and would like to get into it someday. I've told him, "Want to make a small fortune in motorsports? Start with a large one." In my opinion, all the big-time financiers who spent their way into the sport over the last two or three years, thinking they're going to make a killing, will not be in the sport in five years. They don't have the soul. This sport is going to go back to its roots in the next five or six years. Not because it wants to, but because it has to.

I can talk this way because I've been around a long time and seen a lot, and without boasting, I feel I have a strong sense of historical perspective. I've always been a student of history, whether of World War II, America, or racing and the automobile. Almost nothing makes me happier now than playing with my hot rods and old cars, all of which get driven. When I'm beginning to restore an old car, I'm thinking about its history, too. I'll disassemble it, then take some individual component apart down to its smallest pieces, and examine it. I'm trying to envision what the guys who built it were thinking. I really appreciate the way things were done in the past. They were built to last.

Your sense of the past, hard work in the present, ability to think in the abstract and your personal integrity will all combine to construct your life. That's what I mean when I say "everything counts." Ultimately, this is a story about truth, honesty, hard work and respect. The racing is almost secondary, but if that's what you hope to do in life, I can give you the straight word about how I did it.

2
Sweet Home Chicago

AFTER EMIGRATING TO THE UNITED STATES around the time of the First World War, my father's family (originally named Mueller) worked its way from New York to Chicago, where there was a big German population, and settled there.

My grandmother opened a bakery on what we Chicagoans call the Near South Side. She and her husband Frank had a son, George, who married my mother, Alice Cronin. I'm their oldest child, born June 30, 1939, under the cloud of war. That's probably part of the reason I'm so deeply interested in World War II history.

We lived in a working-class German Catholic neighborhood on the Near South Side. My mother was a nurse at Little Company of Mary Hospital. She continued taking classes for years to keep her nursing certification current, even after my sisters and I were born, and even after my family moved to Saint Charles, well west of Chicago. My Mom was also very involved in a whole range of neighborhood activities and in the local Catholic school, Saint Sabina, where my sister Pat and I went. Pat was two years younger than I, and my second sister, Mary Alice, was eight years younger than Pat.

My father was a very smart and truly gifted engineer who worked for Western Electric. If you're of a certain age, you know that at one time Western Electric made about 90 percent of the telephones used in the United States, the kinds with rotary dials on them. My Dad worked in a giant manufacturing plant that Western Electric opened in 1904 in Cicero, Illinois. As late as the 1970s, more than 25,000 people still worked there. Western Electric was a pioneering firm in the development of radar, one of the most critical technological advances of World War II, and my father

This is one of my favorite photos of my Mom in her nurse's hat. It doesn't take a rocket scientist to figure out why my Dad married her. (Don Miller Collection)

was assigned to work in that department. Dad was a legitimate, self-taught electrical wizard.

I can't say specifically that my father was interested in cars, but he was a good mechanic. However, my Uncle Bill Kalal, whom you've read about earlier, was a car guy, a total hardcore gearhead, on what was then the very cutting edge of automotive enthusiasm and knowledge.

Uncle Bill, who was involved in the operation and design of military aircraft while in the Marine Corps, had been stationed for a while near San Diego. After the war, San Diego was a hotbed of hot rodding that was probably second only to Los Angeles itself. Like a lot of newly minted ex-GIs, Uncle Bill had a lot of money, since there weren't too many opportunities to spend it on military bases. When he re-entered civilian life, he got himself a new car, a 1947 or 1948 Mercury with a flathead V-8.

There was already a wide variety of speed equipment available for that legendary Ford-built engine, most of it produced in California and a lot of it produced by guys who had been working with aircraft during the war, either as civilians or military personnel. Uncle Bill loaded up on this stuff, bolted it up to the Mercury, and returned home to Chicago.

There was no system of Interstate highways yet, so on the way back from California, Uncle Bill would surely have taken that classic trip across the American West that dozens of travel books today instruct people on how to re-create. Route 66 had its eastern terminus right in the middle of downtown Chicago, near the Loop. He rolled through little adobe towns, past gas stations, mesas, truck stops and

My Dad once owned this car, a Mercedes-Daimler, although I know next to nothing else about it. (Don Miller Collection)

grain elevators, rumbling along behind a full-house flathead. His Mercury was a coupe. It was also a hot rod, the first such hopped-up car I'd ever seen in my life. I was already fascinated by cars, reading what car magazines I could get into my hands, when Uncle Bill rolled up with his Mercury.

This '48 Mercury looks almost exactly like the one that my Uncle Bill owned—the car that started me on my journey. (Chuck Dobson Photo)

    As far back as I can remember, there was never a time—never— when Don didn't have his head under the hood of a car. When we were little kids, Don was always building cars from anything he could get his hands on, from cardboard boxes to shipping crates. It was funny because everything he found always had value as a potential component in his next invention. One day, when we were walking home from grammar school, he said, 'Let's cut through the alley and see what kind of parts we can find.' That particular day, we stopped by one of our neighbors' trashcans and Don found a piece from an old disassembled washing machine. He picked it out of the trash and inspected it closely. Then, he looked at me with this big smile and said, 'This is perfect. It's just what I need for the steering on my new race car.'

    The following day, Don showed me his new steering on the race car he was building, which was an assemblage of wooden rails with four wagon wheels mounted on curtain rods, topped off with a baby buggy seat. The washing machine shaft was mounted on

My sister Pat and I taking a break in our back yard in Chicago. This was around the time I built my first hot rod from washing machine components. (Don Miller Collection)

wooden blocks. The pulley end had clothesline wrapped around the pulley with each end connected to the opposite end of a board, mounting the front wheels. A single bolt through the center of the two-by-four served as the pivot. When you turned the shaft, it pulled the rope and turned the wheels.

He looked very serious. 'Tomorrow we can test it,' he said, which only meant one thing to me: Tomorrow, our neighbor Eddie Collins and I would be pushing Don down the sidewalk as fast as we could run while he pretended to be winning the Indianapolis 500."

PAT WORLEY
Don's sister
Yorkville, Illinois

In Chicago, lots of hot rods got parked during the hurricane-force snowstorms that lashed along Lake Michigan during the winter. Then, and right through my young adulthood, it was a big deal to roll into a Midwest springtime in a hot car. Another rite of spring was listening to the Indianapolis 500 on the radio, the live broadcast during the race on Memorial Day. If you were a kid in Chicago around 1950, the 500 was a very big deal, certainly on a par for many of us with how the Cubs and the White Sox were doing early in their seasons. Even before the interstates, Indy was still only a couple of hours south of Chicago by car. We also had homegrown Chicago guys in the race, professionals who'd toughened up in Midgets and Sprint cars. Guys like Duke Nalon, Emil Andres, Tony Bettenhausen and Paul Russo.

I can't remember the exact order of things anymore, but on Memorial Day in 1949, I listened as Bill Holland won the Indianapolis 500, and that was the day that Uncle Bill dropped in at our house for a holiday visit and took me for my first ride in a true hot rod.

I was nine years old and I was thrilled beyond my ability to express it in words. Everything in my life that was of any consequence from then on can be traced back to that cruise through the Near South Side on Memorial Day. That's where everything in racing really began for me. My life went on from there, but first, of course, I had to go to school and get some homework done. That's part of the story, too.

3
Being Bud Crayne

TO SHOW YOU HOW HOOKED I was on cars, let me tell you the story about a book report that I had to write in fifth grade when I was 10 or 11 years old—my very first such project.

At that time, a book report meant going to the library with your library card and taking out a book on some subject. Of course, I had no interest whatsoever in doing a book report at all, on anything. But off I went, to the Chicago Public Library branch location that served our part of the South Side, and inside, through the huge doors, where a librarian was sitting at a big wooden desk. There was a large sign right above her that said "QUIET." Right next to her desk was a long, wooden case with drawers full of index cards for each title: the Dewey Decimal system. It was the typically silent, solemn, old-fashioned library, the whole building looking like a big vault.

The librarian asked, "What is the subject you're looking for?" And I responded, "I'm looking for a book on cars."

She stared at me for a couple of moments and then said, "Manufacturing?" I said, "No, how about hot rods?"

"What's a hot rod?"

I was trying to be patient. "Well, you know, it's a souped-up car." Finally she understood. Using the drawers and cards, she found a book. It was a little hardcover called *Hot Rod*, and the author was a man named Henry Gregor Felsen. It's likely that you never heard of the author of this very important book in my life. Henry Gregor Felsen was a pretty prolific writer back when I was growing up. During his lifetime, Felsen probably wrote at least 50 books, most of them novels and most of them aimed at younger readers like I was around this time. Many of the stories were about being aboard a U.S. Coast Guard cutter, aboard a submarine or in the cockpit of a fighter. But most of all, Felsen really liked cars. He wrote a story about stock car racing, and he wrote a lot of books about hot rods, including the one I found in the Chicago library that day.

I checked out *Hot Rod* and took it home. I wasn't a big reader when I was 10, but thanks to Uncle Bill, I was already seriously fascinated with cars. I was always sketching them in my notebooks at school, ideally when the nuns weren't watching. I started reading *Hot Rod* that night after supper, and just kept at it, turning pages as I ripped through Felsen's story. My mother finally came into my room and said, "Look, it's late. You're going to have to get some sleep. You have to go to school tomorrow." It was probably about 9 o'clock at night, pretty late for me at that age. I grabbed a flashlight, got into bed, and kept right on reading *Hot Rod* with the flashlight held discreetly underneath the covers. I don't know how late I stayed up, but I think I read that whole book in two or three days, definitely a first for me.

Felsen's book just infected me. I don't know how else to express it. *Hot Rod*, as the title implied, was about a young rodder named Bud Crayne. It tells a tale about how obsessed he was with cars, building them and working on them, and it included a life lesson. As I learned later, many of Felsen's books contained that sort of lesson, a moral, even though the cover typically showed a couple of young kids in a hot rod speeding along.

Crayne was continually doing this and that to his car mechanically, trying to make it better, faster. He even recorded things on a pad strapped to his thigh, just like the military pilots did during the Second World War. Crayne would jot down things like the maximum RPM when he'd run his car at full speed through town, which was illegal, obviously. As the story went on, he got in trouble with the cops but managed to work his way out of it. The climax is a race with another guy. He wins, but for all the right reasons. The life lesson that Felsen was imparting was that if you're interested in something, and you really want to be good at it, whatever it is, you have to work hard at it. You can never stop trying to improve or you'll never reach your goal.

Hot Rod affected the way I thought about everything after that, especially anything automotive. That one episode really set me in the direction that my life ultimately would take. Literally, honestly, I wanted to be Bud Crayne.

I still have that book. The cover artwork is a well-detailed painting of a young guy—Bud?—up to his elbows in the engine of his dramatically channeled roadster with cycle fenders, his girlfriend waving

The book that started it all, Hot Rod *by Henry Gregor Felsen. (Jim Rigney Collection)*

at some pals roaring by in a three-window coupe and a '34 Ford road-ster, kicking up plumes of dust. About 10 years ago, I saw a whole boxed paperback Felsen collection in a store, and I bought it for my grandson for his second birthday.

A happy ending to this little story was that my book report actually got an A+, probably the only time in grammar school that I ever got an A+ in anything. As with most of the Catholic schools in Chicago during the 1950s, all of the teachers at Saint Sabina were nuns, dressed in long, black habits trimmed in white. My teacher was Sister Mary Catherine, who taught all of my subjects, including English.

We wrote on loose-leaf lined paper with three holes punched in each sheet, which we then put into a three-ring binder. After you handed your work in and got it graded, you put it back in the binder and kept it there. That way, when the nun would give you your report card at the end of the marking period, you and she would go back through your work, and she'd point to it and say, "This is why you got such-and-such as your mark on your report card."

My book report was only three or four pages, handwritten on that loose-leaf paper in Number 2 pencil. I can tell you straight up that the nun had no idea what a hot rod was, or who Henry Gregor Felsen was. She told me she wanted to see the book, so I brought it in. I'm guessing that she was making sure that I hadn't copied anything.

Sister Mary Catherine told me that if I applied myself to the rest of my subjects like I did to the book report, I'd be a straight-A student, which I was anything but. She also said she gave me an A+ because the book report was very well composed and very well written, and had no misspellings. From what I know, the last reason may have been the most important one of all.

4
Losing My Ride

I WAS ALMOST 15. I loved cars and wanted be around them so much that in my free time, I'd hang around our neighborhood gas station, Ashland Sinclair. It had four pumps, two islands, with a roof over the pumps that came out from the building. Like the typical city gas station, it also had a pair of mechanics' bays plus an office and a semi-paved washing area.

Over time, I got to know the guy who owned it. He had a 1946 Plymouth convertible with a souped-up L-head straight-six—as much as a flat-head Plymouth could be souped up, I should say—with dual exhausts. It also had flamethrowers, which lots of people put on their exhaust systems to make them more, shall we say, noticeable. A flamethrower consisted of a Ford Model A ignition coil that was mounted back in the trunk and controlled by a cockpit switch. A regular automotive spark plug was wired to the coil and placed inside the tailpipe, way back by the echo can. When you'd hit the switch, it would heat the coil up, then light the spark plug along with the excess fuel vapors mixed in the exhaust. When the whole thing fired, huge rooster tails of flame whooshed out the tailpipes. For the time, this was very big stuff.

Before long, the station started giving me some things to do besides stand there and stare at everything. First, they let me pump gas and wash windows. The arrangement was that if I worked three or four hours after school, and all day Saturday, I would get a dollar a day. That was my first automotive job. I thought it was fantastic. I could save all that money, my six-dollar weekly salary, and eventually use it to buy a car, of course. What else?

My co-worker at the station was named Jimmy—I can't recall his last name. He was probably 25, stood maybe 5 feet, 10 inches tall, was kind of lean, always wore box-toed shoes and had a DA haircut. He was a really precise type of mechanic, and always kept his own car perfectly clean. All the tools in the station were kept on a pegboard wall in the bays, with loops from which to hang them. Jimmy used to get very mad if you left a tool on the shop floor. He'd go ballistic and yell, "Tools are expensive. They get lost if you leave them on the floor. When you're done using one, put it back on the wall." As strange as it probably sounds, Jimmy didn't have a toolbox. Everything he owned was hanging on that wall. You know, I don't even know where Jimmy lived. To me, he lived at the gas station.

Jimmy showed me how to fix cars, how to change their oil, and a lot more. Back then, gas stations and neighborhood garages didn't have lifts, they had pits. You'd pull the car over it and have to climb down a little ladder to go underneath. The station also had two grease guns, one hanging down above the pit and another down inside it, both attached to a barrel full of grease. The air compressor that powered the guns was inside the garage, because it got so cold in Chicago that you couldn't keep it outdoors—the thing would have frozen solid.

It was always noisier than hell inside with the compressor running. I had to put head gaskets on the compressor after scraping the tops of the pistons. The rings would wear out, and when it was spinning, the compressor would suck the lube out of its own crankcase, leaving carbon deposits because it got so hot. So every so often I would have to pull the head off, clean the deposits and replace the gaskets. It was the first time I ever used a torque wrench. It was huge, like a breaker bar, with a metal scale on it and a pointer.

I was saving my money. Not long after I turned 15, I started looking for a car and finally found a 1936 Ford roadster. It was raggedy but it was still a Ford, and a roadster. Jimmy looked the car over and said, "That's it. That's what you need, because it's got a flathead in it. If you come down here on a Saturday, after we're done, if we're not too busy, I'll teach you how to do some things on it." That was terrific, especially since the Ford didn't run. I finally talked the guy who was selling it down to $50 and bought it right there. A neighbor helped get the Ford over to my house.

There was still a small problem: I had no driver's license. In the 1950s, the minimum driving age in Illinois was 16, and I was just barely 15. My Mom and my Dad made it absolutely, unmistakably clear that they would not let me drive that Ford without a license, even the couple of blocks to the gas station. This had already been a matter of family discussion for a while, because I had been actively looking for a car to buy since I was about 14.

I talked my Dad into letting me put the Ford in our garage and

Unfortunately, I don't have a photo of my actual '36 Ford roadster, but it looked a lot like this car. (Daniel Strohl Photo)

keeping his car on the street. It was nearly spring, so having his car buried at the curb by plows wasn't an issue anymore. The Ford's body was in pretty nice shape, but it didn't have a top and it didn't have roll-up windows. From what I could tell, somebody had begun working on it, maybe trying to make a hot rod. It was a light tan with a black fender on the right rear. My Dad, who was not only an engineer but also a damn good mechanic, told me, "Let's try and turn it over and see what happens." He and Jimmy managed to get the flathead running. It didn't have any exhaust system at all. With my savings, I had to buy one piece of the system at a time from Warshawsky's in Chicago, the auto store that eventually became J.C. Whitney. Eventually, I also got a pair of headers for about $14.

Within perhaps four months, with Dad's help, I'd gotten the Ford to run consistently. It had some decent used tires on it. The rod-actuated mechanical brakes weren't as desirable as more modern hydraulics, but I had them operating pretty well. But I still didn't have a license. When my parents decided to go away for a couple of weeks, trouble wasn't just brewing; it was about to spill over.

Every year, my parents would go up to my Aunt Marie's, all the way up in northern Wisconsin, and stay at her lakefront cottage, where they had moved when my uncle retired. As my family was getting ready to make their very long trek, I begged them to let me stay home. By then, I was able to work all day long as summertime neared. I was going to turn 16 on the 30th of June. They agreed, which meant I would stay home with my grandmother, who lived with us upstairs along with my Aunt Mary and my Uncle Harry. It wasn't like I was

Circa 1956. I had a job working on cars and that's all that meant anything to me at the time. (Don Miller Collection)

going to be left unsupervised at age 15 while they were a couple of hundred miles away.

Before they left, my Dad took me aside, and told me, very bluntly, "Look, there's only one thing I'm telling you right now, because I know how you are with that car. You better not drive that damn car while I'm gone, sneak it out or anything like that, because if you do, I'll sell it and you won't have a car." I have to make it clear right here that my father didn't object to me *owning* a car. The much more important matter was that he'd have nothing to do with my driving it without a license—or registration, license plates or insurance. He told me that when I was 16, he would help me get the right paperwork and the plates, and that I could then start paying for my own insurance.

They were gone two weeks. Of course, despite his stern warning, the temptation was just too great. One day, there was hardly anybody around except my grandmother, but she never paid any attention to what was going on outside. My aunt and uncle were off shopping or something. So I fired the Ford up in the garage, like I used to do all the time. Only now, I looked both ways, didn't see anybody in the alley behind our garage, and I backed it out. I drove it down to the end of the alley, turned around, and put it back in the garage. Even with the mufflers I'd bought from the catalog, it was still window-rattling loud. I never noticed, and I was flush with how great it all was: I'd just driven my own car. In another eight weeks or so, I'd get my license and could drive that Ford anywhere. The problem, of course, was that I had just driven it against my father's express command.

I figured I'd gotten away with it, too. They got home from Wisconsin, nobody said anything, and everything was fine, I thought. Three days later, my father came home from work and said, "I need to talk to you."

He took me aside again. "I want you to tell me something. I want you to tell me about your car." So I started rattling on about everything I was doing to it, but he stopped me. "Tell me about driving your car." It all spilled out even faster: "Oh, I didn't drive the car, and . . ." He cut me off. "Don't lie to me, because I know you drove that car, and I told you not to drive that car." "Oh no, no, I wasn't, I didn't . . ." "Yes, you did."

Later, I learned that the neighbors had ratted me out. They saw the Ford going down the alley, not that they needed to: A guy with a potato sack tied over his head would have known as much from the racket. I tried to say I was sorry and got sharply interrupted once more: "You shouldn't have lied to me. You shouldn't have driven it. I told you not to drive it. We let you stay home, we tried to treat you like an adult, but I can't treat you like an adult. I made you a promise that if you did this, I was going to sell the car."

I think what happened was that some of the older ladies in the neighborhood didn't like Don, because he was so successful even as a kid, and they told on him, to our grandmother. But Don learned a terrible lesson, a lifelong lesson. You knew that if you got our Dad upset, you were in big trouble. He rarely raised his voice. We both went to Catholic school, and in our house, if one parent told you something, you didn't go to the other to try and work something out. No was no. You didn't try to work the system."
PAT WORLEY

Cold panic began to grip me. "Oh, my God," I blurted out, "You can't sell it. It's my car." He answered, "You live in this house. It's *my* car. I'll take the money I get for it and I'll put it in the bank for you, but you're not going to have a car."

That was it. Within two weeks, the Ford was gone. I was absolutely devastated and enraged. I wanted to run away from home, everything else. It was as if the world had ended. You know how teenagers get; they think the whole world is picking on them and out to get them. But my Dad was the one who had the title to the Ford. He never told me who he sold the Ford to; he did put the money in the bank for me. But I wasn't allowed to buy a car. I would lie in bed at night gazing at the ceiling and simply couldn't imagine why this had happened to me. My sister would tell me, "You better just cool it, because Dad's really sticking to his guns on this."

June finally came and I got my license after my birthday. After some time had passed, I came to realize and acknowledge that Dad was right and I was wrong. I'm still not sure just what made me smarten up—I guess I had to work it all out in my mind, lose my conviction that nobody could tell me what to do, and start being rational.

Much later on in life, especially at Penske Racing, I was called "The Iceman," not completely in jest. I didn't let things get me rattled. Believe me, I was a long way from being that way as a teenager. When I came to my senses, I finally realized that my anger and attitude over losing the car was never going to work. It's not necessarily bad to be wrong: You eat a little crow, apologize, get your act back together, start over again and hopefully, get it right the next time. I sat down with Dad and we talked about everything that had happened. He told me, "I hope you understand that I didn't do this because I don't love you. I did it because I do love you. I want you to understand that there are rules in this world. Everybody has to follow rules. Even the president of the United States has to listen to somebody." I said, "Who's that?"

Dad answered, "His wife."

I traded a Vincent Black Shadow motorcycle and $70 for this car, which Ray Tracy and I customized. She was beautiful in black primer. (Don Miller Collection)

He said something else that's stuck with me forever. "Listen to me and remember this. A man is a man whether he's wealthy or poor. The only thing that any man has got that has any value is his reputation. If you get a reputation for being a liar, your life is going to be miserable. So don't lie. If you're wrong, okay. You're wrong. It's not bad to be wrong. Let people know you were wrong, and that maybe there's another way to do something, because life is a negotiation."

It sank in. He told me, "We'll get you a car, and you can start driving it to high school." Well, it wasn't two days later that he came home with a 1947 or 1948 Chevrolet sedan, a six, after selling my cool Ford roadster. I said, "Dad, I hate that car. It's ugly." He replied, "It's transportation. You paid $25 for it. You've still got $100 in the bank. It runs beautiful. Just drive it. Take it to school and later, we'll find you something that you really like."

The truth was, just having a car again felt like a million dollars. I hated that Chevy and I drove it for two or three weeks while I kept looking for a Mercury. My father knew I hated it. I traded the Chevy to a guy down the street for a motorcycle, which made my mother absolutely out-of-her-mind mad. But my Dad stepped in and said, "It's his money, he doesn't like that car, he wants that motorcycle. I think he made a really poor choice, but it's his choice."

The motorcycle was a legend from England, a Vincent Black Shadow. It looked vicious. The guy who owned it wanted a car because he had a family, even though the Vincent was only a couple of years old. He could never get the thing started, either. You could never use the kick starter; it would snap back and break your ankle, so I had to push start it before I took off for school in the morning. I think I had the Black Shadow for about a week and a half. I traded it, plus $70 in cash, for a 1949 Mercury coupe before I managed to kill myself. God only knows what that Vincent would be worth today.

5
Going Straight, Going Faster

AGE 16 DIDN'T COME quickly enough for me. Neither did 17, which, to be precise, was in 1956. But it was a measurably better year for me from the dual standpoints of having my driver's license and having obtained my first 1949 Mercury—one of the most storied American cars ever—in which to exercise my long-in-coming privileges. It was a two-door coupe, a thoroughly used car, but nevertheless, a very nice one. When I got hold of it, it was stone stock. It was a stick shift because pretty much everything was a stick shift then, a three-speed manual transmission with overdrive. It was arguably better looking, and considerably safer, than the old Vincent that I'd traded for it.

Naturally, as a kid who was deeply into hot rods already, I had to get right to work on it. The first thing I did was add a pair of duals. I was holding down two jobs by this time, at the Sinclair station after school during the week and I also had a job working at Burke Ford, a Ford dealership on the South Side. Burke Ford, of course, had all kinds of old parts lying around. One that I spotted immediately was a four-barrel intake manifold for a 1953 Mercury, with a four-barrel "haystack" Holley carburetor attached to it. I asked the parts manager what they were going to do with it; after checking with the boss, he said, "We'll sell it to you for $10 and deduct it from your pay." That was probably about one-fifteenth of what it cost new, but it was still 10 bucks, a fortune to a young kid back then.

I worked that whole Saturday for no pay, in exchange for the manifold and the four-barrel, but I had scored some heavy parts for my Mercury. They definitely worked, which was good because I couldn't afford a lot of engine parts. I was just busting wide open with pride over what I'd done, believe me. At the dinner table I was bragging about the deal to my father

when my mother suddenly blurted out, "Ten dollars! That's ridiculous. You only paid 50 dollars for the whole car!" Obviously, then as now, value is in the eyes, or perception, of the beholder. Nevertheless, those modifications that I made, starting with the cheap Mercury parts, really transformed the car's performance.

When I graduated from high school in 1957, I wasn't sure what I wanted to do, so I enrolled in two different schools at the same time. One was the American Academy of Commercial Art and the other was the Art Institute of Chicago, where I took an Industrial Design course. I also signed up for the Illinois National Guard.

Right around this same time, some guys I knew were beginning a new hot rod club in Chicago. They called it the Tappets. Becoming one of them was eternal for me. Right here in my Mooresville shop, where my buddy Razoar and I play with old cars today, I've still got my original cast plate from the Tappets. The 1949 Mercury became my entrée to the Tappets, and thereby, into the social world that surrounded fast cars. As it unfolded, the Tappets provided an intensive learning experience about the mechanics of cars, and membership in the group led, eventually, into my life of racing.

Some of the guys in the Tappets were from my own neighborhood and some were from surrounding areas in Chicago, probably 15 or 16 guys in all. One of my closest friends back then was a fellow Tappet, Ray Tracy, who is still a really good friend to this day. Ray was an excellent body man. He was only a year older than I was, but even at 18, he was just supremely gifted. Ray was standing next to the Mercury one day, eyeing it and taking in its fabulous lines. Finally, he said to me, "You know, we ought to make a custom out of it." For the first time, I was involved with a guy who had a critical eye, trained on a car's outward appearance. Just by looking at the car, Ray was teach-

I built a killer flathead engine for the Victoria but I was getting my butt kicked by the small block Chevys. (Don Miller Collection)

ing me. I not only became aware of bodywork issues, which I might otherwise have ignored, but wanted to actively work on them.

Ray became an important early mentor to me. His verbal tutoring, when combined with the sketches that I'd been learning how to draw and detail while I was going to art school, allowed the two of us to work in close concert on changing the Mercury's appearance. He'd suggest that we weld on the headlight rims from a 1952 Mercury, or stretch the quarter panels, and I'd be able to rough out how they'd change the Mercury's overall looks, right on my sketchpad.

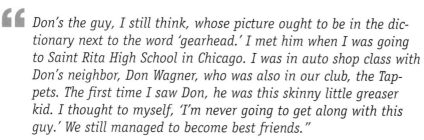

Don's the guy, I still think, whose picture ought to be in the dictionary next to the word 'gearhead.' I met him when I was going to Saint Rita High School in Chicago. I was in auto shop class with Don's neighbor, Don Wagner, who was also in our club, the Tappets. The first time I saw Don, he was this skinny little greaser kid. I thought to myself, 'I'm never going to get along with this guy.' We still managed to become best friends."

RAY TRACY
Chicago rodding pioneer, Don's lifelong friend
Pentwater, Michigan

Working together, we shaved the hood and the deck lid, took off the door handles, doing the period custom stuff you'd expect. We went to a junkyard and found an old Lincoln Continental from the 1940s. The Continentals from those years used to have mechanical pushbuttons on the outside of the doors instead of conventional han-

Going Straight, Going Faster   **23**

dles. We removed the buttons from the Lincoln, filled in the Mercury's doors and put the buttons in. Ultra slick. Of course, we lowered it with blocks and put fender skirts on it. The Merc was in admirable shape with no rust, even though it had probably been in Chicago since it was new. It wore black primer, like any number of other 1950s customs that never got completely finished. Ray, on the other hand, had a 1951 Oldsmobile convertible that he later turned into one of the most absolutely beautiful, award-winning customs that you'd ever see. It was finessed down to the last imaginable detail. He repainted it gold, molded in Packard taillights and all that kind of thing.

Taken as a group, the Tappets really had some neat cars, Fords and Mercurys and Oldsmobiles, mostly, customized and with souped-up engines. Against all expectations, one of the guys came from a pretty well-off family and had a brand-new 1956 Plymouth Fury hardtop. The club had real longevity, and it was still going strong when I finally got drafted in 1959.

The cars weren't all hot rods in the purest sense, like '32 Ford roadsters and such, because this was Chicago, and in the winter the weather was terrible. That meant that closed cars, custom sedans and hardtops, were preferred.

I'd had the Mercury for maybe a year when I sold it. Next, I bought a 1951 Ford Victoria coupe, which became my entrée into serious, hardcore drag racing. I thought the 1951 Victorias, with their no-pillar roofline, were really slick looking. This time, I even had some money left over, because I sold the Mercury for a lot more than I paid for the Victoria. That allowed me to build a full-race Ford flathead, put it in the Ford and go racing.

My very first venture to any drag strip was at Oswego Dragway, the strip that was closest to us when I started and about 35 miles west of downtown Chicago. There were still plenty of hot cars with modified flatheads around in 1957, but we were running the Ford in C/Gas and were getting our heads beaten in by cars with overhead-valve engines, especially the new small-block Chevy. But being a true-blue

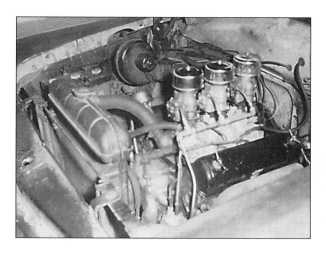

Ford guy, I opted to swap in a Y-block Ford engine, a 292-cubic-inch OHV Thunderbird V-8 with dual quads. I'd read in *Hot Rod* magazine that it was a weekend job, but it ended up taking me three weeks. Ray Tracy wasn't impressed with that, but the performance improvement proved very rewarding. Within a year, though, I sold the Ford, too.

About a week later, I bought a 1951 Studebaker convertible, for transportation. It had the overhead-valve V-8 that Studebaker had introduced for 1951 and a three-speed manual. Of course, I couldn't leave it alone. I put a dual-carburetor Edmunds intake on it with a pair of two-barrel Carter carburetors, finned aluminum Almquist valve covers and overdrive, plus dual exhausts and a Spaulding Flamethrower ignition. Ray and I spent a ton of time working on this car.

 Don had bought this beautiful little Studebaker convertible, and he started souping it up. I became extremely intimate with the underside of this particular car, because every time Don really flogged it, he would knock a rod bearing out of it. Back under the car we'd go, drop the pan, put new bearings in it, put it back together. But one time that remains crystal-clear in my mind was when he finally decided he was going to sell the Studebaker, even though it was beginning to develop another rod knock. We pulled the pan once more. This time, though, we discovered that the crank throw on the number-five cylinder really needed to be turned. We arranged to have a machinist come out and turn down the rod journal while the engine was still in the car, something that mechanics actually did back in the 1950s. We had it done with the Studebaker in Don's father's garage. There was only one problem:

Left: Several of the Tappets members' cars were powered by 292-312-cubic-inch Ford V-8 engines. This tri-power engine resided in Joe Okon's '54 Ford. (Don Miller Collection)

Right: This photo of Ray Tracy's beautiful '51 Olds doesn't do the car justice, but on this day, we were there to race. (Don Miller Collection)

I loved this little Studebaker convertible despite the fact that I spent as much time working on it as I did driving it. (Don Miller Collection)

It was December, it was 29 degrees inside the garage, and the only heat we had was from a 60-watt light bulb at the end of the extension cord under the car. I was never so glad to see that Studebaker sold."

RAY TRACY

By this time, I was grabbing cars and selling them in one big blur, including a Model A Ford, a 1930 five-window coupe. Somebody had already started making it into a hot rod, but I finished it, with a big-inch flathead. We built a tow bar to get it to the strip. The rules dictated that with the 296-cubic-inch flathead, we had to run in D/Altered against, you guessed it, the Chevy small-blocks. As a result, about three or four months later I pulled the flathead and stuffed that Model A full of my own small-block, a 283 Chevy, which I'd bought out of a wrecked 1957 Corvette. It was a hot engine, the small-block with dual four-barrels and a Duntov cam. By the time I got it into the Model A, it was 1959. I had two sizzling cars, a V-8 Studebaker—no lie, Studebakers were hot cars—and this Corvette-powered Ford coupe. I was ready, man.

Except for the fact that about then, I got drafted. But until I got my "Hello, Don" letter from Washington, I was building and driving these cars. No matter what car I was considering, I always thought first about how it was going to perform in a straight line. Drag racing was exploding everywhere in the second half of the 1950s. I followed it obsessively and read about it constantly. I had seen my first race as a spectator when a racing mechanic and fabricator named Fred "Jeep" Kirschner, who ran a 1950 Oldsmobile with a 331-cubic-inch Chrysler Hemi in B/Gas, took me to the strip at Cordova, Illinois, around 1955. Besides Oswego, a really popular Chicagoland strip, there was Half-Day, a smaller place just north of Chicago and pretty

This coupe was my first traditional hot rod. Originally I installed a full race flathead, but quickly converted to a 283-cubic-inch Chevrolet. If you can't beat 'em, join 'em. (Don Miller Collection)

much at the end of its rope when I first started to race. Farther north was Rockford Dragway, which has a special place in drag history as the first four-lane strip. It was on a grand scale. All these were quarter-miles except for Half-Day, which was an eighth.

 I think that when I met Don through racing, it was actually at a track. I go all the way back, all the way to Half-Day, even back when the Granatelli brothers ran it, where they had what was probably the first organized drag race in the Midwest. It was an eighth-mile, concrete surface, on a Nike missile base. I ran 78 mph in my 1940 Ford with Navarro heads and a 1949 Mercury four-inch crankshaft. It was a Tudor, which I liked better than a coupe because of all the weight back there.

Half-Day was pandemonium. Andy Granatelli was right when he wrote about it in his book. There had to have been 10,000 people there, going nuts, all over the place, no guardrails. It was unbelievably wild. There was one guy there with a car that was just a bare frame—the word 'dragster' didn't yet exist—with a box, a crate, for a seat. We had shorter seasons in the Midwest, compared to California, but we made the most of them. We were usually only about a year behind the guys out there that ran year round."

ED RACHANSKI
Chief Technical Officer, Oil-Chem Corporation
Founding Indy Racing League team owner
Henderson, Nevada

I met Vance Ferry, one of my best friends to this day, when I was racing at Half-Day. We were both working at Sears at that time, Vance as auto center manager up in Fox Lake. Vance was a total, hardcore, flat-out drag racer. He ran a bunch of roadsters called *Compulsion*. Even though we didn't run in the same classes, we became fast friends and began traveling to races together. One destination was in Wisconsin, a very famous track named Union Grove Dragway. For decades, Union Grove had a legendary promoter, Broadway Bob Metzler, a terrific character. There was also U.S. 30 Dragway, which was in Indiana, outside Gary. We'd run all those places plus Muncie, Indiana; Martin, Michigan; and even all the way to Kansas. We raced at Topeka and at Great Bend, where the very first NHRA Nationals were contested in 1955.

" *Even though I've known Don for a long time, I still remember meeting him for the first time at Half-Day Dragway in northern Illinois. He was the city slicker from Chicago and I was the farm boy from out in the country. I found out that we both worked for Sears, and we both loved cars. We were both very competitive in our racing efforts, and though we didn't agree on everything, we formed a very long-lasting relationship.*

Don is contagious. Beyond that, he's an extremely good mechanic, but he's a hardheaded German, and in many cases, had to learn the hard way. I was very deeply into drag racing, so it was a given that Don and I would get together, combine our knowledge and develop some very innovative racing solutions. We did it even though Don was hooked on doorslammers, and my race cars have always been roadsters. His theory was that you could move a house with enough cubic inches, but I was into real light cars, small-cube motors and lots and lots of RPM."

VANCE FERRY
Compulsion Race Cars owner/driver
Gurnee, Illinois

Even though Vance and I became terrific friends, he never joined the Tappets, probably because he lived 30 miles north of the city and our meetings were usually in our South Side neighborhood. The club had several excellent drag cars. My real education in building high-performance cars, and turning wrenches in general, was honed while working shoulder-to-shoulder with my fellow Tappets. The process of learning to make horsepower never slowed for any of us.

I believe I'm correct in saying that in Chicago we were just as avid a bunch of car and racing enthusiasts as all those guys in California who became world famous. We, however, didn't receive any attention

from the car magazines because almost all the magazines were head-quartered in Los Angeles. The indisputable truth, though, is that some of the quickest, fastest and most brutal drag cars of that entire era were in the Midwest. We had a lot of cars and teams back then that eventually became members of UDRA, the United Drag Racing Association, as well as AHRA and NHRA.

Another reality was that Chicago had horrendous winters and most of the work had to be done outside because hardly any of us had garages of our own. I can remember putting a camshaft in Bobby Lewandowski's 1950 Ford two-door sedan in the alley behind Ray Tracy's house in Argo in March. Those terribly cold and snowy winters meant we couldn't race all year like the California guys who got all the stories and photos in the car magazines.

Despite our long, blizzard-enforced off-season, there were a lot of scarily good Midwest racers who could go to California, big races like Bakersfield, and just blow those cats off. One excellent case in point was a guy called Gabby Bleeker. Here was someone who worked with literally nothing, and he still had one of the most wicked Altereds in the country. Another one, who's much better known than Gabby, is Arnie Beswick. He was a farmer from southern Illinois—in addition to being a Midwest drag legend and a hero to Pontiac fans—and won his class several times at the U.S. Nationals. He usually drove in Stock, Super Stock, A/Stock—a great guy. Yet another was Larry Teeter, who had a '32 Ford with a Chevy in it. Then there was the team of Pat Minick and John Farkonas, who later formed the *Chi-Town Hustler* team with Austin Coil. We had a Chicagoan named Corvin Latus, who was probably one of the biggest innovators in drag racing, from any time. You may have never heard of him but you've heard of

the car that he built. It was a dragster called *The Hun*. And it was tremendously, frighteningly fast. It started off as an AA/Gas car, and then eventually he ran fuel in it.

In Chicago we also had Romeo Palamides, who built a lot of famous piston-powered and jet Funny Cars and dragsters. Mike Marinoff—he had a fantastic series of Gas coupes, beautiful cars. We had a local car that was always advertised in the Iskenderian camshaft ads in the 1950s. It was a 1951 or 1952 Cadillac four-door sedan, and it had a very souped-up Cadillac engine—with an Isky cam, of course—owned and raced by the McKenzie brothers. Vance Ferry bought "Ohio George" Montgomery's old car, the 1933 Willys Gasser, took the Ford cammer out of it, put in a four-cylinder motor from a Chevy II—which is a torque monster, made it ridiculously light at something like 1,500 pounds and set all kinds of national records. I could go on and on.

> The Midwest had some of the hardest-charging drag cars in the country. I bought Ohio George's 1933 Willys Gasser and put a 151-cubic-inch four-cylinder "Iron Duke" in it, making 297 horsepower. I can do a body, and by the time I was done with it, the car weighed 1,515 pounds. For a doorslammer, that's almost nothing. The studs that hold the wheels on were titanium. I put them on my lathe and hollowed them out. Same thing for the hinge pins on both doors. I went to this huge Gas coupe and sedan meet and ran almost two seconds quicker than the national record, right out of the box."

VANCE FERRY

Top left: Ray Tracy built this wicked Olds-powered '40 Ford coupe that we nicknamed "Grumpy" after its owner. (Ray Tracy Collection)

Top right: Ray Tracy with his friend Patty Barber and a trophy for C/Gas at Oswego, Illinois. (Don Miller Collection)

Bottom: I painted this cartoon on the quarter panels of Ray Tracy's '40 Ford, reminiscent of the nose art that was used to decorate bombers in WWII. (Don Miller Collection)

Ray Tracy, the Wagner brothers, Bob Lewandowski, Mickey Gratchner and I, Chicagoans every one, would all go on Sundays to the races. We won class trophies, won Street Eliminator a couple of times, and we traveled to all those tracks I mentioned.

I got drafted before I could really campaign my Chevy-powered Ford coupe, but I sold it to one of the guys in the club, Donnie Wagner, who raced it.

> ❝ *Don comes by one Sunday wearing a really nice sweater. I mentioned it, and he says his Mom had picked out this brand new sweater for him, and how much he likes it. He also tells me he's having a problem with the Model A Ford hot rod coupe he had at the time, which had a small-block Chevy he had extracted from a '57 Corvette wreck and had rebuilt himself. Unfortunately, the engine wouldn't start under battery power. Don tells me that if I give him a pull with my car, he can let the clutch out and loosen the engine enough so it will catch and start. All we had was a 10-foot rope, so that's what we used. As I'm pulling him along, the engine fires and belches some flames out the top of the carburetors.*
>
> *Don started waving for me to stop. He jumps out of the coupe, blows out the flames in the carburetors, twists the distributor a couple of degrees, and jumps back in the coupe. You have to remember that this car had no exhaust system, only cast-iron headers. We pull it a few feet and it fires up. We stop, and then I see him jump out of the car, pull this brand-new sweater off, rip the sleeves off it and stuff them into the exhaust headers, one sleeve for each side. I'm standing there, and he just tells me, "The cold air is going to warp the valves otherwise." I finally said, "But I thought you liked that sweater." He says, "Yeah, but I like this car better."*

JOE OKON
Long-time family friend,
Custom car and performance engine builder
Oak Forest, Illinois

My racing was starting to get really serious in 1959. And then, following a series of blunders on my part, a plain white envelope came in the mail, informing me that I'd lost the big Selective Service System lottery.

6

In the Army, Wow

THE STORY OF HOW I became government property is, I guess, somewhat amusing. I had a deferment for a while because of my enrollment in the American Academy of Commercial Art in Chicago. I belonged to the Illinois National Guard, which meant that I was supposed to go to monthly meetings, and there was also a summer Guard camp for two weeks every year. I joined as part of my deferment, thinking it would keep me from getting drafted.

My military occupational specialty—what vets like us call MOS—was radar. As I've mentioned, my father was an engineer with Western Electric in Chicago during the war. Western Electric was the largest producer of these radar sets, so I had a pretty good home schooling in how they worked. Deferment for school or not, I still loved going to drag races. All I wanted to do was race, race, race. I was working two jobs—at Burke Ford and for Sears as a part-time mechanic and tune-up guy—going to school, working on my cars and racing. I was getting really competitive, and I didn't want to miss anything, so a couple of guys in the Guard and I worked out a system by which we could skip out on the required meetings and cover for each other by signing each other in as if we had actually been there. For a while, it worked out OK. I really thought I was getting away with something.

Wrong.

I went to the strip one Sunday when I was supposed to be at a Guard meeting. This time, I didn't bother to cover myself with the other guys. And of course, this was the one time the officer of the day happened to notice I wasn't there. They checked further, going back through the records, and it didn't take them long to figure out that I had skipped a whole bunch

Home on leave after basic training at Fort Leonard Wood, Missouri. (Don Miller Collection)

of other meetings, too. The commanding officer called me into his office for a special meeting, which was when I first realized I was in trouble. He barked, "We turned your name in to the local draft board. You're no longer draft-exempt." I just went, "WHAT?"

I couldn't believe it. I told my Dad, and he listened and simply said, "Look, you're going to have to pay the piper now." Maybe six weeks later, right in middle of prepping the coupe for drag racing, I got the letter. I was hoping that something would happen to change my fate, but when they call, you've got to go. My sister drove me downtown, put me on the train, and I went to Fort Leonard Wood, Missouri, and through Army Basic Training.

> ❝ *That was a horrible, horrible day. Our Dad had just had a major heart attack the day before Don left, and he was a long time recovering from it. I volunteered to take Don down to the train station in Chicago, except that he drove. I had no sense of direction, even though we'd lived in the area for years. I remember that I dropped him off at the recruiting building somewhere, and then I was supposed to go back to work.*
>
> *"I drove around lost in Chicago for what was probably the next three hours. I couldn't figure out where to go. Finally, I ran out of gas. I'd given Don all my money, and asked somebody in the neighborhood I was in to lend me 25 cents' worth of gas. It was*

lunch time by then, and I remember that I passed the same police-man about five times. He practically took me where I needed to go all by himself."

PAT WORLEY

I remember that we only had perhaps two days off in the whole Basic cycle, which lasted eight or ten weeks. Ray Tracy drove all the way down from Chicago in his Olds, brought my sister with him. It was a long drive; the base is about halfway between Saint Louis and Kansas City. I'll never forget, it was in the dead of winter. It was colder than hell there.

Toward the end of Basic, we had the Airborne test, and I took it. I thought it would be really cool to be a paratrooper, and what do you know, I passed. It was a physical; you had to run, jump over picket fences and so forth. I was already a really good marksman because my father had taught me how to fire a rifle from the time I was 10. He would take me out every two weeks, first with a .22 pump Winchester that I still have, then shotguns and even with a .30-30 Savage rifle. When I went into the Army, I qualified as an Expert on the range almost immediately. I was on the rifle team. So here I am, all ready for paratrooper school, and I hear, "You can't go into Airborne." The commanders said that since I already had an MOS in radar and the government had already spent all that money to train me while I was in the Guard, they were going to send me off to another radar school.

I still think they were just trying to punish me for missing the

My trusty '57 Plymouth Fury made many trips to Chicago and many more to Alamogordo, New Mexico. (Don Miller Collection)

Guard meetings. I tried to file a protest, but that was useless. They sent me to Fort Bliss, which is out in the middle of nowhere in rural Texas. Remarkably, in the middle of all this, I took the Officer Candidate School test, and I passed that, too. Now I'm about to go to Texas, but my Dad, from his work at Western Electric, knew all these senators. He managed to arrange it so that if I passed the OCS tests, I might be able to get an appointment to West Point. But in the end, even though I'd passed, I decided that I didn't want to go or become an officer.

My father just about disowned me. He practically yelled, "You're passing up the chance of a lifetime here." He didn't talk to me for, probably, three or four months. Only my Mom would speak to me—she didn't want me to stay in the Army, either. At this point I was not happy to be in the Army. But I made the best of it, and waited to get out and return to racing. As it turned out, I still had some things to learn.

A lot of people who know me—probably even most of them—think my background's purely connected to circle-track racing. It might be due to my longtime association with Rusty Wallace and Bobby Allison, especially after I joined Roger Penske. They don't realize I was a committed, serious drag racer long before I ever even saw any kind of oval race. It was actually my Army days that marked my first exposure to any kind of oval-track competition—and as a driver, no less. That major transformation of my motorsports orientation, and ultimately, my whole life, came in 1960, mainly because there was no drag strip in El Paso, the nearest major city to Fort Bliss.

There was, however, a sports car course. El Paso, which is right on the Rio Grande along the Mexican border, had a real SCCA-type road racing facility. There was a guy down there named John Bull who owned a couple of dealerships, one of which had an Austin-Healey franchise. John had a pair of small Austin-Healeys, what became known as the Bugeye Sprite, which he raced around Texas. I met him through another guy, a semi-pro racer, I guess, who was trying to promote sports car events. John asked me, "Have you ever tried sports car racing?" I told him I'd driven Corvettes, but never a European sports car. Next thing I know, he's actually offering to let me try one of these Healeys in a race.

Off and on, I'd already been sampling some dirt racing just across the border in Mexico, in Modifieds. It was at a tiny little dump, a real dive, outside Ciudad Juarez, strictly an outlaw thing. When I met John, I'd probably driven there a half-dozen times, actually winning a couple of Modified races in the process. My Modified was an old Chevy coupe with a six-cylinder Chevrolet engine, running—honest—snow tires. About the only thing it had in common with today's Mod-

ifieds was a lack of fenders. I don't remember who any of the other drivers were; some were from Texas and some from Mexico. The track was extremely primitive, more like a rodeo or bullfighting arena with some planks around the outside to form a guardrail. Amazingly, nobody got seriously hurt or killed, at least when I was there. I don't think there was even an ambulance on hand during the races.

When John offered his Austin-Healey, I visualized a 1500, the typical Big Healey, as it's called now. John's, though, was a Bugeye. Tiny car, tiny engine, about 975cc of displacement, but I agreed to drive it and see what happened. Believe it or not, I raced it maybe 10 times, winning about five outings, despite having never seen a sports car race before in my life. The first time, I had to start dead last because the promoters lined up the races based on driver points. I'd had perhaps two hours of practice. To me, the Bugeye was totally anemic. I kept saying to myself, "This thing doesn't have any power at all." But it cornered really well. I started getting the hang of how to enter and exit the corners, where to brake and accelerate. At once, I was winning, partly because I'd learned how to drive like hell on back roads in Wisconsin. Besides running the Mexican Modified, it was my only non-drag experience.

So here I was, a winning race driver on real race tracks, and my winnings were . . . zero. The Modified owner would take us all to Juarez, me and the one or two guys who made up the crew, pay to get us in the pits and pocket whatever the car won, which might have been enough U.S. currency to buy a hamburger and shake back in Texas. I drove it for fun. Things were very different then, and I was coming out of drag racing, where we didn't race for money in the first place. We got little plastic trophies for winning our class at the drags. I've still got some of them. You paid your own money to tear your own stuff up.

Despite my responsibilities as a soldier, I managed to make time to fool around with cars, and not just racing, either. While I was assigned to Fort Bliss, I owned a 1940 Ford coupe. I put a souped-up flathead in it, took it to Mexico and got the whole interior upholstered. The guy in Juarez who did the upholstery was just terrific, and the Ford was beautiful inside, even though it only cost me about $150 to get the whole interior done in the tuck-and-roll treatment that everybody had to have in 1960. Dirt-cheap.

I also bought a 1957 Plymouth and drove it back and forth from Chicago to Texas a whole bunch of times. One thing about that car that I never liked was those huge gold-anodized side spears that we so closely identified with the early Fury, so I pried them off, and painted the sheet metal underneath them in light green. After a lot of searching, I managed to find a drag strip in Alamogordo, New Mexico, about 80 miles from El Paso. I met a really beautiful girl in Alamogordo, and used to drive back and forth from Fort Bliss to see her.

Later I was assigned to White Sands, New Mexico, where the U.S. military still has its big missile range and where the first atomic bomb, Trinity, was tested during World War II. We went there to fire off the missiles, so it was exciting in a way, but I didn't really like it.

I've already admitted that I resented being in the Army, but I still have to give it some credit, because I did progress as an individual while trying to be a soldier. As my enlistment went on, I became an

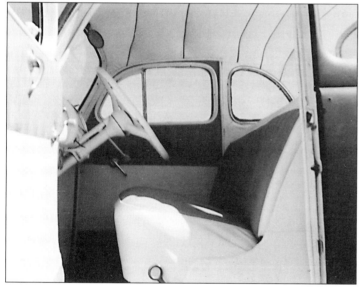

Despite my military responsibilities, I managed to make time to build this '40 Ford coupe. The beautiful rolled and pleated interior was done in Juarez, Mexico for the grand total of $150. (Don Miller Collection)

acting radar officer. I climbed in rank to Specialist 5, a buck sergeant in today's Army. Despite a noncommissioned rank, I was still considered a radar officer even though the Army was starting to bring in warrant officers to do that job. In the early 1960s, when you got out of the active-duty Army, you still had two years to go in the National Guard and then another six in the Army Reserve. I finally made warrant officer when I got back into the Guard.

Weeks of total boredom while on duty at White Sands proving grounds were punctuated with moments of unauthorized laughter. We were looking for a better way to steer this 2.5-ton truck. (Don Miller Collection)

All of our equipment was mobile. Here, we have dug in our acquisition radar trailer for our Nike Hercules missile battalion. (Don Miller Collection)

White Sands military exercise included construction of perimeter defenses, including this .50 caliber machine gun nest. (Don Miller Collection)

The Army taught me a lot about leadership, and what it means to have esprit de corps. As a young soldier, I finally started believing in concepts such as individual responsibility and its relationship to organizational objectives. I resented what I'd call the "oppression" of the Army but I came to see that in order to move a mass of personnel in combat, you *had* to have discipline. Long term, I used those lessons to understand the importance of chemistry between yourself and others, and between other individuals. That's remained with me throughout my business and racing careers: Be a people person. Understand your people. Move them by example, not intimidation. You'll always get a lot further. So for me, the Army wasn't a worthless adventure. I disliked it, but learned to respect it.

> *I know that Don was in the Army and sometimes, when we are just sitting around talking about things in general, he inadvertently refers to his time in the service. He makes some reference to how much he really didn't like the structure. But, he always goes back to some point in time where this experience helped shape his view of what life should really be. Don has taught me a lot about friendship and, from what I can garner from our many conversations, some of these guidelines came from what he learned in the Army. Don is big on loyalty and strength through trust. He always says, 'When the bombs start going off, you need someone you can trust in the foxhole next to you,' and I believe that you can take this lesson with you through the rest of your life."*

RYAN NEWMAN
Driver, Penske Racing, 2001-2008
Mooresville, North Carolina

BACK IN THE REAL WORLD

I, and my new attitude, returned to Chicago in January 1961. I entered the world of automotive sales, first back at Sears, where I worked my way into the buying department. I finally deduced that there was an actual, legitimate business side to the world of fast cars, not just building or driving them. I was a lot smarter about that, though I continued to drag race.

By the time I got out of the service, a lot of the guys in the Tappets had moved on, and the club, for all practical purposes, was dead. I really wanted to build a drag car, however, and decided that at that point of my life, I really didn't want to get married like many of my friends, but race. So I tracked down one of my friends, Don Warren, and in 1962, with some major assistance from another great guy, Ray Tracy, we built a 1955 Chevrolet as a pure drag car. It was the original *Big Noise*. And to put it in plain, frank English, it was an absolute, bona-fide ass kicker. Don and I just won and won and won with it. To support my habit, I had the job with Sears and was making good money there, especially in the sales end of it.

The Sears Auto Centers were already recognized as extremely successful in the accessory retailing business by the early 1960s. I supplemented my pay by working on cars, then by buying and selling them. I became the resident 1957 Chevrolet guy in my part of Chicagoland. If you lived there, and you were looking for a good '57 Chevy, I was the guy to see. In the early 1950s I'd been known as a

BIG NOISE

Don Warren and I campaigned this Chevy all over the Midwest
and set many class and track records. (Don Miller Collection)

One of the many engine
combinations we ran in
the Big Noise during the
early-to-mid '60s.
(Don Miller Collection)

hardcore Ford guy, but by the late 1950s I'd been beaten up so badly by the small-block Chevrolet that I decided to join 'em instead of fight 'em. I'd buy these cars, fix them up and sell them, sometimes two and three '57 Chevys at once. By this time, my parents had moved from Chicago to Saint Charles, Illinois, about 40 miles west on the Fox River. I didn't really want to live in Saint Charles, so I kind of bunked in with one of my pals, Larry Nowak, and we worked on cars. Larry was in Oak Lawn, on the near southwest side.

 Don and I had a great friendship. We worked together at Sears during the week, and hung out together on the weekends. I think that the common bond was cars—fast cars—and the faster the better. In the early days, Don, Joe Okon, and I were real dyed-in-the-wool Ford guys. Joe had one really slick 1954 Ford with a souped-up Y-Block 312, and I had a super nice 1958 Ford two-door sedan with a Y-Block that was mildly warmed over. Don was driving his 1951 Ford Victoria with an early T-Bird engine. But we were always building something in the garage. I remember Don was building a Model A Ford with a killer flathead and I had just started working on a Buick-powered 1951 Dodge pickup . . . We were consumed with the car thing at that point in our lives, and we were always helping each other."

LARRY NOWAK
Lifelong friend
Las Vegas, Nevada

I also found a 1957 Corvette sitting in the back of a lot nearby. It was pretty rough but I bought it, telling myself it was going to be my car for the street and strip. For openers, I made it into a real tire-smokin', fuel-injected four-speed car, just the ticket for B/Sports Stock.

Top: This was my first Corvette with fresh paint and mag wheels. We called it The Teakettle *because the fuel injection whistled so loud. I won a lot of races with this car—on the street and the drag strip. (Don Miller Collection)*

Right: Back in the day, it was all about the trophies. These were the first two that the Corvette won. (Don Miller Collection)

Now I had this hot Corvette, in addition to *Big Noise*, so I was racing two cars. *Big Noise* started out as an ordinary 1955 Chevrolet two-door sedan, a 150 or 210 instead of the heavier Bel Air. We immediately put a much stronger Pontiac rear in it and a four-speed Muncie. Don and I had at least three or four engine combinations that we would swap in and out so we could run the car in various classes. It had everything from a relatively tame 265 all the way up to a 352-cubic-inch small-block, a bored and stroked 327. We had carburetors, fuel injection, all kinds of different combinations. We ran in all kinds of classes, and we won in every class we ran. It could run in D/Gas or E/Gas, depending on the size of the motor and the type of induction or fuel system that we used. It was a typical Gasser, just as that category was starting to become monstrously popular.

As to the Corvette, I was driving it every day, and also was dating my soon-to-be wife, Pat. When we got engaged, the Corvette was our car.

> When I met Don, he was still living with his family in Chicago, where they had a one-car garage. He met all the people I knew through working at Sears, and they used to come out to my neighbor Les McVeigh's house in my family's neighborhood to work at his garage. These guys were Larry Nowak, his brother Ronnie, and Joe Okon, among others. Les' sister, Clarice, was my best friend.
>
> Don came over to Clarice's house one night back in 1958. He brought over his other girlfriend, Patty Barber. I think it was Les who actually introduced us. Clarice and I gave going-way parties

and coming-home parties for guys who were going into the service. Don didn't show up for either one of his parties, but we still had a good time. So it wasn't love at first sight. We'd all go to the drive-in movie theater, park in the first two rows, and the guys would gather in one car to talk about what they were going to do on Sunday at the drag strip, and the girls would be together in another car.

Cars were it. I really don't know when we actually first talked about getting married. We knew a guy named Tommy Mroz who'd just come back from the Army in 1961 and had a new Max Wedge Plymouth. Don had his Corvette and he'd raced Tommy on State Road, and beat him. Tommy complained he couldn't get the car into second. Don told him that even I could drive that car, and told me to get in and take off like I was coming off the line. He said it had a clutch just like the Corvette. I ended up blasting the Plymouth down Central Avenue.

When I came back to where he and Tommy were standing, he proposed. Don said, 'I'm going to marry you. You can drive my car.'"

PAT MILLER
Don's wife of 47 years
Mooresville, North Carolina

That Corvette was also pretty damn notorious at the drag strip. I'd taken it up to run in B/Modified Sports, and I was winning a lot with it. A lot. Many of those wins, or most of them, came on all those aforementioned Chicagoland strips. But a bunch of them didn't. The ones that I got elsewhere formed the elementary courses of my education as a professional racer, emphasis on "professional," as in "paid."

7

Busted

T O HEAR THEM TALK, everybody thinks that street racing only existed in California or New York. The Beach Boys sang about Colorado Boulevard in Pasadena. New York City had the Connecting Highway between Brooklyn and Queens, which was so famous that when you go to some swap meets today, you can find vendors selling fake Connecting Highway winner stickers that look like NHRA decals. All that's certainly true enough, but Chicago in the early 1960s was an absolute hotbed of street racing—even though we were buried under snow there for months. There were three or four prime—and illegal—racing spots in the Chicago area, and I won my share of both races and cash. Winning on the street, though, carried its own price. The least expensive was tremendous anxiety.

I was still very much into drag racing—the legal kind—in 1962 and 1963. I was running regularly at Oswego, as well as at U.S. 30 and at Union Grove, a real traveling drag racer. Street racing had its own circuit in Chicago. The biggest location, by far, was adjacent to an old Ford Motor Company assembly plant, an enormous factory that Ford had used during World War II to build B-24 Liberator heavy bombers and engines. It was at 65th Street and covered all the east-to-west distance between Pulaski and Cicero Avenue, several miles, a huge area. The factory had an incredibly long straightaway that ran for miles along what had once been vast employee parking lots. At each end was a large overpass for access from the lots to go north or south on Cicero and Pulaski. The bad part was that once you got inside this gigantic, empty area, there was no way out of it except for one of those overpasses. The good part was that, usually, nobody was out there. The straight was a public street, but nobody used it.

Guys came from all over the Chicago area to race there. The Chicago

The Teakettle *and me, before our infamous encounter with the Oak Brook Terrace Police Department. (Don Miller Collection)*

In 1957, Chevrolet built its first 1 hp-per-cubic-inch production engine—the fuel-injected small block. This one was on steroids. (Don Miller Collection)

police kind of knew about it; they'd come around every once in a while to break it up, arrest a few people. For the most part, though, the racing was spontaneous. Word would get out, say, Wednesday night at around 8 o'clock. I mean, anybody who was anybody in the world of fast cars around Chicago would show up. John Farkonas, later part of the *Chi-Town Hustler* Funny Car team, had a 1957 Chrysler 300 with a four-speed and he used to race it there. There was another guy, Wally Ratze, from the north side of Chicago, whom I knew from the American Academy of Commercial Art. Wally had a 1954 Ford business coupe with a blower over each valve cover blow-

All dressed up and nowhere to go. This baby was soon to become notorious. (Don Miller Collection)

ing into big dual quads. That thing was just a rocket ship. Ray Tracy ran out there with his 1951 Olds convertible with the full-house V-8. Hundreds of people would show up for these totally illegal races. We used white paint on the straightaway to mark off the quarter mile, and there was a guy down at the end that would call the race. It even got to the point where they had two-way radios to announce who'd won.

At first it was all about bragging rights, but it didn't take too long before people began racing for money. That trimmed the fields down quite a bit. I started running my Corvette out there but eventually we all had to move out because the Chicago cops were coming and busting people. At that point, we all moved out to Ridgeland Avenue near 111th street, a spot that was actually in the neighboring city of Oak Lawn. We would race right alongside a cemetery at around 11 o'clock at night, or even later. I was still working at the Sears Auto Center, and right about this time, I transferred to the store in Oak Brook, where McDonald's has its world headquarters.

The Oak Brook Shopping Center, when it first opened up in the early 1960s, was billed as being the country's biggest, most state-of-the-art suburban shopping center. It was built along state Route 83, and the developers kept putting in new roads as it grew and expanded. Behind it was a new piece of straight, fresh concrete that was probably three-quarters of a mile long. It was intended to be an access road, but we had other ideas. I checked it out a couple of times while I was working at Sears, and I thought to myself, "Man, this is going to be an awesome drag strip."

Around then, while I was racing my 1957 Corvette at Oswego, a really rich guy from Minnesota hauled in with a nearly new 1962 Corvette in Honduras Maroon, I'll never forget. We both had fuel-injected engines, and mine was enlarged to 352-cubic-inches, but this new guy was pretty bad-fast anyway. I richened up the fuel injection, really hogged it out, and pulled up to the starting line next to the '62 Corvette. I beat him, but to do it, I had borrowed a pair of drag slicks from Ronnie Nicholson's Altered because I knew I couldn't beat the guy with the tires I had on my Corvette. I beat him by about two car lengths and he was infuriated. He almost yelled, "We need to run someplace where there's not a lot of people around, and I want to run you for some money. Real money."

That didn't faze me because by then I had already been racing for money for quite a while, a lot more than I should have been. I was doing very well, though. Over a recent couple of weeks I'd made more money from illegal racing than at my job. Usually it was $50, some-times $100, which was strong money then. So I told him, "Fine, I'll run you for money." He shoots back, "I want to run you for 500 bucks." And I'm thinking to myself, "Jesus. Five hundred bucks. That's another '57 Chevy." But I borrowed $500 from my pals and told him to come back down and meet me on the Oak Brook con-crete in two weeks.

On the big day, I met him on my lunch hour in the Corvette. I bolted on the slicks, opened up the lakes pipes and went out behind the auto center. The Minnesota motor mouth arrived, towing his '62 Corvette. Despite the weekday, probably 30 or 40 people had already gathered to watch. I got a friend, Lenny Fennel, to hold my $500. The other guy pulled out his cash, something he obviously had in quantity. He had a big truck, a big trailer, and a new modified fuelie Corvette; he had towed it a couple of hundred miles to run in a street race. I was really nervous, probably as nervous as I'd ever been before a race up until that point. I knew full well that if I got busted, I was going to lose my job on top of the $500 and everything else.

I beat him again, this time by about a car length. I was already thinking about how we were going to negotiate, because I knew this blowhard was going to be just livid now. That was when the Oak Brook police roared in, converging at once on both ends of the strip to block us. I didn't have to worry about a truck and trailer, so I just nailed it, pulled off onto Route 83 and kept rolling out of sight. I went maybe four or five blocks, then turned onto a side street long enough to jump out and close the lakers back up. I quietly motored back into the shopping center, then parked the Corvette down at the far end and left it there. I walked back to Sears Auto Center and tried to get back to work.

I was shaking. My hands were trembling so badly that I could hardly write up a service order. My friend eventually came around and told me, "I got the money. The cops nailed him. Nobody told them who you were. But they're going to be looking for that car." So we took the Corvette to his house after work, and everything cooled off after a couple of weeks. The cops still would stop by the Sears store and imply that I was one of the guys in the drag race, so I never ran there again. But all the guys on the inside, in the know, were fully aware of what had happened. It all just made my Corvette that much more infamous. They started calling it the Teakettle because after I modified the fuel injection, it whistled as the air passed through it. I kept driving it to work.

Pat and I were going to get married on October 27th, just at the end of the summer racing season, so I really cooled it right around the local area. The problem was, *everybody* knew that car by reputation. I already had a premonition that sooner or later, I was going to get busted hard in it.

There was a redheaded kid who used to come into my Sears store all the time with a '57 Chevy. It was hopped up, at least by his standards, but no match for my Corvette. He still just thought he was baddest cat alive. On the Friday night before the Saturday I was getting married—*the very next day*—I headed out early for my bachelor party in the Corvette. It was just getting to be dusk. I headed down Route 83 and into Oak Brook Terrace, another suburb. This town was infamous, notorious, for its cops. Additionally, the Illinois legislature had just passed a law that said if you got convicted of drag racing in the street, the sentence was one year in jail. Mandatory. So I was chilling. I wasn't racing the Corvette, or anything else, on the streets anymore.

I stopped at a light in Oak Brook Terrace, and who pulled up next to me but this idiot with the Chevy. He's revving the engine, vroom, vroom. The light changed and I pulled away slowly, but he burned rubber and charged to the next light, waiting for me. I'm thinking this guy's crazy. This was still on Route 83 where the speed limit was 55. On the green, we pulled away but by then, this kid had irritated me so much that I hammered it. I only reached 50 or 55 and then lifted. Meanwhile, he just wailed past. We went maybe another mile when the red lights flashed on behind us.

We were still in Oak Brook Terrace. The police pulled us both over and arrested us. Took us in for drag racing on a public highway. I pleaded, "I wasn't drag racing, I wasn't even speeding." They growled

This is photographic proof that I did make bail and was able to attend my own wedding. (Don Miller Collection)

back, "Drag racing, acceleration test," on and on. They put us in the slammer, me in one cell, the red-haired kid in another. I'm bravely telling them, "Look, you've got to knock this off. I'm getting married in the morning." The cop almost chuckled, and answered, "Pal, you're not going anywhere except to jail. The only way you're getting out is by posting bond." The judge in Oak Brook Terrace had his courtroom right there in the police station and barked that it was going to be a $1,000 bond. Where was I supposed to get a thousand bucks?

I had my one phone call, so I called my Dad. Without blowing up, he said, "Aw, Christ, you're getting married in the morning. You've got to start being a little bit more responsible." He went around to all of our neighbors, borrowed a combined $1,000 from them, came down to the station and got me out. I missed my own bachelor party. It was about 3 o'clock in the morning. And I was going to be married in just a few hours. I also had an obligation to race another guy's car, a front-engine dragster, over at U.S. 30 that Sunday, even though it was the day after my wedding.

Pat and I did get married, I ran the dragster, and while I was out on bail awaiting trial, we went on a honeymoon up to a big resort in Rockton, Illinois.

My buddy Ed Rachanski standing beside his extremely successful '62 Plymouth drag car. (Ed Rachanski Collection)

To My Good Friend Don,
31 out of 33 Wins 1962
Ed Rachanski

> *Don goes where Don wants to go. He did what he wanted to do. But he's got a wonderful wife. Every truly successful man in the business has to have a good gal. Think about all Don's 50, 60, 70-hour weeks, all the weekends away traveling to the NASCAR races. Pat was the queen. He's got a great wife. Right from the start, she worked with him through the uphills and downhills."*

ED RACHANSKI

When we got back, the honeymoon really was over. I started getting ready for my trial, fully aware that if things turned out wrong, I was going to spend the next 12 months locked up. Like I said, my Dad knew a lot of politicians, and he got me a crackerjack lawyer. At the trial, the lawyer proved that I had indeed accelerated quickly but I didn't break the speed limit. Because of that, I couldn't have been drag racing. The other kid, he argued, was speeding but he couldn't have been racing, either, because I wasn't racing, since I was under the speed limit. So how could it have been a drag race?

Ultimately, he got me off scot-free. The other kid got off, too, with a real heavy speeding fine, something like $250, exorbitant in 1963. As far as I was concerned, I'd been represented by Perry Mason. As

you might guess, I learned a critical lesson from this whole sorry tale. I was newly married, and on top of that, Pat and I had learned that we were going to have our first child. Taken together, it all made me decide to clean up my act once and for all. That was my final street race, never mind that my lawyer successfully claimed it wasn't a race at all. That was *it*.

Getting arrested and threatened with jail changed my life forever. From then on, I raced in front of real paying crowds, on legitimate tracks and earning legitimate money. Just that quickly, I was about to become a pro racer. I was also about to experience a crushing blow in my life. About a year after he bailed me out of jail and made sure he got me to my wedding, my Dad died. He was only 52.

8

Turning Pro
(or getting paid, anyway)

BEFORE YOU CAN BE A PROFESSIONAL RACER, you need a professional race car. Mine, the one that made me a bunch of legitimate money—as opposed to the purse two street racers put up as a bet—was the original *Big Noise*, my 1955 Chevy. My whole racing career was built on the foundation of that terrific drag car. As I have described earlier, my good friend Don Warren and I built *Big Noise I* in 1962, with some major assistance from my close friend Ray Tracy. It was a Gasser, which we built in a little two-car garage in Oak Lawn, Illinois, at Don's house. We started out with a 1955 Chevy two-door sedan, either the 150 or 210 series, and stripped it completely. We put in a Pontiac rear, which was much stronger and thus better suited for drag racing than the stock Chevrolet unit. Naturally, we also put a four-speed in it. The first engine was a 301, which is 283 cubic inches with a 4.00-inch bore and dual quads. We built up the entire rear suspension ourselves, drew it up on a big piece of paper. We made the headers by hand.

When we had it all together, we started running in D/Gas at IHRA tracks. We also ran in E/Hot Rod and D/Hot Rod and C/Hot Rod, depending on weight, at AHRA events. There was the NHRA, too, in D/Gas and E/Gas. Those acronyms stood for, respectively, International Hot Rod Association, American Hot Rod Association and the largest drag sanctioning body, then and now, the National Hot Rod Association. *Big Noise* went deep in the 12-second bracket, which was a bullet-fast automobile for that day.

Left: The Big Noise *'55 Chevy coming to the line, ready to take down another victim. (Don Miller Collection)*

Right: Another record tumbles at U.S. 30 Dragway, Gary, Indiana. (Don Miller Collection)

" *Our partnership basically lasted from 1962 through 1972. It was Warren and Miller Incorporated. We were fortunate in that even though we were small fish in a big pond, we had some talent together. We had some good ideas, built these cars in the garage, and also had some good friends who helped us out. Independent of each other, we probably never would have succeeded. We had two cars that ran pretty good. The first one was the '55 Chevy, which became an AHRA record holder in 1964. It was a relatively heavy car, but it was very well built and was definitely competitive.*

It's funny, because I guess at the time, I was more of the engineer, the detail-oriented guy, even though Don is very detail-oriented himself. At that time, though, he was more of a true-blue mechanic with the finesse of a salesman. He really was. He could talk his way into a number of things and on a number of occasions, had to talk our way out of a number of situations. Same thing when we used to race. If we screwed something up, he could talk our way out of it, even when we had to begin to answer to sponsors. Don rustled up several sponsors for our car, including Kendall Motor Oil, Keystone Wheels and Champion Spark Plugs, and several others. I look back on it now and it was a hell of an experience, that's all I can say."

DON WARREN
Mechanical engineer, partner on the Big Noise I & II
West Chicago, Illinois

We took it all over the Midwest: Oswego, Union Grove, Half-Day, Rockford, Martin in Michigan, Detroit Dragway, U.S. 30 in Indiana, Saint Louis International, Topeka. We won consistently, but still weren't making any money with it. That was mainly because the payoff, other than a great time and a great deal of information on setting up for individual tracks, was usually a trophy. When I first started

racing, you did it for the bragging rights and a feeling of accomplishment. My Dad had told me something way back then that really stuck with me: "You know what drag racing is? An exercise in futility." Then he'd snicker.

In 1965, I left Sears and went to work with Ed Rachanski. Ed was from Oak Lawn, Illinois, too. He was a very good mechanic and the hardest of hardcore drag racers. He ran in Factory Experimental—F/X—in the early 1960s, the class that later evolved into Funny Car. Ed had a Mercury Comet, a topless drag car, that he called the *Marauder*. It had a huge 427 Ford engine in it, usually injected on alcohol, and sometimes on nitro, which sounded like a thunderclap that never ended. He ran it in F/X and as a match racer. It was Honduras Maroon with gold leaf lettering, beautiful.

Ed and I decided to start our own company, which we called Rep-Cor Incorporated. We were factory representatives for a lot of the manufacturers in the speed-equipment industry. When I left Sears, I probably had 10 or maybe 12 years in automotive service management. I had sold tires, shocks, all kinds of automotive products, and I had worked with the buying department at the main Sears offices on Ohio Street in Chicago.

RepCor represented companies like P&G chutes and shifters, Hurst, Summers Brothers, Gotha rocker arms and clutches and flywheels, I can't remember how many in all. We sold their products to distributors. Working with Ed, I learned an awful lot about business,

Left: The Marauder *traveled to the races in style. Ed was one of the first drag racers to transport his car on a drive-up hauler. (Ed Rachanski Collection)*

Right: Ed Rachanski and I formed our own company, RepCor, to represent speed equipment manufacturers across the country. Ed's Marauder *F/X car made the cover of* All American Drags *magazine. (Ed Rachanski Collection)*

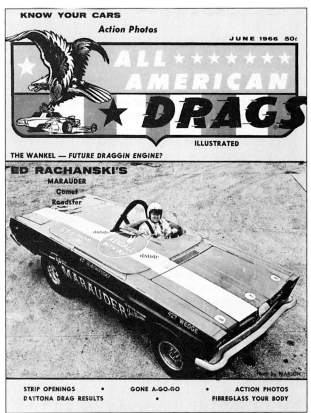

and about how absolutely vital it is to nurture and maintain your own personal credibility. At Sears, I'd developed one-on-one relationships with individual customers, who wanted nothing more than to have their cars run better at a fair price. Later on, as a Sears' buying manager and at RepCor with Ed, I spent a lot of practical hours learning about performance parts from the people who made them, and convincing retailers, such as speed shops, that stocking them would build their own businesses. Ultimately, it was my own credibility as a racer and a reputable individual that was on the line in these negotiations, which pretty accurately described my job.

> *Nobody else probably knows this, but between us, I always called him Duckie. I don't remember how it started, but I always called him that. Duckie. In 1964, Gary Dyer and I got a Mercury deal together from Fran Hernandez at the Ford Motor Company. He and I raced together until he went off to run for Grand-Spaulding Dodge in Chicago. After that, in the latter part of 1965, Don and I formed RepCor. We knew each other, casually, from the drag strips*

but we decided to put our heads together and form the company. At the time, I also was a Kendall Oil distributor, Tri-State Lubricants. I grew up about eight blocks away from him, also.

I was more or less the deal-maker on the high end, but Don was the brains of RepCor. He was the super sales guy, always had a lot of ideas, and made the connections with people like Jardine Headers and others out on the West Coast, Hedman Hedders was another one. We represented Mallory, too, probably 20 products or lines, and we did good, believe me. Don is a PR guy, a swell guy, and he got along with everybody."

ED RACHANSKI

At this same time, Ed started UDRA, whose acronym stood for United Drag Racers Association, headquartered in Chicago. It was a conglomeration of drag car owners and drivers who had said, in effect, that they were through racing for trophies. They wanted money, a notion that caused a lot of people to laugh back then, but Ed proved to be way ahead of the curve on this. Obviously, he knew all the other guys who were racing in Factory Experimental. When they finally disbanded it as a regular class at most tracks toward the late 1960s, they generally either went back to Gas Coupe or Sedan, or else into an Altered class. As an alternative, you could build a Funny Car. When Ed put the program together, UDRA had a nitro Funny Car class, a separate injected Funny Car class, a class for Gas Coupe and Gas Sedans and Super Stock. Each class ran its own UDRA circuit in the Midwest. Usually, they wouldn't all be at the same event, because the way that Ed designed it, each UDRA class would be a stand-alone show. In the case of injected Funny Cars, eight cars would compete against each other, and each driver would be guaranteed a certain amount of dollars just to show up. The winner took home a little bonus.

Left: Ed Rachanski and I turned Midwest drag racers into pros through the UDRA circuits. (Don Miller Collection)

Right: Here's a legit historic photo: The famed Arnie "The Farmer" Beswick at one of the UDRA shows, one of the very few times he drove a Funny Car that wasn't a Pontiac. (Don Miller Collection)

 EXCLUSIVE: The Best, Most Complete Drag Racing Photo and News Coverage

Drag Racer

ontanini Triumphs Thruout Midwest –Flor

I edited this newspaper, which covered a lot of UDRA action. Sadly, Al Fontanini, one of our Injected Funny Car stars who's on the cover, was killed in a towing accident. (Don Miller Collection)

Same thing for the Gassers. Ed would get 16 of them to go to, say, Cincinnati or to Martin, Michigan. Aside from our *Big Noise*, the Gas coupes and sedans featured Midwest stars like the Clark Brothers, who ran a 1933 Willys with an injected Hemi; the Corvette of Wold & Schwartz; and the team of Dombrino, Valentino and Thomas, who ran a tiny Ford Anglia very well stuffed with a big-block Chevy. The Injected Funny Cars didn't last very long in terms of durable popularity, but they really put on a fantastic show. The two who really ruled that class were Fontanini and Nannini, guys from Chicago who ran a Dodge Charger-bodied Funny Car with sponsorship from Grand Automotive. Unfortunately, Al Fontanini was killed in a freak accident while towing his race car back from an event. He was at a tollbooth on the Illinois Tollway when a truck piled into the back of him at full throttle. The whole thing exploded, including the alcohol inside the trailer. It was a terrible loss for the circuit.

The nitro-burning Funny Cars, as you might guess, were headed up by the *Chi-Town Hustler* and Don Schumacher from Chicago. We also had Arnie Beswick, Eddie Schartman, Terry Hedrick in the Seaton's Super Shaker Chevy Nova and one of the touring *Jungle Jim* Chevys—Jim Liberman had several cars stashed around the country for match races—usually driven by Clare Sanders.

I had just started running the UDRA Gas circuit with the *Big Noise* when Ed asked me to become a circuit director. That's when I started to become more heavily involved in the UDRA. Our events were the forerunners of all serious, paid drag racing in our part of the country. The AHRA and NHRA were still handing out trophies while we were awarding cash.

> *This was not an easy job. Don was so good at handling relationships with these guys. We never once had a strike, even though we were doing probably a million dollars' worth of business. I had a lot of good guys in UDRA, but I was closest to Don. UDRA was very successful, and a porcupine under Wally Parks' butt at NHRA. We ran nitro Funny Cars and had 15,000 people show up, when the NHRA wasn't even running nitro in Funny Cars."*

ED RACHANSKI

The *Big Noise* I was running at that time was the second one, a 1962 Chevy II Nova; by the time UDRA began, we'd already sold the '55 Chevy Gasser to some guys in Chicago. It eventually went to Minnesota, where it ran for years. I'd love to find that car and buy it back. The main reason we sold the '55 Chevy was to raise money to compete in the UDRA F/X class with the Chevy II. All of the early Chevy

IIs were very much alike in body style. To keep pace with F/X development, we changed its grille from a 1962 to a 1965 version to make it look more current.

We continued to upgrade the Chevy II throughout its career until we finally retired it in 1969. It started off in B/FX with a 352-cubic-inch small-block, topped with Hilborn fuel injection, on gasoline. Before we were done, it had a 509-cubic-inch Carolina Mountain Motor, as we called it, an injected Chevrolet based on an overbored 454 block with a stroker crank, usually on gas. It would run in the high 9s.

I ended up selling the car, less the engine, to a guy in Saint Louis, and sold the engine to Dickie Harrell. He had that engine in his match-race car when he was killed in Canada in 1971. That same engine then went, I think, to Harry Kalwei, who was on Dickie's drag team. I never saw it again after I sold it. That's another car I badly want to find.

Top left: We stripped the 1962 Chevy II sedan down to the bare shell and then built our own chassis and slipped it under that body. (Don Miller Collection)

Top right: The finished product being pushed onto the trailer for its initial track test. (Don Miller Collection)

Bottom: In front of our house in Oak Lawn, prior to going to its first UDRA event at Cincinnati, Ohio. (Don Miller Collection)

> *I don't know if Don ever tells the story of how he got the Chevy Nova that got built into Big Noise II. I'm the one who found it for him. I can't put an exact year on it, but he was looking for one of those cars, a light Nova or Chevy II. There was a Sunoco station in Argo, Illinois, near where I used to live. A guy would keep old cars parked there, and I must have spotted it abandoned behind the gas station when I was on my way to work. I asked the station owner about this Nova. He said it had been sitting there for a couple of months, and the guy had not paid his repair bill. The owner had taken out a mechanic's lien on the car, so I sent Don down to talk to him. Don gave him maybe $50 to get the car and the title, so he could build it into a race car. The next day, Don and I loaded the car onto a trailer and took it to his house. Don had to go to work, but his wife Pat and her little brothers, who were maybe 10 or 11 or so at the time, stayed home to clean out the car. It was a mess, full of all sorts of paper and trash.*
>
> *Don didn't have a key to the trunk when he purchased the car, so Pat's brothers climbed in, removed the back seat and began to burrow their way through to the trunk, to reach the inside latch and unlock it. Her younger brother Kenny, all of 10 years old, reached in and felt a man's shoe. Not only that, but a leg attached to the shoe. He screamed, 'LET'S GET OUT OF HERE! THERE'S A DEAD MAN IN THE TRUNK!' Pat overheard them and came out to see what was going on. Kenny was warning everybody, 'Don't go near that car! There's a dead man in the trunk!' Pat said, 'Boys, that's impossible. If there were a dead man in the trunk, the car would stink. Let's take a look.'*
>
> *What they found was an artificial leg that someone had left in the trunk. We joked about it for years, but it was an omen, because Don lost his own leg at Talladega in 1974. We never found out who the leg in the car belonged to, but we never forgot about finding it."*

RAY TRACY

In 1969, my life changed again in a major way when I got a call from Bill Genzler of Sears. Bill was the head buyer for automotive products at Sears' main office, and I'd worked with him there before going off to start RepCor with Ed. Bill said, "I've got an opportunity for you. Sears wants to go the way you've been talking about."

He was referring to something I'd been chatting with them about for several years by then. When I was still a service center manager for Sears, we would sell some speed equipment, both out of the centers and through the big Sears catalog. It was a good business, and I knew

that if somebody downtown would listen, it could get a lot better. I'd been advocating, at least to Bill, that Sears expand its performance sales—put a serious and unprecedented marketing push behind it. The market for those products very clearly existed, which I'd known for years through drag racing. My association with Ed only proved to me that I'd been correct.

When he contacted me, Bill said, "I want you to do this job, but I want you to work through National Engines and Parts Company." Around 1970, National Engines was the leading rebuilder of automotive engines in the United States. It was Sears' biggest supplier of hard parts; you could buy a National Engines rebuild through the Sears catalog. Bill's offer signaled Sears' readiness to undertake the major expansion in the performance aftermarket that I'd been lobbying for, however informally. The firm was located in Saint Louis, and as it turned out, moving there was a godsend to me, if not as much for the rest of the family. I met a horde of great racing people there.

So, in 1970, I went back to work for Sears through National Engines as their national sales manager and handled all their performance parts. We even built crate engines, under the brand name of National Eliminator, for both Sears and independent jobbers, long before the term "crate engine" was coined. We sold tons of rebuilt engines, most assuredly by the thousands annually. National Engines had three locations. The home office was in Saint Louis, with big operations in Pennsylvania and in California where the engines were remanufactured. We'd sell them through the Sears catalog, and Sears also had distributors throughout the country that handled parts through retail outlets.

Sears got that growth plan moving, and around this time I met yet another guy who helped me enormously in business networking, another phrase that didn't even exist yet. This was John Scafidi, who

Left: A frequent scene, Don Warren and I prepping Big Noise II *for war in a pit area somewhere in the heartland. (Don Miller Collection)*

Right: If the '55 Chevy made Don Warren and me into names, this Chevy II, Big Noise, *kept us that way. Eventually, it was packing a Hilborn fuel-injected 383-cubic-inch Chevrolet small block. (Don Miller Collection)*

worked for Hurst Performance, of shifter fame, in Warminster, Pennsylvania. I met him when we sold Hurst shifters through Sears. John had been an understudy to company founder George Hurst, and he became my godfather. He wanted to see me race while I was working with National Engines and did so many things for me. There's no way I could ever repay him. Regrettably, he's no longer with us.

National Engines was a terrific time of my life. It was one more climb up the ladder of business, personal experience and knowledge. I learned how to deal both with big corporations and with the individual, traditional parts markets. It taught me all about the American high-performance industry from a different side. I met, and was able to become friends with, manufacturers like Vic Edelbrock, Bob Hedman and Phil Weiand.

Here's an example of a life lesson. Let's say you're trying to get your product line into the system, into the stock of a particular retail chain like a regional auto-parts store. Once you get the chain to recognize you've got a good product, you begin to negotiate your price. There's one line, however, that you never cross. You don't go to one retailer and sell him your product for $59, and then turn around, go behind his back and sell it to somebody else for $54, because word's going to get around fast. In the speed business, everybody knows what everybody else is doing.

At its core, this business comes down to a long, protracted effort of creating a trust with the retailer, or the wholesaler, or whoever it is, and then really working your ass off to ensure you're servicing that account properly. That's what sales were back then. For anyone who values personal credibility, and his reputation, it still is today. It's networking to build and maintain the credibility factor, your personal honesty and record of treating people right, rather than just quoting a price. That's the commonality in what I always did with sales and marketing, stretching from my days selling tires at the Sears auto centers to being a manufacturer's rep for Ed Rachanski, and then with National Engines. The basic requirement of selling yourself has never changed.

Sears' ultimate objective was a trimmed line of fast-moving products it could sell through the catalog so it could capture the youth market early. The logic was that a young guy, still in his teens, who would buy a pair of Mickey Thompson slicks and a set of headers would come back and buy a Kenmore refrigerator and washing machine later on. It was very effective for the company for many years. This was before the rise of the big national speed warehouses, like JEGS or Summit today, and obviously, also before the first gas crisis of 1973.

Sears was already seriously marketing the DieHard battery through racing and performance channels. The person who actually brought the DieHard battery into racing was George Plumb, who was Sears' vice president of automotive and service operations. It was George and a Sears executive named Judd Sackheim who negotiated the first DieHard battery agreement with Roger Penske, who was making a name for himself in Trans-Am and other forms of racing. That connection though Sears, Bill Genzler and National Engines, is how I first met Roger.

In the midst of all this, I continued to work with the UDRA, and watched it flourish. I was also about to begin a new phase in my career, with Roger Penske. My life was becoming a circus act, always balancing and trying not to topple over. I was on the road continuously, just about every weekend in the summer, because the UDRA ran throughout the Midwest. I rarely saw Pat and the kids. The guys in the UDRA, however, because of the business plan that Ed did so much to brainstorm, were making enough money to sustain themselves, which is considerably more than you could say about drag racers in general at the time. The UDRA is still in existence today, I'm happy to report.

Top left: Making the big time—this national ad ran when I worked for National Engines. We were the only non-injected car on the UDRA Gasser Circuit, yet still won many races. (Don Miller Collection)

Top right: I'm accepting the trophy for the Gasser Circuit for the UDRA from Jon Lundberg. (Don Miller Collection)

Bottom right: Late in our partnership, Don Warren and I were still competitive with Big Noise II, *but the responsibilities were getting to be too much to handle. (Don Miller Collection)*

" Back then, everybody was racing with Pennzoil 60-weight. In 1966, I had a nitro-burning engine in my flip-top Mercury Comet. I worked very closely with Kendall's engineering department and told them we were putting 60-weight oil in the engine with a can of STP to make it thicker. Don came up with the idea: Why don't we get Kendall to make a 70-weight oil? That became GT-1, and the first five-gallon can we got from them, we gave to [famed drag racer] Chris Karamesines. That's the kind of stuff that me and Don did, before he moved on to Sears full-time as their parts and racing guy.

His success today proved that Penske saw his intellect, like I did early on. I knew that he'd succeed in anything he did. Don's not a gossip, not a foul-mouthed guy, and can read people extremely well. He's a hell of a good listener. He's humble. He thinks things out. Most of all, Don almost always sways people his way. When we were partners, I never worried about anything Don ever did. Never."

ED RACHANSKI

" I don't know how I coped or managed. I mean, I had to do it. At least once a month, I screamed and yelled and wanted him home, and home every weekend, but this was his job, and we had to eat. There are no 9 to 5 jobs. You just have to adjust. We were a year alone in Chicago when he was with National Engines in Saint Louis, and he had to come home for a weekend out of his own pocket, so we'd have to decide whether he came home or not, but I had my mother and my baby brothers living about six blocks away.

Then we moved to Saint Louis. Don was there a whole two days, with the boxes just brought into the house, and he said, 'I'm going out of town. I'll see you in a week or so.' You never knew. I had wonderful neighbors in Saint Louis, so if I needed anything at the house—and sometimes the women were alone all week just like us—they were there."

PAT MILLER

For me, however, life was just about to change again very drastically. I was about to be introduced to Roger Penske. Nobody who knows Roger, and his habits, will be surprised that it happened at a race track.

9
Roger and Me

My relationship with Roger Penske, as extensive as it's been over more than 30 years, really goes back to a single event. The place that I first met him face to face was at Bryar Motorsports Park, the site of today's New Hampshire Motor Speedway. I can even remember the date without trying hard: May 1, 1969. I'd traveled there with Bill Genzler, my boss at Sears, for a business meeting at an SCCA Trans-Am Series event where Roger's potent team of Sunoco-supported Chevrolet Camaros was racing. I'd spoken to Roger on the phone a couple of times, because National Engines was doing branding programs with him in cooperation with Sears. I learned pretty quickly once we got to Bryar that, indeed, the best place to try and have a conversation with Roger is when he's at a race track. That's not to say it's easy to get him to slow down enough to converse at the track, or anyplace else.

The whole Sears-Penske connection had kicked off in 1967 or 1968, when Sears had Roger go with Mark Donohue to the Baja 1000, the huge off-road race down the Pacific coast of Mexico. They ran an Allstate- and DieHard-equipped entry.

Then, Sears got involved with Roger in the Trans-Am series. Around that time, the company decided it was going to do a full line of Penske merchandise for the Sears automotive centers. It was an agreement of huge proportions that had made millions for Sears, part of the strategic plan to capture the attention of America's youth early on and keep them as customers over time. To that end, Sears had wanted to find a marketing partner that younger customers would immediately recognize and embrace. It didn't take long to settle on Roger Penske, who already had a proven record of success with cars in both racing and business.

Discussing the high performance market at the Presidents Reception Tuesday night were (left to right): Russ Dowling and Erle Keney, National Engines & Parts Co., St. Louis, Mo.; Dick Blind, Carter Carburetor; and Don Miller, National Engines & Parts Co. (JNP Photo)

Don Miller, Director of High Performance for National Engine Parts tells Motor/Age's Stan Stephenson of his new rebuilt engine line. Now a budding drag racer can buy a blue-printed engine, drop it into his car and head for the strip.

National Engines participated in trade shows across the country and used the Big Noise *Chevy II to increase traffic in their booth. (Don Miller Collection)*

Roger Penske became the public face of Sears' motorsports program in just about every way. He put his name and likeness to a line of Sears automotive products that he'd endorsed, in addition to the DieHard automotive battery. The line also included automotive testing equipment, which you still see in use all over the country. I'm a mechanic, and I run into people still using things like inductive timing lights from Penske Performance Products, as we called the line, and those things are over 30 years old.

By 1971, the upper echelons at Sears had firmly decided to get behind this Penske product line in their advertising, the catalogs and retail. They also decided that in order to reach the retail stores, they had to have a liaison person who knew the Sears system, the buying system, and who knew racing. That's when Bill Genzler stepped in and said, "We need to get Don Miller back here. We need to hire him back from National Engines."

Bill Genzler and Judd Sackheim were the automotive prime movers at Sears, and National Engines was their biggest supplier, a huge operation probably doing $3 million a year, a tremendous amount of money in the early '70s. Bill and Judd approached the management at National Engines first before they came to me. The chairman and general manager was Erle Keney, a very prominent businessman in Saint Louis. He told them, "Look, I don't want to lose Don. He's been a big help to us with the engine line, the performance line. We'll pay his salary, and let him continue do some of those

Top left: We flew into New York, where Bill Genzler arranged for us to rent a new Shelby G.T. 500 KR for our visit to Bryar Motorsports Park in Loudon, New Hampshire. (Don Miller Photo, Don Miller Collection)

Top right: This is a photo of the first lap of the Loudon Trans-Am race in 1969. (Don Miller Photo, Don Miller Collection)

Bottom: Mark Donohue on his way to victory in Loudon, New Hampshire. (Don Miller Photo, Don Miller Collection)

projects for you, but we want him to continue to be our liaison for the Penske Products line." So National Engines agreed that it was okay for me to go with Bill to meet Roger, this time at Lime Rock, the lovely road course in northwestern Connecticut.

We flew into New York, where Bill had arranged for us to rent a new Shelby G.T. 500 KR. When we arrived at the track the following morning, Roger was already there, talking to Mark Donohue and to some of the crew members, and Bill introduced me to Roger.

Roger said to Bill, "I read the letter you sent me, read everything you sent me about him. I talked to Judd Sackheim, and now I want to talk to Don by himself." It was kind of chilly, and Roger was dressed in a pair of pressed slacks and a turtleneck sweater. At this point in his life, Roger was pretty relaxed, but he was direct, businesslike. I admire Roger for a lot of things, but what I liked about him at once was that he didn't beat around the bush. He talked to you straight, asked you concise questions and expected the same kind of answers. He's still like that today, except now he has less time than he's ever had. We hit it off right away. I talked to him for a while, then chatted with Mark and with Don Cox. Don had known Roger for a long time. Roger had hired him away from General Motors, where he'd done a lot of the early design work on the Chaparral 2J, the Can-Am sucker car.

We went through the day and they ran in the race. Mark won it,

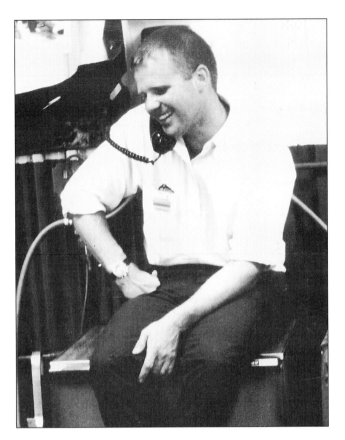

Mark Donohue at the pay phone in the Penske race shop in Newtown Square, Pennsylvania. Obviously, this was before cell phones. (Don Miller Collection)

in the rain, in one of the Penske Camaros. I soon became better acquainted with Mark Donohue. Until I went to work for Roger, our conversations had been limited to light chatter. I'd also visited the Penske shop, then located outside Philadelphia in Newtown Square, Pennsylvania, before Roger moved the teams to Reading, about 60 miles from Philadelphia, in 1973.

Newtown Square was a typical little Pennsylvania village with maybe a couple of thousand people. Roger, Mark and a guy named Chuck Cantwell had converted a former truck service facility into a race shop. It had four bays and a small Cape Cod bungalow in front, which they used for an office. One thing that's always stuck in my mind about the shop in Newtown Square was that there were no telephones. None, except for a pay telephone on the wall. If you wanted to call out, you had to use that phone and have a pocketful of change to feed it even if you were Roger Penske or Mark Donohue. Right above that pay phone was a sign: "Those of you who think you know it all are especially annoying to those of us who do." The shop was located there primarily because Mark lived right down the road in

Media, Pennsylvania, and Roger had his Chevy dealership a little farther away in Philadelphia.

> " The race shop was one block south of West Chester Pike, on a little street called Winding Way. There was the general manager, Chuck Cantwell; Don Cox, the chief engineer; Mary Ann O'Donnell, the secretary; and myself. There was a room upstairs that Mark used as his office, and he ultimately lived there after his divorce, while I lived downstairs on a cot. That was all we did. A very slim operation, but very efficient, as our track record from those days reflects. I was working with the sponsors, the media, various projects with Penske Truck Leasing and the tire company. Then on Thursday night, we'd leave for a race track someplace . . . that was my life."

DAN LUGINBUHL
Vice President Emeritus of Communications, Penske Corporation
Cordillera, Colorado

When I met him at Lime Rock in 1971, Roger was off doing 50 other things, as usual. He says, "I need a guy that can be Roger Penske for this Sears line. I need you to do this, and you're going to have to travel a lot, but we'll work it out. I'll make it well worth your while. You'll work with the race team when we're in locations close by to where you're at. But you'll have to move to Reading, Pennsylvania." And I answer, "That's the deal breaker. I don't want to go to Reading. I won't go to Reading." And he's saying things like, "Oh, you have to go to Reading, it's our headquarters." So I tell him, "Let me tell you what the situation is, Roger. I have a wife and a couple of young kids. I've moved them from Chicago to Saint Louis, and I've just gotten them to the point where they're getting used to living in Saint Louis. Now you want me to move them to Reading, Pennsylvania. I'm not going to do it." Pat hadn't been real happy about moving to Saint Louis in the first place, and still wasn't real warm about it. Our oldest daughter was about 10.

> " I guess I didn't focus very much growing up on the fact that Dad wasn't usually home. That's just the way it was. It was a very difficult thing to try and explain to people, what Dad did, and it was always a joke in our family growing up.
> I told my friends that he was in racing, but we kept it low key. It didn't compare to what a lot of kids' dads did. It definitely had its pluses, though. We grew up with a lot of interesting cars around the house, which made for a lot of conversation with oth-

ers, even when it was a little different. I was able to meet the people when we went to races in the summertime. They were an extension of our family. They knew who I belonged to."

TRICIA MILLER
Architectural conservator
Statesville, North Carolina

We left the conversation where it stood, but about two weeks later, Roger called me up. He said, "I'm up here in Detroit, at the dealership, and I'd like to you to come up here and talk with me." I drove up there from Saint Louis; it took me eight or nine hours. I guess we talked for about an hour. He showed me around the Penske Chevrolet dealership, where I met Walt Czarnecki for the first time, and visited the tire company next door. Roger had just bought Competition Tire West to sell Goodyear racing tires in the Midwest. We talked about business and racing, and he told me, "You know, you've got a really good grasp of business. But you also have an excellent grasp of racing." Roger told me about how he'd been a drag racer, too, at first, and how he'd started off on the wrong foot by taking his Dad's Oldsmobile to the drag strip. He thought he'd lined it up perfectly at the starting line but forgot to take it out of reverse, so when they dropped the flag, the car jumped backwards. It turned out that we'd both owned 1957 Corvettes.

Then he got down to business. "I really want you to do this," he told me. "We can probably put this together in a couple of weeks. You can do this Sears thing during the week, and work with me on the racing team with our sponsors, and then come to the races with us on the weekends. I just hired another young guy, from Ohio, named Dan Luginbuhl, and I want you to meet him. You guys can make a real dynamic duo."

 I grew up in a small town in northwestern Ohio called Bluffton. Roger Penske is from Shaker Heights, an affluent Cleveland suburb. I went to the University of Cincinnati and after I graduated, was working in advertising in Cleveland. Because of my asthma and allergies, I got a deferment from the military. So I went to the credit union, got a home-improvement loan, and bought a race car. Through the Northeast Ohio chapter of the SCCA, I met Fred Marik, whose company, Professionals in Motion, was a marketing and communications firm that specialized in auto racing promotional work with Roger Penske's sponsors, and I was able to work with him and Roger.

I had some opportunity to work with Sunoco, the major Penske

sponsor, when the team was perhaps eight people, including Roger and Mark Donohue. Through the Sunoco association, I was able to connect with Roger and the team just as he started to expand, in 1969. Roger had his Chevrolet dealership in Philadelphia, the racing team in Newtown Square, and he was in the process of buying the truck-leasing firm in Reading, Pennsylvania.

Behind the dealership, he also had a racing tire distributorship, which became Competition Tire East, which at the time was selling Firestone tires—this was the time when Goodyear had first made the decision to get into Indy car racing, and Roger was then able to get the Goodyear distributorship. Roger is marvelous at being able to put together relationships like that. Due to the good job that they did, Goodyear later gave Roger the 10 Midwestern states, too. We finally set up an in-house agency for dealing with the racing sponsors, the media, and Roger's companies, which we called Penske Communications. I was the one-man band. My biggest asset was that I knew how to type."

DAN LUGINBUHL

The job description, as it came to be defined, was for me to be Roger's liaison for the Penske Performance line at Sears, help him with the relationships and paperwork for his personal endorsements, and then work at the races. He hired Dan, too, who was the company's PR guy, or as Roger called him at the time, his Communications Director. When Roger hired him, Dan was a marketing and communications expert for a company called Professionals in Motion in Ohio. I wanted to think more about the job, but Roger wanted an answer. He repeated that he'd make it worthwhile for me financially, give me a company car and an expense account. I was inclined to say yes but when the issue of Reading came up again, I asked him to consider letting me work for him but stay in Saint Louis instead. Still no deal.

It's not that I thought there was anything wrong with Reading. It's actually a historic little city in the mountains of eastern Pennsylvania founded by the sons of William Penn. Pretty brick and frame row houses are everywhere. The dominating geographic feature is a mountain almost right in the middle of it, with a beautiful overlook and a very steep street where the Duryea brothers used to test the cars they built in Reading early in the 20th century. The Fleetwood body company, later part of General Motors, was founded in the town of the same name right next to Reading. It had a racing history, and in the 1970s, the dirt track at the Reading Fairgrounds was one of the most famous speedways in the country. If you were a party animal, Reading, back then, was supposed to have more bars per capita than any other city in the United States. But I needed to keep my home base in St. Louis for my family's sake.

I went on with my job and pretty much forgot about working with Roger, until the phone rang at home several weeks later, at around 10 o'clock at night. It was Roger. "You know, I've been thinking about this. Saint Louis is the center of the country, and you're going to be traveling a lot anyway, so what if I told you that you could have the job and still live in Saint Louis?" The next sentence, basically, covered when I'd be starting, which he wanted me to do the next day. That was impossible, so we made it 10 days. And that was it. I was with Roger. Erle Keney wasn't happy about it, but he was a gentleman. My first day as an actual Penske employee was June 30, 1971.

I went to Reading, where a lot of Roger's operations, including the race team, were based. The biggest entities of what constituted Penske Corporation at the time were Penske Chevrolet in Philadelphia and Penske-Waterbor Truck Leasing, which he had just purchased. The leasing company was based in Reading and had a lot of land and buildings around the area, so Roger just moved his headquarters there. Roger did that several times. When he bought Detroit Diesel from General Motors, he moved the headquarters of Penske Corporation from Red Bank, New Jersey, to Detroit.

In Reading, I had an interview in front of some of the Penske corporate officers and met Dan for the first time. Roger said, "Okay. I know you're a self-starter, so here are your parameters. Here's your budget. This is what you can do. You know more about the business than I'll ever know. So just get going."

> " *Roger Penske talks all the time about the importance of human capital, and he was able to identify it in Don. He was the ultimate car guy. He knew what he was talking about, and as a result, was very effectively able to communicate with the entire Sears organization from the top down. We would put together seminars on the Penske Performance products on a market-to-market basis. It was a two-step deal: We had to sell the automotive department managers, and once we got their blessing, they'd bring in the shop guys and Don would do a demonstration with the products. He was amazingly good at it. Don could tune up anything."*

DAN LUGINBUHL

Despite this being relatively early in the chronology of Penske Corporation, Roger was already doing what he does best. He had a lot of really strong people lined up. One of them was his top executive offi-

cer, Walt Czarnecki. Another was Karl Kainhofer, who started as Roger's chief racing mechanic during Roger's driving days, was later crew chief for Mark Donohue and then built the Indy teams' engines. Of course, Dan was on board. I also came to meet another guy who was instrumental in Roger's success for many years, Jay Signore. Jay went on to manage the International Race of Champions (IROC) series for us, which was a match race among world-class drivers in identically prepared cars, starting with the Porsche 911.

Left: Dan Luginbuhl and I became Roger's dynamic duo. Dan and I were practically welded together, did good work, and had fun on the road. (David Chobat Photo)

Right: I've been privileged to work with some very good people at Penske. Jay Signore is one of the best, and Jay and I remain good friends to this day. (Don Miller Collection)

> *In the very early days, I drove a '37 Ford coupe with a flathead at Wall Stadium, the oval track on the New Jersey shore. I switched to sports cars because the officials at Wall Stadium at the time wouldn't let my wife in the pits. Plus, she had an Alfa Romeo when I married her. I knew Mark Donohue because we used to race together. I drove an Elva Courier with an MG transmission and an Austin-Healey rear end. Mark also drove an Elva Courier and we became very close.*
>
> *I started helping out Roger when he was running his offshore powerboat team when they had the Benihana Grand Prix off Point Pleasant. Roger was the throttle man, I was the mechanic-navigator and Jerry Riegel was the helmsman; these powerboats had three-man crews. Ours was a 40-foot Cigarette, with two 400-cubic-inch big-block Chevrolets, fuel injected. I was driving the truck, doing the mechanical work, first here, and then I went to Reading where we'd pull the engines out and ship them to Mercury Marine in Fond du Lac, Wisconsin. We would put the engines back in at the Reading shops and then my wife Barb and I would drive the truck, all the way to California for the Marina del Rey race and the San Francisco race. Roger wanted me to come to work for him, and*

even though I'd been teaching technical high school in New Jersey, I agreed to do it. I think our only winning race was the 1977 Benihana Grand Prix, and then we sold the boats. After that, I helped Don to get Rusty Wallace going with our stock car."

JAY SIGNORE
Former president, International Race of Champions
Point Pleasant, New Jersey

The Trans-Am and Can-Am teams were based in Reading, in the big brick industrial building so many people have seen right along the Schuylkill River. So was the Indy car team, although it was still in its infancy. The very first race I ever went to, as an official Penske Racing employee was the 1972 Indianapolis 500. Mark won it, but it wasn't easy on any of us. Gary Bettenhausen, Mark's teammate, led 138 laps. I actually knew Gary a lot better than I knew Mark because he was originally from the Chicago area. (Gary went on to have that very bad accident in his dirt car in Syracuse around 1975, when he was still our team driver, even though Roger had asked him not to do any Sprint car or dirt racing.)

At some point, late in the Indy race, Gary's car developed a crack in its overflow tank and the coolant started steaming out of it. His turbocharged Offy finally overheated and Gary fell out. It was shock therapy for us as a team. The McLarens we ran at Penske Racing were very good cars, and we all figured that Gary had everyone covered for the win. We'd had both our cars in the top five all day.

Mark's win at Indianapolis was a win for the team, even with Gary's misfortune. From then on, Roger said I had to come to all the races, joking that maybe I brought the team good fortune.

We moved the Penske Products business ahead, building up Roger's relationship with Sears and the other sponsors. Before long, every major Sears retail store had a performance line. We had a big warehouse in Saint Louis at National Engines' headquarters. We had oscilloscopes, vacuum gauges, compression gauges, oil filters, fuel filters, and a line of heavy-duty shocks, all the equipment you would use in a home tune-up, or even if you were a short-budget gas station.

One day, we were sitting together at one of the race tracks, and Roger said, "We should really capitalize on some of the things that you're doing. I've got all these endorsements, so why don't we put something together where we can go to the race tracks and sell more products? Why not create a souvenir line for Penske Racing?"

In the world of professional racing during the early 1970s, to say nothing of local racing, this kind of proposal was unknown. But I thought about it. I learned that we had an old trailer we'd gotten from

In the early 1970s, Roger was in the process of laying the foundation for a dynamic business empire and one of the world's most successful racing teams. (Don Miller Collection)

Carroll Shelby. The guy who was running the tire company for Roger at the time, Norman Ahn, was one of the original mechanics on the Trans-Am team and also a very good businessman. They had used this trailer to haul tires around once in a while, and when I told Norman about Roger's merchandising idea, he said I should just go ahead and use it. It was a two-axle box trailer, 18 or 20 feet long, pulled by a pickup truck. We figured out that with a trailer to take to the races we could come up with our own line, so we came out first with two Penske Racing T-shirts, one with a picture of the Indy car on it, one with the Can-Am car. Soon, we also had posters, driver cards, and a bunch of other small items.

People were dumbfounded when they saw it. I think the first race we went to was a sports car event at Road America in Wisconsin. We sold that trailer empty. Besides Sears, our other sponsors at the time included Sunoco and Moog, the suspension parts company. After we did so unexpectedly well at Elkhart Lake, we realized immediately that we had to expand the product line. Rolling into 1973, we continued to grow both our businesses and split them. The hard parts that were being marketed through Sears became Penske Products, and the souvenirs and related goods became Penske Equipment. We separated them to keep the whole operation from becoming unwieldy. Both individual entities continued to grow.

Personally, I was interested in Indy car racing, and I was very interested in the Can-Am side, given that we were kicking everybody's butt with Mark driving the turbocharged Porsche 917-30. That German monster had about 1,000 horsepower, probably 200 more than everything else. At the same time, I also had a growing friendship with stock car driver Bobby Allison. Roger had first talked to him when Bobby came out to California to run in a Can-Am event on a NASCAR off-weekend. From that point, I told Roger that he had to do something with the guy. Bobby had showed up cold at a Can-Am race at Riverside, got into a car that was ordinarily driven by Jackie Oliver—a legitimate world-class racing driver—and embarrassed him by qualifying several seconds a lap quicker. Roger talked to Bobby a couple of times after that, and sure enough, in April 1973, he called me and said, "Hey, we're going to put your buddy Allison in an Indy car." I couldn't believe it.

In many ways, the month of May in 1973 was disastrous. A lot of guys got hurt or killed at Indy. Art Pollard was killed in a practice crash as lap speeds edged 200 mph. On the initial start, there was that huge, fiery crash triggered by Salt Walther. Swede Savage had a horrifying wreck in turn four right after making a pit stop. It was unbelievably violent. He lost it coming through turn four, hit the inside wall and the car absolutely disintegrated, virtually exploded in a monstrous fireball. Moments later, one of the crewmen was struck by a fire truck on pit road. The crewman died instantly and Swede died from his injuries about a month later. Pat was up in the suite overlooking the race right above the green-flag pileup and Savage's fatal crash, and saw it all. She was appalled. She said, basically, "I don't want to go to any more races. I don't want our kids to see this. I don't want you being involved in this anymore." I answered, or tried to answer, "Pat, sometimes this stuff happens. It can happen on a street corner. At least this is controlled."

 It was a mess. It was after that race that Judy Allison said to Bobby, 'Please, no more Indy cars.' It was just too much carnage, just horrible."

PAT MILLER

On top of all this, Bobby lost the engine after completing only one lap of his rookie race. So did Mark at the halfway point. Gary Bettenhausen did manage a fifth in our third car, but because of rain, it took three days to complete the race, or more correctly, to mercifully stop it when it rained again on the third day after 332 miles had been run.

We loaded up, headed back to Reading and moved on. We were already well into a project that Roger had begun the previous year when he decided he was going to field a team in the NASCAR Winston Cup Series. Roger already had a partnership with American Motors, and Mark had won the 1971 Trans-Am championship for us in an AMC Javelin. The eligible AMC mid-size car for NASCAR in 1973 was the Matador hardtop. At Penske, we called it the Kenosha Canoe, because it was the ugliest car you'd ever seen, a huge, square thing with this strange, forward-curving C-pillar. When I learned the plan, I told Roger, "I don't know how you're going to do it," but he was confident: "Don't worry, we'll get it all lightened up," and so forth.

I'll say this: Events would prove that Roger was dead right and I was dead wrong. At that point in time, even though I had experience with what the Penske organization could do with the Trans-Am cars, for instance, I was skeptical. That was true even though I knew the thing had a very good engine it, a 366-cubic-inch version of the AMC engine we'd run in the Javelins, built on a stronger 401 block. Good, but not against things like big-block Chevys and Hemis that were still standard in NASCAR. As built by Penske, the Matador had excellent brakes—I bet a lot of people still don't know that our Matador was

The Kenosha Canoe may have been strange to look at but it was a bullet, due in large part to having Mark Donohue in the driver's seat. (Penske Corporation Collection)

the first car in NASCAR with four-wheel discs, which Mark and Don Cox had developed. I was wondering what we were going to do with it against people like Bobby and Richard Petty, but Mark was adamant: "Don't worry about it. With these brakes, we're going to clean their clocks."

Mark, like Roger, was also right. We took the Matador to its first race, the 1973 season's opening event at Riverside, and he just smoked them. Watching Mark drive that car was like seeing an artist at work, an acclaimed violinist or ballet dancer. He was on a lap by himself at the finish. We weren't running all the NASCAR races, and Dave Marcis, who came south from the Modified and Late Model wars of Wisconsin, filled in for us in the ones we did run when they conflicted with Mark's other driving commitments. By the time we got back from Indianapolis in 1973, we had learned that AMC was planning to unveil a radically different, fastback Matador hardtop as a 1974 model. This was the really wild-looking Matador of the mid-Seventies, whose other big visual features were its big tunneled headlights. I took one look at the pre-production prototypes that AMC showed us and thought, whoa, this is going to be a hot rod.

We went from Roger's dealerships in Detroit up to Kenosha to have a look at them. Randy Wittine, who was a wonderful artist and still is, drafted a super neat paint job. Since Mark had to come off the NASCAR program for us to focus on Indy and Can-Am, Gary Bettenhausen drove it in the 1974 opener, again at Riverside, then at Daytona and Atlanta, all decent finishes. Gary took to it immediately, even though the bulk of his history is in open-wheel cars. He was a legendary Sprint car driver in USAC and one half of the fabled Larry and Gary show of the early 1970s with Larry Dickson. Roger discovered him and plucked him from those ranks, so I can't take credit for that smart move.

Gary got the Matador ride and we went to a couple of tests with him. We were actively planning a huge promotion about the upcoming race at Talladega. Sears was going to showcase the Penske products and their sponsorship of our Matador in all of its Alabama stores. I told Bobby Allison we were going to be right there in Birmingham, so we could hang out at his house and shop in Hueytown. I'd been put in charge of our end of the Sears promotion and at the same time, I was going to work with the team on pit road Sunday. This was in May. That's dangerous in Alabama; the risk of violent weather is constant. At the race track, while we set up our pit equipment, the sky was turning black. People were talking about a storm that was coming. They weren't kidding.

10

May 5, 1974

MOST OF THE TIME, rain is just something you deal with, or work around, if you're in racing. The morning of the 1974 Winston 500 at Talladega was gloomy and dank. The 500, incidentally, had been shortened to 450 miles that year as part of NASCAR's response to the first energy crisis, but even with fewer miles, it was constantly under threat from weather. No big deal, right? We set up in the pits, they lined up the cars, and got in the pace laps and let them go, as it continued getting darker and mistier. David Pearson had won the pole for the Wood Brothers, and Gary Bettenhausen in the Matador started up front for us, alongside Pearson. Once underway, it was turning into a good race, despite showers over various parts of the gigantic track. Pearson traded the lead with Bobby Allison, who was in his own Chevrolet, and with Gary in our Matador. Gary was doing great, and actually led the race four different times by the halfway point. Obviously, we were constantly watching the sky, even though Gary was doing so well that everyone's head was spinning. He'd had some starts in USAC stock cars, but nothing of consequence like this. Then, finally, with Gary running hard in the top five, it really started to rain.

Right from the start, when he first hired me, Roger had said he wanted me to come to the races, and when I was there, I worked with the team. In that respect, this Sunday at Talladega was no different from others. My assignment on pit road, years before teams hired specialized people to do these tasks, was to fit the catch can during pit stops. As the race unfolded, Roger, who was there at Talladega, also in part for the Sears promotion, was keeping an eye on the weather like anyone else. On pit road, he told me, "We're just going to do the best we can, and if it rains, it rains. But it might rain the whole thing out, so we need to be leading." Just past halfway, it rained hard. Officials stopped the racing to dry the track, or semi-dry it, but they didn't dry pit road. They had guys out there with big push brooms and stuff like that, trying to move the water aside, but that was pretty much it.

After a while, the green came back out. The rule then in NASCAR was that you couldn't pit under a red flag, meaning that you had to wait until the race officially resumed to do your pit work. Also, there were absolutely no speed limits on pit road, something that didn't come along for close to 20 years. At Talladega, you'd be racing in traffic at something like 195 mph, and even though you started slowing down early to pit, you'd still be doing 100 or 120 mph when you entered the top of the pits. As we stood ready for Gary to come in, it was my turn to handle the catch can, Nick Ollila was handling the fuel cans, and the rest of the guys had the tires and jack. Gary came down pit road on lap 105 of the 160 or so that would make up the reduced race length. I could see that the first couple of cars that came in just before he did were all slipping and sliding on the wetness of pit road. As Gary came to a stop, I had my back to the rest of the approaching cars while we all went over the wall and I fitted the catch can to the fuel overflow vent. I couldn't see any of the incoming traffic.

All I can remember today is that we were doing the pit stop when suddenly I heard this loud "sssshhhh." And then the lights went out.

Later, I found out what happened: A driver named Grant Adcox had come down pit road in the Adcox Chevrolet doing at least 100 mph. He lost control of the car, spun around, and slammed into our Matador, while it was jacked up and we were still doing the pit stop. The impact caught me between both race cars and the pit wall and forced me into the wall. I was pinned between the two cars' bumpers when they crashed together at 100 mph. It just about cut me in half. The impact threw a couple of guys completely over the wall. One of them went flying up in the air, came down on the toolbox and broke his arm. In total, eight guys were hurt. Really a bad, bad wreck. But as Bobby Allison said later, "Well, it killed you, Miller, but you lived."

> *I was working with Harry Hyde on the 71 car, the K&K Dodge. Dave Marcis had just made a pit stop for us after the rain delay. Of course, they didn't pay attention to pit road, because the track was dry. Back then, you could come into the pits at 200 mph if you wanted to. I don't want to ever blame Grant Adcox for what happened next, and I know Don doesn't either, which is why I'm saying all this. We managed to get our own car off pit road, because otherwise, Grant would have hit it, because he slid right through our pit.*

Left: Buddy Parrott, who was a member of Harry Hyde's crew, formed a tourniquet with his belt and saved my life. (David Chobat Photo)

Right: The Talladega accident scene, an event that reshaped my life. (Dozier Mobley Photo)

At this moment, I didn't know Don Miller from anybody. When I looked up a second later, there were people scattered, and people were under the car because it had been knocked off the jack. I saw Don lying by the pit wall, and started screaming for someone to help me. I finally took my belt off and used it to apply a tourniquet and hold it. I worked in a glass company for nine years. When a piece of glass falls, I've seen people get hit and the glass just lays their arm right open, so that was something I knew how to do.

Don was in terrible pain. I think at one point, he was hollering at me, 'Let me die. Let me die.' Instead of seconds or minutes, it seemed like days before the rescue guys got there. Later, the doctor said that if I hadn't applied the tourniquet, he would have bled to death right there."

BUDDY PARROTT
Retired NASCAR crew chief
Cornelius, North Carolina

When the injuries were tallied, it turned out that the accident had just about cut my right leg off, crushed the other one, broken my back, and broken my pelvis in three spots. The impact was so tremendous and sudden that I closed my jaw hard enough to shatter it and crack a lot of my teeth. Oh, my God, I was a mess. When I regained consciousness, I was on the ground, and I remember that Roger was standing over me, looking down. He told me, "Don, don't try to move. You're hurt real bad." But I was conscious, and I could talk to him, so I said, "I know I'm hurt. Just help me stand up." He stopped me, saying, "You can't stand up. I don't want you to even look down. Your leg is torn almost completely off your body."

Buddy Parrott came running, jumped over the pit wall. I glanced around me and noticed that I was between the cars, because after they'd hit, the momentum pushed them farther down pit road. I also noticed that I was lying in a puddle. Of blood. Roger was in control, crystal clear, and kept telling me not to move. Buddy was there, and I can remember him looking down at me and saying, "We've got to make a tourniquet." He was a crew member on the car that was pitted right behind us, whose crew chief was Harry Hyde. He had the sense to take his belt off and make a tourniquet for my leg out of it, and thus kept me from bleeding to death right there. I didn't realize it at the time, but I also had a huge hole ripped in my ass, from where the rear corner of Adcox's car had torn it wide open. This huge laceration in my rear was probably 11 inches long, and that was where most of the blood was coming from, not so much from my leg because the main arteries in it had probably already snapped shut from shock. Even though the scene was total chaos, Roger immediately got hold of the track crew, got the lock off the gate in the fence, and had an ambulance brought right into the pits. They got me loaded into the ambulance, but the guys on the ambulance crew weren't doctors, and didn't really know about major injuries like mine, so they took me to

The Chicago Sun-Times *newspaper carried this report of the accident at Talladega. (Don Miller Collection)*

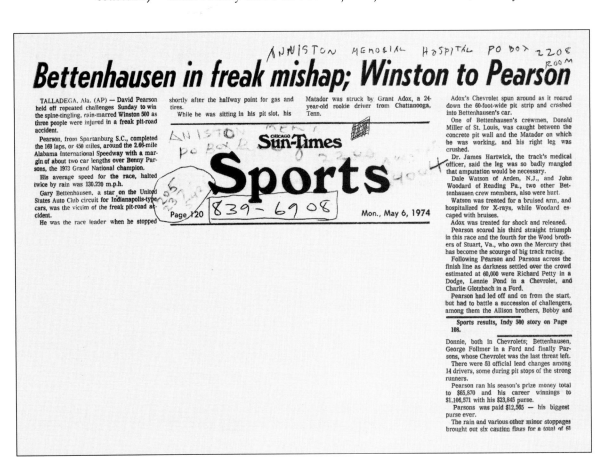

Bettenhausen in freak mishap; Winston to Pearson

ANNISTON MEMORIAL HOSPITAL PO BOX 2208 ROOM

ANNISTON MEARY PO BOX 2 22018 AM 400X

839-6908

CHICAGO Sun-Times

Sports

Page 120   Mon., May 6, 1974

TALLADEGA, Ala. (AP) — David Pearson held off repeated challenges Sunday to win the spine-tingling, rain-marred Winston 500 as three people were injured in a freak pit-road accident.

Pearson, from Spartanburg S.C., completed the 169 laps, or 450 miles, around the 2.66-mile Alabama International Speedway with a margin of about two car lengths over Benny Parsons, the 1973 Grand National champion.

His average speed for the race, halted twice by rain was 130.220 m.p.h.

Gary Bettenhausen, a star on the United States Auto Club circuit for Indianapolis-type cars, was the victim of the freak pit-road accident.

He was the race leader when he stopped shortly after the halfway point for gas and tires.

While he was sitting in his pit slot, his Matador was struck by Grant Adox, a 24-year-old rookie driver from Chattanooga, Tenn.

Adox's Chevrolet spun around as it roared down the 60-foot-wide pit strip and crashed into Bettenhausen's car.

One of Bettenhausen's crewmen, Donald Miller of St. Louis, was caught between the concrete pit wall and the Matador on which he was working, and his right leg was crushed.

Dr. James Hartwick, the track's medical officer, said the leg was so badly mangled that amputation would be necessary.

Dale Watson of Arden, N.J., and John Woodard of Reading Pa., two other Bettenhausen crew members, also were hurt.

Watson was treated for a bruised arm, and hospitalized for X-rays, while Woodard escaped with bruises.

Adox was treated for shock and released.

Pearson scored his third straight triumph in this race and the fourth for the Wood brothers of Stuart, Va., who own the Mercury that has become the scourge of big track racing.

Following Pearson and Parsons across the finish line as darkness settled over the crowd estimated at 60,000 were Richard Petty in a Dodge, Lennie Pond in a Chevrolet, and Charlie Glotzbach in a Ford.

Pearson had led off and on from the start, but had to battle a succession of challengers, among them the Allison brothers, Bobby and

---

Sports results, Indy 500 story on Page 108.

Donnie, both in Chevrolets; Bettenhausen, George Follmer in a Ford and finally Parsons, whose Chevrolet was the last threat left.

There were 53 official lead changes among 14 drivers, some during pit stops of the strong runners.

Pearson ran his season's prize money total to $65,670 and his career winnings to $1,106,571 with his $23,845 purse.

Parsons was paid $12,565 — his biggest purse ever.

The rain and various other minor stoppages brought out six caution flags for a total of 61

the Talladega infield hospital. I remember fading in and out, and telling myself, "This is not going to be good. It's not going to be good."

Roger was in the midst of all this, getting everybody organized. He saved my life that day, and I'll never forget it. At the infield hospital, he was asking the personnel there, "What can you do for him? What can you do?" The doctor or nurse said, "We're giving him blood," but I also remember him saying, "I don't think he's going to make it." And Roger snapped, "I don't want to hear it. I'm not hearing that. Get that ambulance back over here. Get him to the nearest hospital." Roger was actually yelling, something he ordinarily doesn't do. When the ambulance returned, he told the driver, "Get this guy in there right now. We're going to Anniston."

> " On that day, Mark Donohue and I were at the Philadelphia airport, waiting for a plane to go to Indianapolis, where practice was supposed to start the next day. This was before cell phones, so while we were waiting for the plane, I went to a pay phone to call the press room at Talladega and find out how we were doing. Somebody picked up and said there had been a rain delay, but they'd got going again, and then there had been a hell of an accident in the pits. He painted a picture that it had been really been a disaster, which it was.
>
> I couldn't help thinking that if I'd been there at Talladega, it could have been me. NASCAR had had a problem with a couple of fires in the pits from fuel sloshing out of the tanks through the overflow pipe, so they instituted this catch can rule. It's my understanding that originally, they had looked around for somebody to hold this catch can, and it was originally supposed to be Roger's pilot, but they'd sent him off to the airport to change a flight plan or something. So then, Don was standing there, and being the great racer that he is, said, 'I'll do that.'"
>
> **DAN LUGINBUHL**

If you've never been to Talladega, let me explain where it is. The speedway is right off Interstate 20, but it's in the countryside about halfway between Anniston, the nearest city of any real size, and a smaller town, Pell City. In early 1974, it was even more remote, and there was no such thing then as having a medevac or rescue helicopter on standby at the track during a race. No track had that back then. So off we went in the ambulance, and the pain was excruciating, because the thing was just bouncing around on the track access roads. I faded out again, and I can recall coming to, and seeing Roger there next to me, on the bench in the rear of the ambulance. Dale Watson from our team was in the ambulance, too, for the ride to the hospital, and pretty out of it. He had been thrown over the hood of the car and landed on pit road ahead of the two cars. I learned later that the others on the pit stop crew—John Woodard, Frog Fagan, Randy Wattine, and Nick Ollila—had all experienced varying degrees of bruises and broken bones, although miraculously none very seriously other than John, who ended up with a crushed foot and broken ankle.

We finally get out of the track in the ambulance, onto the superhighway, and start heading east to Anniston, which is about 25 miles. The ambulance is wobbling all over the place. Roger's telling me, "Don't worry, we're going as fast as we can," and I answered, "Don't worry? This guy's going to kill us all before we get to the hospital."

We finally made it to Anniston and the hospital, without wrecking the ambulance. It turned out to be the luckiest day of my life, because on duty in the emergency room, was a doctor named Taylor. He was a real no-nonsense emergency trauma surgeon. He stood over me, as if I couldn't hear him, and said to Roger, "You know, this is going to be real iffy. But if we get on it right now, I think we can save him." Roger said back, "You've *got* to save him. This guy's strong. He'll make it." The nurses had been pouring blood into me from the minute they wheeled me into the emergency room, and they took me straight in to surgery. I don't remember this, of course, but I learned later on that Roger got his wife Kathy to call Pat, who was back in Saint Louis, and tell her that I was hurt and hurt really bad. He sent the Penske jet there, and flew Pat to Anniston. Kathy flew in from Detroit.

> *The phone rang and it was Kathy Penske. It was after 5 o'clock, we'd just gotten back from a piano recital and we were just sitting down to eat dinner. I was expecting Don to call. Back in 1974, there was nothing televised and you couldn't get anything on the radio either.*
>
> *Kathy said Don had been working in the pits that day, that there had been an accident and that Don had hurt his leg. Hearing this, I'm thinking that I'll call Mary next door, have her watch the kids, pick up Don at the race track and drive him back to Saint Louis. Kathy said Roger would call me back with details. She didn't say anything more. When Roger called back, he said he was sending the airplane for me. He told me where to meet it, and exactly what time. I called my mother and told her to get on an airplane and come to Saint Louis to watch the girls, and called Don's mother, who was a nurse, and asked her to meet me in Alabama. My neighbor drove me to Lambert Field.*
>
> *I was the only passenger. Nobody said a word to me. We landed, and Roger was there to pick me up. Roger is not a chit-chatter. He*

doesn't sit around talking to you about the weather. He only talks to you when he has something to say. But he chattered all the way to the hospital, and he told me it was the right leg. At the hospital, they started to tell me everything."

PAT MILLER

I guess that first surgery lasted five or six hours. At first, they were going to try and save my right leg. When I came to a day or two later, Doctor Taylor told me, "I don't think this thing's going to take, but we're going to try." Perhaps four or five days passed after that, which was when they told me the leg had developed gangrene because it wasn't getting fed properly by my circulatory system, and they were going to have to take it off. Doctor Taylor told me, "You're not going to have a foot anyway, so we may as well go this way." I didn't argue with that ruling. The leg was crushed. The bones and blood vessels were destroyed. The leg was dying from not being able to get enough blood and oxygen to survive. So they took it off right below the knee.

" Doctor Taylor explained to me that you couldn't build up tissue from nothing, so it was probably healthier overall to amputate the leg. You're subject to so much infection that you really don't want to do otherwise. Don and I had to make the decision quickly. We looked at each other, and he said, 'Get rid of it. We don't need it. Everything will be fine.' That's the kind of confidence he gives off."

PAT MILLER

Before the race started, I had put my chronograph watch into my uniform pants pocket to keep it from getting knocked off my wrist and lost or broken. When I got hit, the impact drove that watch completely through my right femur and took out one inch of bone. So they pulled that bone together and put some steel plates on either side of the break, and then screwed them together. They told me, "You're going to be one inch shorter on the right-hand side than you are on the left-hand side, but the artificial leg they're going to make for you will make up for the difference."

Taken in total, I was completely broken up. There was the huge gouge in my ass, which I knew about by then. My pelvis was broken apart, across the back, and those pieces had to be bolted together surgically. They said that all the other injuries were comparatively superficial, and they could be repaired. But they remained worried about my leg. Really worried. The doctors told me, "If that leg doesn't start to heal soon, we're going to have to take it off right below your hip."

I'd never been injured anywhere near that seriously before in my life. When I was a kid in Chicago, I briefly owned a Harley 45 (after my first short episode with the Vincent Black Shadow), and as with a lot of people who own motorcycles, it cost me a few broken bones. I came smoking around a corner and lost it. The bike went its own way while I slid head-on into a fire hydrant and broke four ribs. So this, by comparison, was the big one. And then Roger said, "They've done a wonderful job with you here in Anniston, but we've got to get you to a big hospital that really specializes in these types of injuries."

Roger had me put aboard the company jet, and he flew me to Barnes Hospital in Saint Louis, which is a huge hospital. So big, in fact, that I had to go through a lot of useless malarkey when they admitted me. They told me I had to see a psychiatrist, etc., etc., and I was telling them back that I just want to get out of there. I got so mad that one time, I lost my temper and told them, "Get out of this room or I'm going to take this goddamn oxygen machine and throw it through the window. You're driving me nuts. I'm going to be fine. There's nothing wrong with me except you people."

Then they told me they wanted to take the rest of my leg off. When he heard that, Roger reached out for Doctor Taylor back at the hospital in Anniston. Dr. Taylor consulted with the Barnes doctors and told them, "There's no reason to take it off. He's going to have a short stump, and he's going to struggle with it the rest of his life, but he'll make it." The internal bleeding had long since stopped. My jaw was broken, and my teeth were cracked. Several of them were bolted together and covered in porcelain. I have two teeth that are still being held together with those original bolts and screws.

> " The other doctor said, 'We need to get rid of this.' Donald said no. He needed his knee for flexibility, to do the work he likes to do—like getting under a car. The pain medication was to be distributed every four hours. They had just planed his bone and he was going through the roof. That's the procedure where they clean splinters and other broken pieces off the bone. Some of them had been working their way out of his butt, following his blood. They had to take the ragged edges off the bone. It had to be done. We all left the room and I drove back home, and Don called me and said in a very calm voice, 'Everything's going to be just fine.' I found out the next morning that when he told me that, he was being evaluated by a psychiatrist. It was after he threatened to throw the breathing machine out the window. I had three young children and a husband in the psych ward. I'm thinking, 'Maybe I should renew my beautician's license.'"

PAT MILLER

There's one part of the story about my accident at Talladega and subsequent recovery that I've never spoken about publicly until now. It's about Benny Parsons and how much he did, under everybody's radar except for his and mine, to make sure that I didn't lose my focus and simply give up after I got hurt. In 1974, Benny was the reigning Winston Cup champion. I didn't know him very well—we'd met a couple of times. But when I was in the hospital in Anniston, he started to call me and to send encouraging notes that he'd written personally.

One day, he stopped in at the Anniston hospital to see me. We talked about things in general, and then he told me that while a terrible thing had happened, I had to work hard to try and get over it, to overcome it all.

"You're going to have to make some changes in life, and learn how to adapt to certain things, get used to being on crutches for a while. But this is also an opportunity for you, believe it or not. Since you have to make so many other changes, this is a chance to restart your life, go forward with a different attitude, and be better at a variety of things than you were in the past. It's up to you alone to make that decision to move ahead."

Benny Parsons visited me at the hospital in Anniston, Alabama. He left me with a new life direction. (Don Hunter/ Smyle Media)

I was grievously injured and somewhat depressed when Benny walked into my hospital room. What he had to say, and the way in which he chose to say it, helped me a great deal. Benny's gone now. We lost him to cancer in 2007. One thing you need to know about Benny is that he was a deep thinker. I know a lot of people may not realize that because of his sunny personality and because Benny always made fun of himself, as he did with his Buffet Benny persona on TV. Later in life, he and I spent a lot of time together, just talking about life and what you have to do to make it work. Benny had been sick with lung cancer but had been told that the surgeons had got it all. Not long after that, we saw each other, and he told me, "Well, I guess they didn't get it all. It's back."

Our family is still close to Benny's widow Terri, who operates their vineyard and winery, Rendezvous Ridge.

Eleven or 12 weeks passed before I was well enough to leave the hospital. Roger sent me to Reading, Pennsylvania, to the Reading Rehabilitation Hospital, where he knew all the people. Norman Ahn from the tire company and Lemar Heydt, the president of the truck leasing company and a wonderful man, watched over me continuously while I was there. The doctors told me I'd have to resign myself to the fact that I'd never walk again without a mechanical aid, a walker or some other thing. An artificial leg was going to just be something to fill out my pants leg, they told me. I had been in the Reading hospital for a week when the second Talladega race date of 1974 came up, the August race. By this time, Gary Bettenhausen had gotten seriously injured in a USAC dirt car race on the mile at Syracuse, New York, so Bobby Allison was driving our Matador. Without me knowing at first, Bobby talked Roger into letting me come to Talladega.

> " *I am sure the events of that terrible day are well documented by others and probably a lot more accurately than my recollections. I had asked Don to handle the catch can for the pit stops so unfortunately that made him vulnerable when Grant Adcox spun. I knew that Don had been severely injured, as were other members of the team. My first instinctive response was to do what was necessary to make sure they were properly taken care of and, in Don's extreme case, to keep him going. It was truly a life-altering experience for all of us involved. I cannot imagine what Don went through at that moment and in the subsequent days. The word that keeps coming back to me when I think of those events is perseverance. Don showed it in so many ways then and has continued to do so for the rest of his life. He is blessed, too, with Pat and the girls whose lives were turned so inside out by what happened but who hung in and remained loving and supportive.*"

ROGER S. PENSKE
Chairman and CEO of Penske Corporation
Bloomfield Hills, Michigan

I had no leg. Bobby and Roger asked me if I really wanted to go, if I could deal with it. I told them, "Sure I can deal with it. I want to go back there. I don't want to be a cripple. I want to be the best I can be." So they flew me down there and took me to the race track. One of the people who came up with the idea to bring me to the track was Don Naman, the president and general manager of Talladega. He and his wife, along with the Allisons and Benny Parsons, had been really instrumental in my care when I was in the hospital in Anniston

I guess the track had gotten a load of letters and telegrams since I'd been hurt. So Don Naman says, "These people really want to know you, so if you don't mind, we want to introduce you before the race starts." This would be during the pre-race ceremonies on the stage they set up in the tri-oval. I told him that I was on crutches and not real good at navigating stairs, which was when Bobby chipped in, "Don't worry. Me and Buddy Baker will get you up there." And they did. Being up there on that stage at Talladega and hearing that crowd did more for my morale than anything else. I realized then, "Wow, nobody's forgotten about this."

The experience made me go back to Reading with renewed vigor and interest in getting better. I really worked hard, day and night. I burst my stump open two or three times; forcing myself to walk on it

Top: The #12 Matador at speed at Pocono Raceway near the close of the season. (Don Miller Collection)

Left: Roger and Bobby took me to the fall Talladega race as part of my recovery program. (Don Miller Collection)

no matter how bad it hurt. The rehabilitation people had to build me a leg that was actually longer than my regular leg. The big problem was the stump, or rather the short distance between where it ends and the start of my artificial foot. That length is what gives you stability when you walk. To compensate, you learn to walk differently. They told me, you're going to walk goofy all your life." I responded, "No I'm not. I'm going to walk how every normal human being walks." And I did it. It took therapy, lots of practice, and a determination to walk that way. I wanted to do it.

My son-in-law is a spinal surgeon, a good one, one of the people who created the artificial spinal disc. He used to use me as a case study in spinal injuries, because when you hear somebody casually say, "Aw, he broke his back," they can look at me. I snapped my head so hard from the impact of the accident that he said it's amazing I can hold my head up. That all came back to haunt me 15 years later, though. I had to have some more major surgeries to relieve the pressure on my spinal cord, and I couldn't use either of my hands for a while. I had a couple of more operations while I was in Pennsylvania, too, minor ones. Wire kept coming out of my leg. It came in through my butt when I was hit and would work its way through the leg, and come out the side of it or by my knee. Wiring off one of the cars, I guess. I kept passing paint chips, too, and little pieces of metal. The edema would drive it outward and force it right through the skin. Infections, too. But by Christmas 1974, I was walking again.

The pain was never gone. It's still here. I have phantom pain from the missing part of my leg probably three or four times a year. When it happens, you would swear to God that you still had a foot and somebody was pounding a nail through it. From time to time, I get bruises on the stump or blisters, from abusing it too much or carrying around heavy things like cylinder heads. I'm not supposed to carry anything heavy, but I do it anyway, all the time. In the medical industry, the attitude sometimes is, "You're a cripple, you better get used to it, you can't do this, can't do that." My feeling is, you can do anything that you make up your mind to do.

Roger, God bless him, stuck with me through all of this, and finally told me, "What you really need is a job." He got Pat and the kids, brought them up to Reading, and put me in the race shop, even though I still didn't have a leg. I had to go to therapy for about three hours a day. The rest of the time, he had me on the telephone talking to all the people I knew from the racing industry, to get sponsorship for this new thing, IROC, that Roger had created, a racing series for superstar drivers from all over the world.

I put all the deals together, starting with the point where we switched the series from using the Porsche 911s that had raced the first year to the Camaro stock cars. Porsche said that they'd done one year of the IROC thing and they didn't want to do it again, despite Roger's pointing out that IROC had been a huge and popular success, so we went to Chevrolet. No matter what anyone says, Roger himself is still the best salesman that he has. He's such a dynamic individual, and has such an extensive record of success, that when he goes into somebody's office and tells them he can do something, they believe him. So he said to me, "We're going to do this IROC thing with Chevrolet, using this engine, with this carburetor, and this transmission. Call up the right people and get us the parts."

So, for example, I call up Bob Hedman, of Hedman Hedders. I tell him, "Look, we're building these IROC cars, and we're going to need you to build us headers to fit them, and we'll need 20 sets of them." He said, "Yeah, I'll do it, just put my name on the cars." We did all this over the telephone. I called Lakewood: They made us the bellhousings. I called Scheifer: They got us the clutches and flywheels. I told these guys that we were doing this project, and they trusted me. The tubular chassis for the race cars were built right there in Reading at the Penske shops. Or more accurately, tubular front subframes and roll cages that fitted right into a production Camaro body in white. I was also helping to get show cars on the road for our sponsors, which provided a good basis for us of what to do—and not to do—once we later began Motorsports International. That's what I was doing while I was recuperating.

Matador Racing Crew Visits

Ste. Genevieve Friday welcomed the famous Don Miller, former racing great who suffered a near-fatal injury that sidelined him, and the crew of the 1975 AMC Coca-Cola Matador prepared by Roger Penske Racing of Reading, Pennsylvania. Miller and the crew were enroute to Florida, where the Matador was slated to race in the Daytona "500" with Bobby Allison behind the wheel.

The Matador boasts a 358 cubic inch AMC V-8 engine, and is sponsored by AMC, Coca-Cola, Sears, Roebuck Co., and the GoodYear Tire and Rubber Company. The Matador has claimed the winners circle in the L. A. Times "500" on November 24 of last year, and the Winston Western "500" on January 20 of this year.

The car has won the last two consecutive NASCAR Grand Daytona "500" set for this past Sunday at Daytona Beach, Florida.

Well-known to racing enthusiasts across the nation, Don Miller (left), and the crew of the Penske Prepared 1975 Coca Cola Matador last week visited Charley Smith Motor Company here while enroute to the NASCAR Daytona "500" in Florida. Kneeling are crew members Chuck Smith and Dave Munari, and at the right is Mr. Clarence Rapp of Smith Motor Company.

> " The thing that really came through for me, with all that Don has been through from the very first time I met him until this day, is his great way with people and his great sense of humor—even under the most dire circumstances—and his ability to get people to cooperate. I clearly saw that when he was suffering his most, after he was hurt. Don never lost his sense of humor.
>
> I don't want to canonize him here, it's not Saint Don the First, and I don't want to be melodramatic. But I think that's the one thing that's carried him through, his engaging personality. Once you get past that, though, you find out that there's some substance there as relates to his understanding of automobiles, performance automobiles. That's part of what made him so effective as we built our racing company. The genesis was, to keep him occupied after he got hurt, Roger had him answering the mail from his bed. That's how the merchandise business really got started, and it turned out to be a really successful business. "

WALTER CZARNECKI

Executive Vice President, Penske Corporation
Bloomfield Hills, Michigan

When I first came back to work at Penske, I did a lot of this. We've stopped at Charley Smith AMC in Sainte Genevieve, Missouri, to show off the race car on the way to the 1975 Daytona 500. To my left are Chuck Smith and Dave Munari. (Don Miller Collection)

All through my recovery process, Dave Munari and I continued to compete in drag racing events in Illinois and Missouri. This station wagon set seven AHRA national records. We used to tell people, "Don't mess with the Wagonmasters!" (Don Miller Collection)

"Don first hired me at Penske to tow Bobby Allison's AMC Matador show car, which I had painted over the wintertime. I put a motor in it, put on big exhausts, just like a real stock car. I was in Clover, South Carolina, on the same weekend as the Rebel 500 at Darlington. We take the Matador off the trailer, and I find out I'm supposed to drive it downtown for some cul-de-sac thing they're doing in the downtown area. Going back to the plant at night after the show, I didn't know that while I was downtown they had dug a ditch about three or four feet wide, for a gas line or something, across the road leading to the plant. I'm going a little faster than I needed to be. I jumped over it in the Matador and ended going about 60 feet down an embankment.

I got a big cut over my eye, and this guy runs up and looks in, tells me I'm going to need stitches. I know there's no doctor open anywhere by this time, and I've got to get the show car either back to Saint Louis or up to Reading to fix it. So this guy tells me he's got a buddy who's a veterinarian, and he can sew my eye up. That's what happened. I loaded the car and headed for Reading, where I'd never been, pull in the Penske gate at 6 o'clock in the morning. I told Jay Signore, 'If you give me a place to work, I can fix this car.' I worked day and night, putting trick parts on the show car that were meant for the actual racing Matador. I got it together, went to the next show, and Don told me that Roger had called and offered me a job painting cars in Reading. Apparently Roger said something like, 'He's a little bit too expensive for me on the road, but I can use him in the shop.'"

DAVID MUNARI

The Penske Indy cars were there at the Reading shop, along with the stock car, which made things really busy. Bobby Allison was still

Bobby Allison brings the CAM2 Mercury in for a quick pit stop. (Penske Corporation Photo, Don Miller Collection)

our driver, and I've got to say that Bobby, Donnie and Eddie Allison were some of the most supportive people I was lucky enough to have during my recovery. Best you could ever ask for. Bobby and I had a wonderful relationship, in part, because we both loved airplanes. Bobby Allison was one of the pioneering high-hour, really expert, pilots in NASCAR, and one of the very best. Bobby was an outstanding, skillful pilot, right up until he had his terrible crash at Pocono in 1988 and nearly died. He'd been flying all over the country to short-track races and sponsor commitments for many years by 1974. Bobby knew all the guys who worked the FAA tower at Birmingham, and when I was first in the hospital, he'd bring his twin-engine Piper Aerostar in real low over the river—very much under the radar—and then he'd pop up in front of the hospital, like, "Hi, guys!"

" *Evil (our nickname for him) had gotten hurt, but was getting back to where we'd see him around the Penske organization. We had a really good friendship right off the bat. We started going to short-track races together on weekends when we didn't have a commitment with the Penske team. I had that Aerostar, and it was low and fast, and I'd take four or five guys with me, including Don, all over the place."*

BOBBY ALLISON
1983 NASCAR Winston Cup champion
1981 and 1988 Daytona 500 winner
Mooresville, North Carolina

Top: Bobby Allison's Aerostar is on permanent display atop a pylon at the International Motorsports Hall of Fame in Talladega, Alabama. (Bobby Allison Collection)

Left: Bobby Allison and I talking airplanes in the garage area at Rockingham. (Don Miller Collection)

I went for pilot training and completed all my lessons, at least for a basic FAA license, but couldn't get it because I'd lost my leg. Later, when Roger, Rusty Wallace and I owned Penske South, Rusty had a little Cessna 172, your basic single-engine, high-wing airplane that a lot of newer pilots fly. Rusty paid a flight instructor to teach me how to fly all over again, only with an artificial leg. I tried it, did pretty well, and I even soloed again, but I still didn't get a license.

One person for whom I have all the respect in the world, maybe more than any other human being, is Bill Brooks, Rusty's pilot. Bill bought me a special apparatus that would fit on my artificial leg and help me work the pedals. He also said something to me: "If you can enjoy it, that's one thing. But if it becomes a safety issue, I don't think it's a good idea."

He wasn't trying to be negative. I respected what he said because of who he is, and what I think of him. I thought about what he said, even during the times that I flew and thought I had really good control of the pedals, because I can drive a stick-shift car really well with an artificial leg, downshift and power shift. But an airplane's a different thing, because you've got to be able to bend your toes forward to engage the wheel brakes, whose pedals are located right above the rudder pedals. I can't do that. I did other things that I wasn't supposed to do, such as landing the plane using the emergency brake to stop it. Rusty is an excellent pilot. Bill Brooks is beyond excellent. He flew generals during the Vietnam War in both fixed-wing aircraft and helicopters. Among pilots, especially pilots associated with racing people, he was the man, and in my book, still is. It didn't take very long for me to realize that I needed to heed his gentle warning.

Bobby, as I've said, came to Penske Racing as our NASCAR driver, but NASCAR was not the major focus of Penske Racing at that time. The Penske NASCAR deal with the Matadors and Gary Bettenhausen was only an occasional-entry thing, because we were also running the Indy cars full time. Gary Bettenhausen was a terrific driver in Indy cars, and having seen him, I can tell you that he would have made a hell of a stock car driver down South, too. Mark Donohue had gone from winning Indianapolis to becoming the first IROC champ, then gone on to annihilate the Can-Am guys with the turbocharged Porsche 917-30. He was clearly destined for even bigger things. Many people, mostly reporters, called him Captain Nice. The guys in the Penske shops had a different nickname for Mark: Charlie Brown. Mark was a very quiet, laid-back guy until he got to know you. He had a great sense of humor, too. He was a gentleman, even though he could be very stubborn in the way he wanted his car set up. But behind the wheel, he changed from Charlie Brown into a predator. Mark told me more than once, "The thing to remember is, when you get in that race car, you have to make the car in front of you go away."

Let's face it, it was largely due to Mark and that all-conquering turbo Porsche that the Can-Am ceased to exist in its original form. He won the 24 Hours of Daytona for Roger in a Chevy-powered Lola T70, and drove the only car Roger had ever entered at Le Mans, a Ferrari 512M that he shared with David Hobbs. The car was extremely fast until the engine failed about five hours into the race.

One thing that I especially remember is getting to go with those guys to Talladega in 1975 when they made their attempt on the world closed-course speed record in the 917-30, which was then sponsored by CAM2, the new motor oil brand from Roger's longtime sponsor Sunoco. They had taken the Porsche to Daytona the first time they attempted the record. I think that was largely to please the France family: the Daytona name, and the history of record runs there in the past, both on the sand and on the superspeedway, including *Mad Dog IV*, the blown Chrysler 413-powered Indy car driven there by Art Malone. *Mad Dog IV* is now in the North Carolina Auto Racing Hall of Fame collection here in Mooresville, by the way.

Left: Mark Donohue and George Follmer shared this Penske Porsche 917-10 during the 1972 Can-Am season.

Right: In 1974, Penske debuted the new Can-Am Porsche 917-30, which was so dominant that it soon earned the name "Penske's Panzer." (Penske Corporation Photos)

Left: Mark Donohue being interviewed by members of the press after setting a new world closed-course speed record of 221.160 mph at Talladega, Alabama. (Don Miller Photo, Don Miller Collection)

Right: Mark Donohue relaxes in the driver's seat after his record run at Talladega. (Penske Corporation Photo)

You can obviously get a car up to speed at Daytona, but it's a lot bumpier than Talladega. The track was rough enough that the engineers had to raise the 917-30's ride height, which slowed it down, and the car finally fell victim to burned pistons. The turbochargers were constantly running at maximum output, which leaned the mixture out and cooked the engine.

We were motivated to get that speed record. Besides the promotional angle of it all, Roger wanted to knock A.J. Foyt off the closed-course record, which he'd set in one of his Indy cars at 217 mph and change at the big Goodyear test track in San Angelo, Texas. After the burned pistons at Daytona, the Porsche engineers looked at the whole mapping for the fuel injectors and the turbocharger setups, and that's when the decision was made to take the car to Talladega and try again with lowered ride height.

Dan Luginbuhl and I got there the day before and the weather was really threatening. We had arranged a little deal for the local press to come out, along with anyone else who wanted to, but there was still almost nobody there. Mark got in the car and did a couple of warm-up laps. They made a few adjustments and sent him back out. This was a car whose engine made a consistent 1,100 horsepower in Can-Am trim, and some 1,500 horses on the dyno. Mark laid down three awesome laps—his warm-up laps had been over 200 mph. The best was 221.160 mph. That was the record. I'd never seen Roger so excited, even though Mark was almost nonchalant. When Roger asked him if there was any more left, Mark replied, "Nah. I can't hold my breath any longer."

I got to know Mark pretty well. By this time, Roger was already working, very quietly, on creating a Formula 1 team. He really wanted one. No American had done anything in Formula 1 since Dan Gurney. Roger had lined up sponsorship from First National City Bank, and opened a new race shop in Poole, England, which became Penske Cars. Mark and Don Cox, the Penske team engineer from Reading, worked with designer Geoff Ferris to produce the team's first F1 car, the Penske PC1. Longtime Penske stalwarts Heinz Hofer and Karl Kainhofer became the team manager and chief mechanic, respectively. After turbocharged engines were banned from Can-Am, Mark had retired as a driver, though he had re-emerged for IROC and the Talladega record runs. Roger's first driver choice had been Peter Revson, who was killed before he could join the team. Mark was unhappy with retirement so he came back to drive the last two F1 races in 1974.

I only wish this chapter had a different ending. The week after the Talladega record run, Mark left for Europe and the 1975 Austrian Grand Prix. A revised Penske PC1 was used, along with a March 751 that Roger had purchased during the F1 season. In the morning practice session, Mark crashed with tremendous force after he apparently punctured a tire. He did not die immediately at the scene, as a lot of people still report. He actually walked away from the accident. As the guys on the team described it to me, Mark went back to the pits, sat down and was talking to everybody when he suddenly said he had a really bad headache and passed out. It turned out that the impact had shaken loose an embolism in his body, a blood clot, which traveled to his brain and sent him into a coma. The damage was done, and Mark died without regaining consciousness.

Roger was at the track in Austria that day. He was devastated. He decided that he was going to quit racing, but later changed his mind. John Watson, of Northern Ireland, took over the seat and brought Penske its first F1 win, ironically, a year later in Austria. Roger's decision to stay in racing opened the door for people like Tom Sneva, Rick

Mark Donohue at speed in Penske's new PC1 Formula 1 car at Watkins Glen, New York. (Penske Corporation Photo)

Mears, and the whole later cast of Penske characters that also came to include Rusty and Ryan.

Roger left Formula 1 not long after John Watson won that race. He'd proven his point. The subsequent PCs from Penske Cars were all Indy cars. As for Mark, I believe that if he'd lived, he would have eventually come over to stock cars full time. He'd already won in the Matador at Riverside, and had several superspeedway starts besides Daytona. He was good at it, and I know that he enjoyed it. It was terrible that we lost him.

11

Raising Rusty

A T THE RISK OF CONFUSING YOU, let me go back a couple of years before the accident, to another important set of circumstances that helped set the direction my life would take. Before I was really selling a lot of tires for them—when I joined Roger later on in his Competition Tire business, which I'll tell you about in a bit—and watched them at the track, stock cars really weren't my thing. I worked with them, but I was into drag racing. When I come down to click off the life-changing experiences that happened to me, I credit one of them to John Woody, who took me to my very first NASCAR stock car race.

Before he and I came aboard as partners with Roger at Competition Tire, John was what we called a tire jockey. He was a mechanic, and had mounted tires for Huggins Tire Company, which owned the Goodyear distributorship in the southeastern United States. Very much an honest, straightforward guy. One day, John says, "You know what? You need to come with me." We end up going from Detroit to Dover, Delaware, and a NASCAR Winston Cup race at Dover Downs, the high-banked mile. Even back then, the race was already known as the 24 Hours of Dover. I think the race went on for something like six hours, which is probably an exaggeration on my part, but it definitely felt that long. Richard Petty finally won it after what seemed like forever. In spite of everything, I kind of liked it. It was that day, in the garage area at Dover, when I first met Bobby Allison.

By this time, I had also met Rusty Wallace, when he was an incredibly young but amazingly eager kid. His Dad, Russ Wallace, was a really accomplished Late Model driver, especially on dirt. Russ had even worked for a while in a Sears auto center, like me. I already knew a little bit about

stock cars, even on short tracks, when I met Rusty for the very first time in 1972 or 1973. That was when I was building my 1934 Ford two-door sedan, a hot rod with an AMC Pacer front suspension, in Saint Louis. I needed the rear axle housing narrowed, to get it underneath the car so I could fit a Frankland quick-change center section in it. I went to the shop owned by a guy named Glenn Bopp. The last name is pronounced "Bope," but a lot of people also said it as "Bop." He was the proprietor of Bopp Chassis outside Saint Louis, which made some winning Late Models during the 1970s, including a memorable Ford Granada that Dick Trickle drove for awhile. When you talk to guys who know short-track stock cars, they'll tell you that a Bopp was a car to have. So I walk in there, and Rusty's working for Glenn, who promised that he could narrow up my Frankland rear end without a problem.

We're talking, and Glenn says to me, "You should meet this kid who works here with me. He's been dying to meet you." Glenn knew that I worked for Roger Penske. He told me that the kid, whose name I didn't know yet, also knew I worked for Penske and was an aspiring race driver. I'm listening and thinking to myself, I don't need any more of this. Glenn kept urging me, saying that this kid was different, that he was really something, so I went over and introduced myself. If you can imagine how in conversations, people imitate someone who talks really fast or is really hyper all the time— "Rahrahrahrahrahrahrah"—that was exactly how Rusty talked. When he finally slowed down enough so I could actually understand him, he blurted out, "I even know where you live!"

I'm eyeing this teenaged kid, maybe 16 years old, with a face full of pimples and this wild, frizzy, flaming red hair. He goes on, "Yeah! I know! You live on Summer Haven Drive! I saw that little trailer out in front that said Penske Racing Products on it! I deliver the papers to your house!"

I'm still listening. "Really." Rusty's chattering on, and now he practically yells, "Do you know Charlie Chase?" Well, yes I did. Charlie was then a captain in the fire district in Creve Coeur, the suburb of Saint Louis where we lived. The Wallace family, parents and sons, delivered papers to his house, too. And he was a racer, not just a firefighter, who owned a Late Model of his own, like the Wallaces. They became acquainted with each other while pitted at various tracks, and in 1975, combined their teams. So when he dropped Charlie's name, I interrupted him: "Oh yeah. Wallace. You're Russ Wallace's kid." And Rusty starts rattling again, "Yeah! My Dad! He kicks everybody's ass!"

I finally manage to get in, "That's cool." And he goes, "Hey! You ought to come out and see me run, at Valley Park!" Then, to Glenn Bopp, "Does he know Kenny Schrader?" "He" being me, and I told him, yeah, I know Kenny Schrader.

Rusty tried to get me to promise to come out to Valley Park that weekend, when both he and Schrader were going to be running. I halfheartedly promised to do so. As it turned out, I actually was home that weekend and I did go to the track, taking Pat with me. Valley Park was a third-mile paved oval whose official name was Lake Hill Speedway. Russ Wallace was already a big gun there, and Rusty had become immediately famous locally by winning his maiden outing there in 1973. Ken Schrader and his father Bill, from nearby in Fenton, were also regulars. Lake Hill, or Valley Park, was a hotbed of Late

Left: Young Rusty Wallace takes a victory lap at Lake Hill Speedway, Valley Park, Missouri. (Don Miller Collection)

Right: Rusty Wallace celebrates in Victory Lane, sporting his ever-popular nuclear hairdo. (Don Miller Collection)

Model racing, pulling drivers from a wide area around Saint Louis. Larry Phillips, the fabled dirt and asphalt Late Model champion from Springfield, Missouri, visited frequently. Another periodic visitor was Pete Hamilton, whose journey had taken him from running Modified coupes on bullrings outside Boston to victory in the 1970 Daytona 500, after which he built and raced Late Models from his new home turf in the South. Bobby Allison ran there sometimes, too; he could show up anywhere in the country on any given night, flying in at the controls of his twin-engine Piper Aerostar.

The Wallace kid did win his heat race at Valley Park that night. But what struck me a lot more was the fact that he was just so . . . pumped up. I'd never seen a kid in racing with more fire blazing inside. At the track, he was racing on again: "You've got to help me! You've got to help me! We've got to become big-time stock car racers! Maybe someday, you could introduce me to Bobby Allison!"

I was friendly but noncommittal, and time ticked onward. It got to the point where Rusty had gotten himself his own shop, a rented place, and told me I could bring my hot rod over and work on it if I wanted. That wasn't a bad deal. His new shop was only a couple of miles from my house in Creve Coeur. I thought about it, and later talked to Charlie Chase, who called Rusty a pain in the ass, though pretty affectionately. But I did move the Ford over there and we all ended up working together. As a result, I became interested in what Rusty was doing.

By the time I met Rusty, Bobby was already driving for us at Penske, having run our car at Indy beginning in 1973 and then taking over the NASCAR ride when we were still running the Matador. And by the time our Winston Cup car was the CAM2 Mercury, Bobby was our full-time driver. We were really good friends at that point, traveling together to Winston Cup events, and our kids were hanging around together. I was also traveling with Bobby to a lot of short-track races. We'd be at a Cup track, run practice, jump in his airplane and go to some race somewhere on a Saturday night before heading back to run the Cup race the following day. We did this a lot because, as I've said, Bobby was an excellent pilot and mechanic and was even a development guy for Piper at that time.

After seeing Rusty drive, I knew he was already a pretty good chauffeur. He was always asking me to introduce him to Bobby Allison, so I finally did give Bobby a call and mention Rusty to him. Bobby agreed to keep an eye on him, and over a period of time, he became one of Rusty's mentors. That was especially fruitful once Rusty began his move out of the relatively light short-track Late Models and into heavier cars, particularly in USAC, where the cars had similarity

Bobby Allison became one of Rusty Wallace's chief information sources when it came to track setups. (Kenny Kane Photo, Don Miller Collection)

to what NASCAR was running. Bobby provided Rusty with a lot of setup information for these cars that allowed him to start off fast, which was invaluable.

When I first got involved with Rusty, he was probably running three or four different cars at once. One belonged to him, another belonged to Charlie Chase, and the others belonged to various guys in the Missouri and Illinois areas who'd hired Rusty to drive them. A lot of those cars were built by Larry Phillips. Others were built by a really nice guy from Arkansas named Larry Shaw. A Late Model back then, in that part of the country, was really anything that wasn't a USAC stock car. It could be a tube chassis, a Camaro snout, or something else. Rusty got some enormously broad experience, running all kinds of cars at all kinds of tracks for a bunch of owners, and no matter what, he did very well.

> ❝ *Don Miller was everything in the world to me. Don was the guy who was guiding my racing career. If I wanted to do anything, I called Don Miller. If anybody wanted me to do something, they called Don Miller. Any questions I had, I called Don Miller. And anytime I got lost, or was trying to find sponsors or anything, I called Don Miller."*
>
> **RUSTY WALLACE**
> *1989 NASCAR Winston Cup champion*
> *Mooresville, North Carolina*

During this period, Roger said, more than once, "What are you guys doing back there with this guy Wallace?" I'd explain that Rusty was a young guy, he's coming on, and he's going to be a really good race car driver. Roger would answer, in essence, "Ah, you don't need that; you don't need to mess with that." Regardless, Bobby and I kept building our friendship and our support of Rusty.

Rusty was getting a reputation really, really fast. He was completely in control, at least when he was in the race car. Very flexible, very adaptable, always used his head. I always noticed, whenever we went someplace for a big-dollar Late Model race, maybe Rolla in Missouri or Fort Smith in Arkansas, Rusty watched what everyone was doing very intently. He'd learn who the fast guys were, sit them down and talk to them, pick their brains, then come back and change the car. He was a good mechanic and very good setup man who understood the cars. If it came that he'd have to turn the car from loose to tight, or vice versa, he knew how. We'd be in the middle of a 100-lap race and Rusty would come on the radio—we were the first team to have radios—telling us how to adjust the car. He was always in the hunt. As time went on, Rusty built his own cars, then ran Bemco and Dillon cars, anything he thought would be faster. Finally, people were getting in line to have him drive their own cars.

My relationship with Rusty was basically as his agent, his personal adviser. I helped him do everything. I got him sponsors, dealt with them, did his contracts, even wrote his press releases. I never took a dime from him the whole time I worked with him, because he never had any money then anyway. I liked him. I knew he was going to be what he eventually became. Rusty definitely wanted to be a famous race driver. I told him I'd make him a household name like A.J. Foyt if he followed what I told him. I told him where he needed to start running next. I told him to go to ASA, which was the premier group for short-track pavement Late Models in the country, and to not just win races, but win the championship. Then I told him, we'd go to USAC, and then after USAC, we'd get in side deals like ARTGO and All Pro. I explained to him that he couldn't bring the movers and shakers to Valley Park and Missouri, so he'd have to go after them to show them who he was.

" *During the seventies and early eighties, we all worked on Rusty's cars for next to nothing. Don said we were volunteers, but I think we were more like slaves. We would work all night long and then take a shower, jump in the truck, and go to the track, and this went on for two weeks straight. At the time, Don would meet us at the track on weekends and he would end up driving the truck back home to Saint Louis. He would then change clothes and jump on a plane and go halfway across the country for Roger or Goodyear, whichever was on the schedule."*

JEFFREY THOUSAND
Original crewman for Rusty Wallace
Car chief, Penske Racing
Mooresville, North Carolina

Rusty won 202 short-track races before he went to NASCAR, plus the ASA title that he won over Dick Trickle. I always referred to that kind of background as developing your own schematic, building ever-higher tiers of races, series and championships that would elevate your career. The plan I helped Rusty develop was for him to run as many races as he wanted, but never miss a championship-series event, and make absolutely certain he was prepared to kick butt once he arrived at one of them. If ASA wanted him to do some PR for its series, I had him do it. He would be doing the same things Trickle was, so Rusty became associated in people's minds with Trickle, and they both became big names. ASA used them both in all their advertising.

This was stuff I had learned through drag racing with UDRA—if you didn't promote yourself, nobody else was going to do it for you. In UDRA, we went out well in advance of an event and promoted it through the newspapers and on the radio. When I came to Penske, and got hooked up with Dan Luginbuhl, Dan taught me a tremendous amount about the promotional aspects of this sport. I took what I already knew, added what Dan had taught me, and helped Rusty become better at his craft. I made him cut that nuclear hair of his, wash up, press his pants, wash and press his shirts. I'd already learned from Roger that if you look like a slob, people are going to assume that's what you are. Don't use the f-word when you're talking in front of the press. It's not acceptable. Be gracious toward your competitors. Perception is everything.

Two other guys were also important to Rusty's early success. One was Nicky Prejean, a fire-equipment supplier from Gonzales, Louisiana, who owned a big company, Southland Fire Equipment, which sold fire trucks. He was really into Late Model racing and had put some money into Rusty's operation, bought some of the cars for him, and gave him money for travel and tires and such. Nicky, who also owned some drag cars, was a part owner of Rusty's team during that time. Mostly, it was for the big Southern races, such as All Pro. The other guy was John Childs, who owned a tire company in O'Fallon, Missouri, near Saint Louis. John was a big race fan but he also liked to participate, including working on the cars. He was a good businessman and realized that with Rusty's popularity, people would buy tires from him if he put his company's name on Rusty's cars.

We had the whole package: an excellent driver, very good sponsors, and good cars from all the top chassis builders. We had outstanding engines, built by Don Kirn in Saint Louis, and a consistent crew, which a lot of people didn't have, even though many of them were volunteers. That crew consistency did a lot to make Rusty a threat every time they raced. The core of the team was Dave Munari and Jeff Thousand, two really good guys who have a long history with me, and with Rusty. Dave's association with Rusty came through me, through my drag racing partnership with Dave in the Munari & Miller AHRA car. Jeff's relationship with Rusty came through Charlie Chase. Jeff was an excellent welder and fabricator, which led me to later hire him when Roger established Motorsports International. Charlie, I should add, was probably as big a mentor to Rusty when he was coming up as I was. He was as crusty as they came, and always on Rusty's case: "If you can't get out of bed before 10 o'clock, call me and I'll come take my name off the car." There will only ever be one Charlie Chase, a prime mover in the development of Rusty Wallace.

I had never managed another driver before Rusty. I never wanted to. What brought me to Rusty was his incredible fire, this blaze in his gut. I knew he would be successful if somebody gave him some guidance, because he gave 140 percent, always. It was amazing. I had never met anyone up to that point who wanted to win as much as Rusty did. Now, having said all that, I don't think anyone can actually manage a race driver. What you do, more accurately, is give them guidance. I like to say that they're a lot like fighter pilots. Once they're out of your sight, they're on their own. At that point, nothing you've ever told them means anything. You don't teach them how to drive the car. They either know that or they don't. They get better by getting seat time.

" My Dad is very patient. He listens to both what people are saying, and what they're not saying. I've learned from him over the years that it's not just what people are telling you, it's what's around them. He gives people direction and leadership so they can carry their own momentum."

TRICIA MILLER

Back then, and now, still, I can go out to a race track and watch 40 guys, and tell you pretty quickly who the three guys are with the best car control. In this sport, car control is everything. If you have that, you can learn the rest of it. You don't even have to be brave if you've got car control.

What, you ask, is car control? Go to your local speedway some night, and I guarantee you'll see some guy who goes down the straight like a rocket ship, but then gets all over the brakes going down in the corner, gets the car half sideways and is on and off the gas and brakes and jerking around until he hopefully comes out the other side. It looks pretty stylish, like, "Look how that guy throws that car around." Well, that's exactly what he's doing, throwing it around, because he has no control over it. Some people say that in this situation, you can't tell if it's the driver or the car, but trust me, it's the driver. Even if the car's bad, anybody who lets a car get that far out of control isn't a good driver. If it's that bad, bring it in and fix it. If it's that bad during the race, slow down. That's what the brake pedal is for. If you don't slow down, you're going to crash. If you crash, you're not going to finish. If you're not going to finish, why did you bother going to the race in the first place?

It may sound rough, but that's the way it is, maybe not 100 percent of the time, but certainly 85 percent, at least. That's what I first saw in Rusty Wallace, car control. The ultimate car control guy, in my opinion, is Ryan Newman. Go watch Ryan. If you ever get a chance, watch some tapes of his open wheel stuff. It's phenomenal. That guy has more car control than anybody I've ever seen, anywhere. There's another guy out there now with extremely good car control, and that's Carl Edwards; another in that category is Jimmie Johnson. Mark Martin is another racer with superb car control. I don't care how fast you are. On a given day, my grandmother could have been fast in the right car. Being fast consistently, and bringing the thing home at the end of the day, makes a good race car driver.

Rusty had another attribute pretty early on, after I got involved with him, a grasp of business. The Late Models that Rusty drove early on were based on the chassis that Pete Hamilton had developed for Sportsman cars. The cars worked really well, and I suggested to Rusty around 1975 that he consider building some cars based on that design. That, in turn, led him and me to form the Poor Boy Chassis Group at Rusty's first shop in Des Peres, Missouri. Besides Dave Munari and Jeff Thousand, we also added two guys from Saint Louis, Paul Andrews and Dave Wirz. People started buying the Poor Boy cars, led by Mike Allgaier, who owned a Hoosier Tire distributorship and speed shop in Springfield, Missouri, and who then started selling them to customers. Mike's nickname has always been Alligator, and his son Justin is a rising star today. Justin came out of dirt Late Models and Midgets to win the 2008 ARCA championship and take on a full Nationwide schedule for Penske Racing, beginning in 2009.

In the early Poor Boy days, when I was freshly screwed back together—mostly—after the Talladega mess, Bobby Allison used to crack that I had more metal in my body than Evel Knievel. I probably didn't, but he started calling me "Evil" anyway. As a result, Poor Boy

I drew this cartoon and Rusty framed it and hung it on the shop wall at Poor Boy Chassis. Rusty would simply point to it when anyone asked for a credit account.
(Don Miller Collection)

Chassis Group became known as The Evil Gang. We even had a patch embroidered with that name and an outline of the state of Missouri, imitating the famed Alabama Gang patches that Bobby sometimes wore. Other Evil Gang regulars were Don Kirn and Dave Wirz.

> **“** We had an All Pro car Glenn Bopp built that Rusty won several races with. The first time Rusty ever went to Bristol, which was for an All Pro race, we sat on the pole. Just blistered them, set a new track record, and it was several years before that record was broken by Randy Sweet with that outlaw dirt Late Model with all the wings on it.
>
> We flew around that place. Rusty led something like 160 laps of the race and had to come in for a right front, and we had a lug nut rounded off and couldn't get it off. So we had to send him back out with that tire, and Mike Eddy won the race. Rusty was third. I was sick.”

DAVID MUNARI

I said that Rusty won 202 races, and some of them were huge, regardless of the track length. He beat Larry Phillips in Springfield. He finished first ahead of Trickle in a Wisconsin ARTGO race. At Rockford Speedway in Illinois, Rusty topped both Trickle and Neil

Bonnett. He went down to Bobby's home track, the Birmingham Fairgrounds, and took a 400-lapper over Darrell Waltrip. We were traveling and winning consistently. For 1979, Rusty and I decided to take on USAC. Rusty was a legitimate star by now, and this time, he got a chassis that wasn't from Pete Hamilton, but instead from Tom Hamilton—no relation—who at the time ran Stock Car Products in California. Rusty fitted a Pontiac Firebird body to the chassis, which was narrower than the more typical Chevy Camaro. In USAC, pony cars and compacts like Chevy Novas could run against larger, NASCAR-type cars. This was a very important race car, because Rusty ran it on everything from dirt to the biggest superspeedways, and it was the car that really got him into NASCAR.

So did a couple of glasses of wine. Roger and I shared them at the Penske Racing holiday party in Reading just before Christmas in 1979. You know how that goes. I had a couple in me when I brought up this old Chevrolet Caprice that had been sitting, I don't remember how long, in the corner of the Penske Racing shop. I told him we ought to drag it out, fix it up and let that kid from Missouri try it. That's how I referred to him. I'm not sure Roger would have even recognized Rusty's name at that point. He was a little dismissive of the whole idea at first, but later in the evening, after a couple of more glasses of wine, he agreed to let us do it.

> " When I met Don, I was looking for a guy who knew people, who could actually help me guide my career. My father was busy running the family business and didn't have the time. Nor did he have the kind of connections that Don had. Don had a lot of business background, the business of racing. Eventually, he told me, 'I'm going to call up Penske and tell him I've got this hot-shot new young driver,' and that's what he did. We went to meet him; he told me he had this old car, take it to Atlanta and test it. Don spearheaded the whole thing, we took it to Atlanta, and in my very first race I finished second (to Dale Earnhardt)."

RUSTY WALLACE

The Chevy was one of the cars that we still had around from when we had previously planned to get back into NASCAR. It had been sitting there for a year and a half, at least, but it was still a brand-new Banjo Matthews car that we hadn't even completely finished when the Penske NASCAR effort ended in 1977. I think it originally had had 1978 Monte Carlo sheet metal on it before we made it into a Caprice.

Let me backtrack for just a moment. As I said, Rusty had that Firebird and was running it in USAC, a series that was probably second only to NASCAR in the late 1970s. Rusty ran the full USAC schedule in 1979 and did extremely well, finishing third in points to Foyt and Bay Darnell. It's also become folklore as to how he asked Foyt for a setup at the dirt mile at DuQuoin, won the race, and then kind of got vocal about it. Foyt and his people really disliked that, and there was some heat between them and us all year long.

Rusty was still the USAC Rookie of the Year and won four races. USAC ran big tracks, including the Milwaukee Mile and the old Texas World Speedway, while ASA ran at extremely fast, banked short tracks like I-70 in Missouri and Winchester. Rusty took the same Firebird to Talladega for a 300-miler in the old NASCAR Grand American series, which briefly combined superspeedway Modifieds with older Late Model Sportsman cars. He qualified third and ran fourth in the race. Then Bobby put Rusty in his own Sportsman car at Charlotte, where Rusty finished sixth. Early in 1980, Jay Signore let Rusty test one of the IROC cars at Daytona. So Rusty was getting to know his way around some very fast speedways.

Left: We worked on that Caprice every night following our regular jobs at Penske, sometimes until 11 p.m. (Penske Corporation Photo, Don Miller Collection)

Right: Don Kirn was the engine builder for our first race with Rusty at Atlanta. (Penske Corporation Photo, Don Miller Collection)

For a while, Roger was actually referring to Rusty as "Dusty Wallace." He was originally going to try him out at Daytona, but I convinced Roger that going to Daytona with the blocky Caprice would be like going there with the box you'd ship it in. We put together a team that included Don Kirn, Kenny Wallace and Jay Signore, and I hired Tex Powell as crew chief. Tex had been around for a long time and had been a crew chief for several teams, including Foyt's. We both believe that we actually met for the first time in the Trans-Am days, when I first joined up with Roger, and when Tex was working on the Mustang team that Bud Moore was running for Ford. Tex is also, and I really believe this, one of the great, unsung geniuses of NASCAR, especially when it comes to drivelines. Tex worked for years to improve the standard Borg-Warner Super T-10 transmission, cut his own gears for them, started making casings and finally founded Tex Industries, making what became a standard transmission for guys in NASCAR.

> *I was running the shop for Roger at the time. We worked on the Indy cars and whatever else during the day and then worked on the Caprice—which everybody said was a dog sled and would never do anything—at night. Don and I would finish at 7 or 8 o'clock at night and then get to work on the Chevy. I only vaguely remember how we got it together, because we weren't even into stock cars at the time. Don's a hard worker, a good soul, but I don't know how we did it because in the midst of all this, he was doing his Sears traveling for Roger, too. We had Roger's blessing to build the Chevy but I'm not sure how much of a blessing he actually gave us."*

JAY SIGNORE

In February of 1980, we headed down to Atlanta for Rusty's test. He did well, nudged the wall a little on one of his laps, but no problem. He was fast. Jay had the IROC cars there to test and Rusty got some additional laps in with them. Donnie Allison had also given him some impromptu coaching on getting around Atlanta in one piece.

Even in its original configuration, Atlanta was one of the fastest Winston Cup tracks. We all thought Rusty was ready to attempt the Atlanta 500, though, his first Winston Cup event and his first 500-mile race of any sort. But once we got to the track for opening practice, we started having problems. Not with Rusty, who qualified seventh, astounding everybody. The problem was that the engine Don Kirn built for us was chronically leaking oil. (Don was an outstanding engine builder, who powered Rusty in both USAC and ASA, and is sadly gone now.) We couldn't correct it. That's when Tex really came

Left: Rusty and I discussed some chassis changes prior to his first practice during the Atlanta test. (Penske Corporation Photo, Don Miller Collection)

Right: Tex Powell was the crew chief for our Atlanta adventure. Rusty and Tex communicated extremely well. (Penske Corporation Photo, Don Miller Collection)

through for us, probably saved the race, and provided an object lesson in how important relationships really are in racing.

I had actually worked for Tony Foyt, A.J.'s father. One of the things I really cherish about it was that I was able to promote some harmony between the crews. That's because Rusty had been in a really tight point battle with A.J. in USAC. If they'd have had guns, they'd have shot each other, right there in the garage area. And yet, we ended up running an A.J. Foyt engine in the car that day at Atlanta. Roger agreed to pay for it, but I made the deal and it was partly because Ron Puryear, Foyt's engine builder, and I had worked together for Ray Nichels and Paul Goldsmith up in Indiana and at L.G. De Witt's. I have a lot of respect for Ron, a very creditable engine builder and human being, who went on to work at Bahari Racing and later at Morgan-McClure.

That Kirn engine was making some major horsepower, but it was running at a real high temperature. Then, when we took the cover off the Oberg oil filter, we found metal flakes in there, more than there should have been. We'd been running really high temperatures. We had no spare. I went to Ron, we got the engine, took everything over to the airport next door next to the track and when we were getting it in, realized we had to change oil pans, after taking most of the top end off the Kirn engine. And Don hung in there with us while we did it. Me, him, Red Man, Don Kirn, David Munari and Mike Mitler. Larry Penn was there, too."

TEX POWELL
Team consultant, Red Bull Racing
New London, North Carolina

We took the Caprice outside the track to a little airport next door, put it in the hangar, and let Tex go to work. He started putting our pieces on the engine he'd gotten from Foyt. One of them was a trick oil cooler we'd cobbled up in Reading, with two cores, back to back. We built it that way so that during qualifying, we could drop a steel plate between the cores to block off the airflow and add a little speed and extra downforce for qualifying. The cooler was part of the reason Rusty qualified in the top 10. Looking back, I figure that when we started having the oil leaks, we probably just forgot about the plate. Tex put the oil cooler onto Foyt's engine with the plate still in it, and none of us caught it.

Roger was there for race day. Rusty strapped in and the green dropped. It was, and I'm not exaggerating, a shocking day. I don't think we were ever lower than 10th or 12th. Rusty was on the hammer all day. The only problem we had was when Rusty lightly hit Benny Parsons on pit road, bending the front sheet metal a little. That led to a, shall we say, animated discussion on pit road between Roger and me. Roger wanted to bring Rusty in under the green and fix the damage. I told him no way, that we'd lose a lap. It went back and

We qualified seventh and knew that we had a good shot at a top-10 finish. All we had to do was survive. (Penske Corporation Photo, Don Miller Collection)

Rusty ran in the top 10 all day and finished second to Dale Earnhardt in his very first NASCAR Grand National race. (Penske Corporation Photo, Don Miller Collection)

forth until he finally agreed with me. The race unfolded with Dale Earnhardt and Cale Yarborough going at it up front, until Cale had a distributor go sour on him near the end. That moved Rusty up to second, which was where he finished. It was incredible. Here's this practically unknown driver out of the Midwest, a short tracker, making his first Cup start on this blindingly fast superspeedway and he finishes second to Dale Earnhardt. That's still the greatest debut performance ever in Winston Cup.

> " *Jay Signore had suggested that Dave Marcis be the driver and Frog Fagan the crew chief. Don wanted me to have it. He said I was open-minded and liked to get things done right away. I've said for a long time that the three most important tools in racing are a hammer, a screwdriver and flat black paint. What's the most universal tool? The hammer. What's the most beautiful color in the world? Flat black. What cannot be used as a hammer? Nothing. We did not take each other seriously but Don and I were deadly serious about our racing. Don Kirn was the engine man, and I still believe to this day we could have won that first race with Rusty if we could have continued to use Kirn engines. But the result that day, second, wasn't all bad. It was pretty bold to run a car as square as that old Caprice at Atlanta in the first place."*

TEX POWELL

Roger had committed to five Cup races with Rusty in 1980. We also got him a Monte Carlo, and took it up to Michigan for the USAC race. Rusty was a bullet on that race track. He came in for either his first or second pit stop, running in the top five, but when he let the clutch out, the driveshaft broke and put us out. We ran it later at Charlotte with Norton sponsorship and finished around 15th, as Rusty then realized that maybe this Winston Cup thing wasn't as

Penske Racing built Rusty a new Monte Carlo and we ran it at Michigan and Charlotte. (Don Miller Collection)

Rusty narrowly edged out Richie Evans in the NASCAR Grand American race at Talladega, Alabama. This was one of the most exciting motor races I've ever watched. (Don Miller Collection)

easy as it looked. Roger ultimately decided to stick with Indy cars, at least for the moment. Rusty was disappointed, even though Roger offered to give him the Chevy. The leftover Mercury stuff that we had from the post-Matador days, we sold to Bill and Ernie Elliott. Rod Osterlund bought the rest of our Chevy stuff for Earnhardt.

Working with Don, and Rusty, was really an opportunity for me to do a little upgrading. I remember when Benny Parsons came by the shop right after I told Don that I would participate in this. Benny came by, and he said that to work for Roger Penske and Miller was a wonderful opportunity, that I should be thankful for it, and that he hoped Miller would keep me from doing some of the cruder things. That deal was recognized, certainly, as very upscale racing. The Penske group was really big. To be with them was a learning experience.

One thing that I know Don and I have in common is pride in what we do. I would regard Don Miller as being one of the least political people down here that's ever had success. In this sport, he has done things in his own way, with honesty. Nowadays, it's about marketing, public relations and salesmanship and all that. Don got the job done in a more direct, legitimate fashion. I've got tremendous respect for him, because he was able to accomplish what he's done in a realistic fashion, without the bullshit."

TEX POWELL

Raising Rusty   **117**

Rusty finished second in USAC points in 1980, to Joe Ruttman, winning both races at Milwaukee. That was in the Stock Car Products-chassis Firebird, the same car he'd used to win on dirt at the DuQuoin mile. Then, with the same car, he went back to Talladega for the Grand American 300. The only significant changes made to the Firebird were springs and flaring the front fenders to keep the air out of the wheel openings.

I was there. The race was incredible, still one of the best I've ever seen. Rusty put this smoothed-over dirt veteran on the outside pole at 202 mph-plus. Again, the race was heavy with radical superspeedway Modifieds. One of them was this wild orange Camaro driven by the great Richie Evans, the Modified megastar out of upstate New York. Richie had run the thing as a superspeedway Modified at Daytona with this monster big block, but he put in a 355-inch small block to make it Grand American-legal. It came down to a tremendous battle between him and Rusty. They went at it right into the final lap, which was clocked at 202 mph. Rusty snookered Richie going into turn three and won it. Rusty was now a winning superspeedway driver.

He was also now becoming a national star. Rusty could truly say he was competitive with the very best stock car drivers in America, from Larry Phillips to Dale Earnhardt to Richie Evans. We both knew he would eventually make it in Winston Cup. I had a partner and a buddy, and a racing legend in the making.

12

The Eagle Flies

B Y EARLY 1975, I had begun my life again. I was on the road for Penske, going all over the country with an artificial leg, visiting stores, holding sales meetings, building the business. My title was vice president of Penske Products, with Roger as the president. Pretty soon, Roger comes up to me, and says, "You've done an outstanding job with all of this. Would you be interested in getting into this business even further?" Sure, like what? "How would you like to buy into Competition Tire West, and become my partner?"

"I'd like that. I really would." Roger's plan was that John Woody and I would actually run the company. I'd handle sales and John would manage the day-to-day operations. I took my Sears stock, converted it into cash and bought into the tire company. The Goodyear Tire & Rubber Company has always handled its racing business through third-party distributors; Competition Tire West was a one of those distributors. Back in the 1950s, a company called Triple R distributed Goodyear racing rubber in the Midwest. When it went belly up, Roger bought into it and moved it to Detroit, renaming it Competition Tire West. Roger had also owned a sister distributorship, Competition Tire East in Reading, Pennsylvania, for a long time. Huggins operated the Goodyear racing tire distributorship in the Southeast, and Shelby was the distributor in the Far West.

My new title was vice president of Competition Tire West, but I continued to have the vice president's title for Penske Products, and was still managing all Roger's endorsements. I also had responsibility for the real estate for a while. So, I was building the tire business, running Penske Products, managing the souvenir business, doing all kinds of other things. Nobody at Penske had just one job at that point. I was going to the races,

119

to boot. We had the Indy cars, we had IROC, and we continued to run the AMC Matador in NASCAR through 1976.

And right at that particular point, Goodyear approached us at Competition Tire and said, in essence, "You know what? We only have about 5 percent of the short-track racing tire business in the Midwestern United States." That may be an impossibly small number to comprehend today for giant Goodyear, but at the midpoint of the 1970s, it was painfully accurate. To put it impolitely, Goodyear was getting its ass kicked. By everybody. The competing brands were Firestone, McCreary, Hoosier and M&H. Also, there was Towel City, with its racing retreads. Everybody had a big slice of the short-track pie, except for Goodyear. So, off we went to Akron, Ohio, where Goodyear has its world headquarters, and met with Leo Mehl, along with another person for whom I have enormous respect, Phil Holmer. Or, as I call Phil, "Buddha." Phil was almost like a Dad to me. Leo went on to become Goodyear's worldwide director of racing operations, and at this point, he and Phil were the company's two top racing managers in North America. Phil told me, "We need someone here to help us figure out how to get this business back." And I said, "Well, let me take a look at it. Because, you know, it's going to make us a lot of money if we do end up getting it back."

Phil was Leo Mehl's deputy. He was in charge of all stock car and full-bodied racing for Goodyear, which, in this era, was pretty much everything except drag racing. Eventually, Goodyear gave Phil sports cars, too, and then added short-track cars, Modifieds, that sort of thing. Phil told me to think about it and see what kind of ideas I could come up with. By this time, I had met Rusty and was becoming seriously hooked up with him as a friend and a mentor. I had a pretty fair idea of what was going on with short-track racing and a general notion, at least, of what the competitors sought when they spent money on tires.

So after the meeting with Leo and Phil, I call Rusty and tell him, "Hey, let's go to an ASA race." And Rusty, all full of vinegar like he usually is, is blurting, "Yeah, yeah, yeah! Let's go to an ASA race!" So we tow the car to this ASA event, which as I remember, was at Indianapolis Raceway Park. Even though I'd met him before, I'd never spent any time seriously talking to Rex Robbins, the founder and director of the American Speed Association tour in the Midwest for Late Models. This time, I decided to correct that oversight, and I'm very glad I did. Rex and I became instant friends. We just clicked. I asked him, "Rex, what's it going to take to get into short-track racing with Goodyear?" He thought about it and said, "Well, one thing is getting the price down, and they're not going to do that. You've already got Hoosier and McCreary making these tires cheap."

I listened, and then I asked Rex a question: If I could get Goodyear to make a special spec tire that could be run at all the ASA race tracks, and run safely, would he entertain making it the spec tire for ASA? He answered, "I don't know. Let me think about it. But it would be a big endeavor." No kidding.

I went back to Akron and talked to the people there, again and again. They told me, and I agreed, that such a deal would be a major undertaking because it would involve a lot of testing before we could sell a new tire to anybody, to be sure it was safe. This was the second half of the 1970s, and most everybody had some kind of a tire rule then except the outlaw tracks. Typical parameters included circumference, width and wheel size. At the time, a lot of the asphalt touring series was flirting with the $10\frac{1}{2}$- to $11\frac{1}{2}$-inch tire, and they were really getting expensive. I told Phil that he and I should go to Leo and explain that the way we were going to make our money would be by making inroads through the ASA, which was already a famous Late Model series with some stellar drivers.

Leo sat, listened, and finally said, "Listen, Don, I believe you, but it would cost a fortune to develop a special tire like that." I gave Leo my word that I was going to work harder than anybody ever had before to create this tire, and make it work. Leo gave the go-ahead.

I traveled with Bobby Allison all over the country to short-track races, which gave me a good understanding of short-track tire requirements. This photo was taken at Oswego (NY) Speedway, helping Dick Berggren in the pits. (Don Miller Collection)

Until we got the racers to trust us at Competition Tire West, you never saw this sight, Goodyears being unloaded at a Midwest short track. Soon, this tough market belonged to us. (Don Miller Collection)

> " I've known Don just about as long as I've known Roger Penske himself, and that goes back pretty deep into the early 1970s, because I first started with Goodyear in 1962. Don was at the race track with Penske, and like me with Goodyear, we were both over-the-wall guys with our respective employers, even though by the late 1970s, I was in charge of all racing for Goodyear.
>
> Don is kind of unique in the sport, in that he's done most everything you can in racing, starting as a mechanic. He's raced himself, been a sales professional, helped us with the design and marketing of Goodyear tires for the Late Model and Modified guys during his days running Competition Tire West. He has a very complete resume of racing experience. He's a leader, and especially effective as one because he knows all aspects of the sport and its complexities.
>
> I like to say that when guys like Don and I first started out in this business, racing was a real rough-and-tumble activity. Since then, however, the level of knowledge that you need has expanded enormously, including the tires, the engine development and the aerodynamics. The people who work in racing expect to have managers who, I guess, will have more than enough knowledge of these technologies, and how they work, to avoid asking them a dumb question. On top of everything else that Don has as a leader and motivator, he has that kind of knowledge. I know it, and obviously, Roger Penske knows it, too.
>
> With his skills working with people, his knowledge of the constantly changing technology of automobile racing and his ability to adapt to those changes, Don was a natural go-to guy at Penske. He's the kind of person you can hand an assignment of any sort over to with confidence, knowing that the job's going to get done. Throughout Don's career, it's been pretty visible that he's a natural leader, who can take a project, and the people he works with, and see it through.
>
> After as many years in racing as he and I have, there's almost a point where you can start to become burned out, but I don't know that Don's reached it as yet. You know what they say about what to do when something absolutely needs to be done: Give it to the busiest person. Roger's done that with Don for a long time."

LEO MEHL
Retired Director of Worldwide Racing
Goodyear Tire & Rubber Company
Hudson, Ohio

So Goodyear took the plunge and made this new tire, with a 10½-inch tread and a code number that I still remember: D2542. It was

called the LMS Eagle, for Late Model Stock, to be mounted on a 15-inch wheel. We got the first couple of sets, and I took some over to Rusty. We mounted them on his Late Model and quietly took them to Valley Park, a real tight quarter-mile paved track. Rusty ran them, came in and said, "You know, for as small as this tire is, it's got a lot of bite. I don't know how long it's going to last, but for 10 or 20 laps, it's pretty good."

It was a start. We demounted the tires from Rusty's wheels and I took them back to Akron. The engineers looked them over and were pleased with what they saw. The tires showed little in the way of wear, and I told them that we'd run maybe 30 laps on them, at the most. The next step, they said, was to bring in Goodyear's test driver—Dick Trickle, whom I already knew. Dick listened to my pitch and mused, "I'd really like to do this, because, you know, we really need this. Not only in ASA, but also in the Central Wisconsin Racing Association. I don't think anyone really realizes how big this short-track thing is in this country."

That was especially true for Wisconsin, and especially at that particular time, when short-tracking was almost religiously important. There was a major Late Model event somewhere in the state almost every night of the week during the season. Just to name a few venues, the Late Models ran at Kaukauna, Milwaukee, Slinger, Wisconsin Dells, La Crosse, and I know I've missed a bunch. But they all ran under the same rules, largely as set by the CWRA. I asked Dick how many cars he thought were in Wisconsin. "Mmmm, maybe 200 Late Models. Plus there's all these little tracks around here that aren't part

Goodyear built a special tire for asphalt Late Model stock cars called the LMS Eagle. We tested it, refined it, and then sold it all over the country. (Don Miller Collection)

of our thing, but they run the same rules, too. And then there's ARTGO, which runs a slightly different rule, but we can be competitive with them." I asked, "Who runs ARTGO?" Dick answered, "John McKarns. Want to meet him?"

We went to Madison, Wisconsin, where ARTGO was based, and met with John McKarns and his wife, Sue. He listened carefully, too, and said, "If we could make this work, it would be great." I asked John who was in a position of authority with CWRA, and John immediately said, "Clem Droste. He's hard core. He's a racer, he knows his business and nobody's going to put anything over on him. He doesn't particularly care for Goodyear because they're way too expensive. My biggest problem now is that the guys who have a deal, like with Hoosier, can get anything they want made with the right D-number, the stock number, cast into the tire even though it's twice as soft as what they're selling to everyone else. I've got to stop all that. I don't think Goodyear would do that, would they?" I gave him my word that they wouldn't.

The next step was a series of tests that had never been done before, open to the public so that people could come and watch. Trickle did all the driving. We started at Golden Sands, a track that had been closed, up near Wisconsin Rapids. We cleaned it all up, Trickle came in with his Late Model and we started running. We ran 300 laps. Mike Miller was there, too, a really good Late Model driver who at that time was running the #16 Dairyland car. Mike, Boomer Bohmsach and Trickle, in conjunction with Clem Droste and Jimmy Back, an absolutely legendary Wisconsin driver, had come up with the 9:1 rule for Late Model racing in Wisconsin, because they didn't want to keep wearing engines out. They went to Chevrolet and developed the whistler, a detector that you stick in the spark plug hole; if the compression ratio is any higher than 9.0:1, it'll whistle.

Now that they had the 9:1 engine, they wanted a more affordable tire. We tested our new spec tire all over Wisconsin that summer. We knew we had to be ready for the annual promoters' meeting in December, where they would vote on their tire rule for the following season. The drivers would be at the December meeting, too, since they were the ones who were going to have to buy the tires. We tested at a bunch of different tracks, went back to ASA and tested for them, then drove to Capital Super Speedway in Madison and tested for ARTGO. Trickle had told me, "Man, this thing is holding up a lot better than I thought it would."

After all the testing, we went back to Akron to go over the results with Goodyear. I had Jeff Thousand with me from Rusty's crew. To a man, everybody was convinced that the tire would work, but then came the big hurdle: Could we get the price down? Back then, a typ-

ical Goodyear racing tire cost about $110, whereas the Hoosiers were about $80. We pleaded with Goodyear. We took a smaller margin as the distributor, and Goodyear also agreed to take a smaller manufacturer's margin. We got the retail price down to $89, and I went to every race track and sanctioning body in the Midwest to sell the tire. Ultimately, we went from 3 or 4 percent of the race-tire business in the Midwest to nearly 70 percent of the asphalt track business in about 18 months. Think about that. The D2542 became the tire of choice in Late Model racing because nobody got anything special, on the sly. Goodyear made one tire, and one tire only. It was phenomenal. I was a hero.

Ray Dillon built this Avanti race car for the 24-hour race at Daytona. Ray shocked everyone by choosing the Goodyear LMS Eagle, usually run on oval tracks, for this race with excellent results. (Richard Gallatin Photo)

There's a sidebar to this story. After accepting the 2542, the officials and promoters then asked us to develop a new, superspeedway tire for the long Late Model events at places like Winchester, Indiana, which is a paved half-mile but has corners as steeply banked as Daytona or Talladega. Winchester has long had a very demanding 400-lap race for Late Models. The ASA also ran on the two-mile superspeedway at Michigan.

We used the same approach; Goodyear developed the D3311, a harder, longer-lasting tire than the 2542 for speedways. Then we had all kinds of dirt racers switching to Goodyear. We took the 3311s to Michigan International Speedway, where they ran fine. Shortly thereafter I was talking to Ray Dillon, of Dillon Chassis, who was building Rusty's cars at the time. This is late in 1982. Ray calls me at home late one night—that's how I usually heard from him—and he tells me, "Hey Don, I made this deal with Stephen Blake, who's restarting the Avanti sports car as the Avanti II. Blake wants to build an Avanti II-bodied race car, using one of my chassis, and run it in the 24 Hours of Daytona. I don't know what tire to put on it."

I said, "Ray, let me tell you something. If you put on a regular road race tire, it'll cost you a fortune. They'll wear out fast. You'll be stopping before you need gas. Why don't you put on the 3311? I'll send you four free, and you can test them." He said, and I'm moderating the quote here, "You're kidding me." Ray ran them for something like 80 laps in a test at Daytona, and called me again, saying, "It's incredible. They don't wear and the lap times don't fall off." Ray built the car and installed a small-block Chevy built by Bo Laws. The drivers were Joe Ruttman and the chassis whiz, Herb Adams. They had mechanical problems in the actual race, which slowed them down somewhat, but Ray still only used about two sets of tires for the entire 24 hours. That just blew everyone's mind.

To get everything executed properly on these deals was pretty challenging. I had to work with executives at the world's largest tire company, track owners, the sponsors that they had to work with every season, and a bunch of drivers, many of whom raced for a living under intensely competitive conditions. Most of those also probably started out thinking I was going to cheat them somehow by trying to shove a tire down their throats. On top of it all, I had to answer to Roger for the way I ran his business. That said, it was an enormously enjoyable and satisfying time, although I spent a huge amount of time on the road with the various ventures.

> " *When I hear people complain, I feel like saying to them, 'Hey. My husband has one leg, had all kinds of broken bones. He was put back together, and works seven days a week, sometimes 14 hours a day. Tell me how hard your life is.' He's proud of what he does, and he doesn't want to fail. Donald has the charisma to succeed, and Roger has the confidence to let him. Roger Penske never tells you how to do something. You're already supposed to know that.*
>
> *I'm not saying it was all roses. But when you have a boss like Roger, you want to work hard for him. Don loved his job and was able to make a living at it. He asked me once, 'Would you rather I stay home all the time and hate what I do?'"*
>
> **PAT MILLER**

13
Trinkets and Trash

THE SPEC GOODYEAR SHORT-TRACK TIRE, even beyond its intended applications, was a huge success. All the while, we had continued building up Competition Tire West, building up the souvenir business, and maintaining our Penske endorsements as well.

Late in 1979, Roger once again came to me with a question. This time, it was, "How big do you think the souvenir business could be?"

I told him, "It can be as big as the drivers that you have." He explained to me, in some detail, how our race team sponsors were saying that they wanted to get additional exposure, something that went just beyond the racing itself. Roger asked if I had any ideas, and if so, he wanted me to implement them by creating a new business venture for Penske that dealt with sponsor issues alone.

I agreed to do it, but told him that for it to work, I needed to be excused from all the other things that I was already doing. Roger didn't miss a beat. He offered, on the spot, to buy my share of Competition Tire West. We came up with what I thought was a fantastic price. Roger offered to give me all of the value in Penske Corporation stock, which turned out to be a good deal as the stock has split several times over the years. He said I could still keep working with the race team. Then Roger conversationally laid out the framework for a company that would do what Penske Products did with its promotional lines—although it was apparent from the start that we couldn't call it Penske Products; we had to take a neutral position if we were to represent other clients with connections to racing.

Ticking off pieces of his idea, Roger was confident that we could immediately get Norton Company and Gould, who were sponsoring the Penske Indy cars, plus a couple of others, like Sunoco, as customers. We figured that we'd build a marketing and souvenir business on a scale that hadn't been seen before in the sport. We decided to name the company Motorsports International, and it began business in 1980 as a subsidiary of Penske Corporation.

This was a very busy time. I was still finishing up at Competition Tire, and Rusty was beginning his Winston Cup career in earnest, starting our Chevrolet at Atlanta and finishing that astounding second to Dale Earnhardt, who was on his way to his first Winston Cup title. As we've seen, Penske was already in the souvenir and the racing products business, but when Motorsports International first opened for business, the souvenir operation had been moved to the race shop in Reading. We started out with $60,000 in obsolete inventory sitting on the books. So, as much as I like to say we started Motorsports International with nothing, that's not accurate. On the balance sheet, the obsolete stuff was less than nothing. "Trinkets and trash," some of the bookkeeping people called it.

The first decision I made as president of Motorsports International was to move the whole operation to Saint Louis, that location thing again. Let me summarize here what we accomplished with that company: We created, and perfected, the concept of full-service marketing for race sponsors. We conceived and built the first show cars, a standard thing in racing sponsorship today. We designed and built the traveling souvenir trailer. We had a business that handled timely, effective national programs for teams and sponsors in every discipline of motorized racing, including boats. It was a terrific success—to the point where NASCAR eventually came to us to buy it for themselves—and generated profits that formed the foundation for Penske Racing South.

Before I agreed to go into this with Roger, I was confident it would work, for what's really a pretty simple reason: I watch people, and watch what they do. By 1980, millions of people wore clothing and bought souvenirs every day that supported some kind of pro sports team. If you're on the street and some guy comes walking your way wearing a Pittsburgh Steelers T-shirt, he obviously got it from someplace. In 1980, it was pretty clear to us that racing, especially at its top levels, was ready for the same kind of phenomenon. We already had pretty strong evidence of that by selling out of the little souvenir trailer that we'd bought used from Shelby.

We started out with a single truck and trailer. We also, I should add, pioneered the design of the modern souvenir trailer with the flip-up side panel that becomes a sales window, years before every NASCAR team had one. Within 18 months, or by mid-1981, we had built a brand-new building in Saint Peters, a suburb of Saint Louis, and we had 60 people working in various capacities to maintain

growth. We had show cars traveling all over the United States. Besides the original sponsors that Roger brought aboard, we also had Pennzoil and the Miller Brewing Company, plus a bunch of others. We put on a Legends of Drag Racing tour that included guys like Dyno Don Nicholson, Arnie Beswick and Phil Bonner, all storybook guys from the early factory Super Stock and F/X wars. In a year and a half, we became the marketing arm for all motorsports sponsored by Miller, including unlimited hydroplanes, the big racing boats. By about 1986, this was a multi-million-dollar business. From that single truck-and-trailer rig, we went to having close to 40, and our trucks were traveling a million miles a year. That's two round trips to the moon, and we rolled up all those miles without a single accident.

> " *When I started working for Penske Products, the company was tiny, with only six full-time employees. We were primarily a merchandise-fulfillment company specializing in auto racing clothing and souvenir items. Most of our merchandise was Penske Racing-related, either for the sponsors or event merchandise for the fan. We produced our own catalogs for mail order and began sending souvenir trailers to some of the Indy car events.*

Motorsports International represented many high-visibility corporations, including the Miller Brewing Company. Shown here is the Miller Porsche 962 show car. (Don Miller Collection)

Trinkets and Trash   **129**

We quickly outgrew our original facility in Saint Charles, Missouri, and moved to a new location not far away in Saint Peters, Missouri. The new facility was huge by comparison, about 30,000 square feet. Shortly after we moved in, I was talking to Don and remarked that I thought the new building was beautiful but I questioned the need for all of this space. What were we going to do with it all? Don looked at me and said, 'We are going to fill it up with new clients and lots of new business. In 18 months, you're going to be telling me we need more room.'

Obviously, he knew more than he was telling us at the time. Shortly thereafter, the business just exploded. Don had more energy than anyone I have ever worked for. He was always there to suggest a solution or solve a problem, but he wasn't a micromanager. He instilled confidence in his employees and encouraged them to take charge. It was obvious to everyone that he enjoyed doing his job and he was very good to his people. I stayed with Motorsports International until Penske moved it to Michigan in 1993. By then, Don was already down in North Carolina with the race team.

In terms of his leadership abilities, I'd say his strongest one, ironically, is his wish not to be a leader. He tries instead to bring out each individual to grow into a leader in his or her own right. That's how you build a team. Whatever Don gets involved with, you know it's going to turn into something good."

CELIA BENNETT SMITH
Former Logistics Manager
Motorsports International
Saint Charles, Missouri

Our controller, or head accountant, at Motorsports International was Dave Hoffert, a razor-sharp guy when it comes to cost control. He emphasized, again and again, that a very important element in determining our profitability would be our ability to control our insurance bills. Dave kept telling us, "You guys can't be crashing the trucks." And despite those miles, we never did.

" *I told Don more than once that he ran a business like a Mom and Pop operation, but somehow the numbers always seemed to work. He had a sense about accounting: Accountants are the people who clean up the messes that marketing people make. Don has a great sense of humor and whenever things got a little testy between us, he would always revert to his favorite Don-ism. He would look you straight in the eye and say 'What the hell, Dave. If it wasn't for guys like us screwing things up, guys like you wouldn't have any-*

thing to do.' We would both have a good laugh and then settle down and resolve the problem.

Don and I were a bit of the opposite. He was into cars, where I didn't have any background like that at all. Yet somehow, we always seemed to make things work."

DAVE HOFFERT
Chief Financial Officer
Penske Racing
Mooresville, North Carolina

We assembled a great team at Motorsports International, and I think that was the key to our success. Richie Rubinstein led the marketing department. If you're from the Northeast and his name rings a bell, give yourself an attaboy. Richie had previously worked in upstate New York for Glenn Donnelly, founder of DIRT, the big group that sanctions dirt Modified racing, including Syracuse. His team also included Wally McCarty, previously of CATO Marketing in Atlanta, and Steve Stubbs, who was one of the promoters of ASA. We also had two or three other very successful marketing people from the racing fraternity. The logistics director was Celia Bennett and the fabrication and maintenance section was managed by Jeff Thousand, who'd started out wrenching with one of Rusty's early Late Model teams. These were all gifted people who were dedicated to this operation.

Dave Hoffert was our Chief Financial Officer at Motorsports International. Dave considered my accounting skills to be somewhat lacking and often said I ran things like a Mom and Pop operation. After 25 years of working together, we are still good friends. (Jim Donnelly Photo)

> *Motorsports International didn't invent the show car, but the team there certainly perfected it. I can remember that before that time, if the show car driver got sick or if we were stretched too thin, Don and I would take a show car wherever it needed to go, all the way from Reading to Saint Louis, or the other way. We had a pickup and a fifth-wheel trailer, and we'd just drive straight through, no problem. We had that kind of relationship."*

DAN LUGINBUHL

The guy in charge of all the mechanical stuff, including the very first Winston Cup souvenir trailer, was Jeff Thousand. Let me say this again: We built everything. If you've ever seen a show car at your local auto parts store, it's not a former Winston cup car that just got stuck in a trailer. Not with us at Motorsports International, anyway. We had a huge fabrication shop at our headquarters, where Jeff and his guys would build them from scratch, specifically as show cars. Like everything else in racing, it's purpose built.

It's hard to describe the magnitude of what we did, but at its high point, Motorsports International operated 20 show car teams in just about every category of professional auto racing. We actually built the show cars, plus modified the trailers to facilitate souvenir sales as well as transport the cars between display locations. In addition, the marketing department developed promotional events for 10 major corporations then involved in premier racing series. While all of this was going on, the souvenir fulfillment division was growing by significant proportions each quarter.

I told Roger from the outset—another guy who called it "trinkets and trash"—that if this was done right, the drivers would make more money than guys in the NFL. I told him that if a driver was making a million bucks now just from driving, had a merchandising program that was done properly, and kept winning races, he could make that million dollars a year from racing and *$10 million* from souvenirs. Roger's response was, "You have lost your mind." But five years later, Dale Earnhardt was making $5 or $6 million a year driving for Richard Childress, and $10 million on souvenirs. (The drivers typically net 10 to 15 percent of retail as a royalty.) Think about that. And the retail sales through his endorsements were probably over $150 million a year in the same time frame.

Obviously, any operation of this size produces its share of remarkable stories. One that will always stick in my mind involved an amazing accomplishment by the Indy car team of Penske Racing. In 1987, Penske Racing had three teams entered in the Indianapolis 500, all scheduled to compete with the new March-Cosworths produced

by Penske Cars Ltd. in Poole, England. Due to some mechanical difficulties—plus a practice crash—the Penske Team found itself short one race car. Jay Signore, then the president and general manager at Penske Racing, called me directly and asked if we still had this old March 86C that the team had loaned Motorsports International the previous year for conversion into a show car. My answer was yes, but I added that the car was then on display in a hotel lobby in Reading. Jay told me, "Get it back quick, and bring it directly to Indianapolis, because we're going to be forced to race it this month." We got it there. Al Unser then drove it to victory in the 1987 Indianapolis 500.

We were so effective that I finally realized that one day, we'd have to go out of business at Motorsports International simply because we'd never get big enough to supply the Kmarts and Wal-Marts of the world. Yes, honestly, I really believed it would get that big someday. And really, that business doesn't have much of anything to do with auto racing per se.

You know what? Right now, we're at the point where it's all gone over the top and is on its way back down. Everything in sports is cyclical. I don't care if it's road racing, Indy car racing, stock cars, baseball, football or anything else. It grows and shrinks. The NASCAR-driven souvenir industry isn't selling T-shirts now like they used to. It got so big that they finally did end up putting T-shirts in the Wal-Marts. Joe the Plumber or whoever can now go there and buy a Jeff Gordon or Kasey Kahne T-shirt and pay 12 bucks for it. At the race track, it's going to cost him $30 to buy it off a souvenir trailer. What's the economics in that? The only way to make this souvenir thing work any-

This Penske March show car was called in as a replacement vehicle for Al Unser, Sr. at the Indy 500. Remarkably, Al won the race in this car. (IMS Photo)

more is to go back, rebuild the dealer network, and make this stuff really hard to get, exclusive, like it used to be.

When I look back today, I still can't help but conclude that Motorsports International was both a tremendous challenge, from a business standpoint, and a monumental organizational achievement. During the first few months of operation, Dave Hoffert asked me how I intended to generate the operating capital to grow it at the rate I'd predicted in my formal business plan. I explained that the object was to contract our services to as many existing sponsors as possible and be innovative, to stay on the cutting edge of the business. He looked at me, and then pointed to a photo I had mounted on the wall behind my desk. "Kind of like that guy," he said. The photo was a black-and-white picture of Albert Einstein. It was captioned, "Imagination is more important than knowledge." I nodded to Dave and answered, "Exactly."

 If Don says you can do it, you will do it. Look at what we had to pull off to keep all those trucks and trailers rolling when we were in Saint Louis. Look how he first sold that track tire to ASA for Goodyear. His vision, in terms of making things happen, is incredible, his ability to see something through. There were a lot of hours with him, round-the-clock, but the satisfaction of seeing something finished, done right, was well worth it. Especially when you, yourself, were the one with all the doubts about whether you could pull it off."

JEFF THOUSAND

We rode that cutting edge for years. Ironically, 12 months after we started the business, Dave visited us to formulate our first annual financial report. I'll always remember what he said: "Believe it or not, Miller, you are going to break even this year, which I believe is fantastic." As it turned out, Motorsports International became hugely profitable, generating millions of dollars annually, and hundreds of thousands in profit. We did all right, I'd say.

14

MBA (Management by Ability)

I LIKE PEOPLE. I like to be able to say, "This person, right here, can do something." I've known lots of people I can say that about, like Jeff Thousand, for instance. I knew he had intelligence and leadership ability and only had to be given some responsibility. The same thing's true for the Dave Hofferts and John Woodys of this world. You surround yourself with good people and build them into a team. That's exactly what Roger Penske does in his various organizations. Roger is a people person, too, as well as a great leader. In my way of thinking, there are two types of leadership: by example, and by intimidation. Roger is a leader by example.

> After a couple of days of working really long hours, when you might start feeling sorry for yourself, you'd look over and there would be Roger, going flat out. Nobody in the company was above doing anything, including Roger. He set the standard. If you're going to be in the racing business, you'll find out it's very time-intensive, and that there's a sense of urgency involved. Roger would always say, 'Look, the Indianapolis 500 starts at 11 o'clock, and they're not going to wait for you. You've got to be there. You've got to be ready to go.' That's true at any race track. When it's time for the green flag, it's time to go. We always considered ourselves the best in the business. Don and I always had a saying: Proper Prior Planning Prevents Piss-Poor Performance."

DAN LUGINBUHL

Exercising proper leadership, in any endeavor, is vital to success. Leadership by intimidation will work for a while. Ultimately, though, it falls apart because people get tired of it. They'll grumble among themselves, "This is

135

what that guy says to do, but he never does it." Richard Petty told me one time, "You know, racing is like any other sport, or any other business, but instead of all the other forces from the outside getting together to destroy you, you destroy yourself from the inside because your ego gets too big. All of a sudden, nobody knows anything but you."

If you make up your mind to do something, you have to tell yourself if it's going to take a lot of effort and you can't do it by yourself. So what do you do? You look around and find someone who can help you. They don't necessarily have to know everything, because you're going to learn together. What you know, you can teach them going in. You're going to get better together, and that's when you're at your strongest. No matter what you do, if you don't have the chemistry to make the circle complete, you're never going to get there. In all kinds of businesses—and for sure, in all kinds of racing—you can take money, just pour it in, and never achieve a damn thing, because you have no chemistry. Some people don't care. *They don't care.* It's just a job. That's why some of these big businesses are failing, because their people just want a paycheck, or a bonus. They don't care about the company. If you have a set of circumstances like that—you have a 30-man crew and you're trying to reach a certain goal, and nobody really cares—you'll never get there.

You make them care by showing them that whatever you're going to ask them to do, you will do yourself, too. You might possibly tell them, "I can do it probably better than you, but I'll let you try." You don't have to actually say it, you can just let them figure that out. And you have to be patient at the start, because otherwise you'll never get to the point where they'll believe in you. At Penske South, Dave Hoffert, our chief financial officer, said one day, "The reason we made it here in spite of everything . . . is because you've got these people believing in you. They'd eat ground glass for you. They know you'll do the same for them."

My philosophy is to get a central core of five or six individuals and build on it. Let them pick the guys they want to work with, while you oversee their choice. Never tell them, "This guy's a jerk." Instead tell them, "I don't know that this person's going to work out. I know you'll do your tasks the right way, but I don't think this guy will do that, because of A, B, C. So before you make a choice, sit down and think about it because you've got to live with him for a while." Ninety-five percent of the time, they'll make the right decision.

When you're going to go after a big challenge, do it with the understanding that when you go to war—which is what we do every weekend—you take your best planes, your best bombs, your best tanks, and you play it like war because at the end of the day,

Nobody in Late Model racing believed their tire supplier would be honest with them. I proved otherwise. In this business, personal credibility and accountability are utterly indispensable. Here, Darrell Waltrip, Bobby Allison and I talk tires at the Milwaukee Mile ASA race. (Don Miller Collection)

there's only one winner and everyone else is a loser. You put your best army together, so you really have to know your people.

I went out of my way to get to know my people. I wanted to know who their families were, how many kids they had, did they want a house, or were they overextended. It didn't stop at the job interview process. Life is a job interview process. It never stops. When you're going down the road, you're always thinking about the next step, or next question, and the one after that. When they come through the door, you've got to ask those questions so you can know if that person can even get to Step One. The big thing, and this may be an over-simplification but I've found it to be true, is that everything is built on relationships. You build them first with the people, and eventually, those individual relationships become a relationship with the company, and it's always based on one thing: Can they trust you? For me, it went all the way back to being a factory rep for Ed Rachanski at RepCor. If you get a reputation for being square and trustworthy, then you can achieve your objectives.

Here's another example: Another tire manufacturer was going for the same CWRA contract that we were. It was a huge potential contract, since the CWRA guys raced six nights a week. We were all shooting for a specification and pricing point. Every time, it would come down to, "How good is this guy at keeping his word?" The reason we got the CWRA business every year with the Late Models was that we never lied to them, we never cheated them, we never low-balled them, and we told them, "This is the price that everybody pays all over the country." At a CWRA meeting in the dead of winter, one of the suppliers had about a $15-per-tire advantage over Goodyear and almost got the contract, but they didn't get picked. The racers didn't believe that the code number on their tires meant anything. Too many times the previous year, they'd showed up with soft tires for their selected teams that had a bogus code number stamped on them. Their word was no good, and their reputation had preceded them to this meeting. Phony promises don't work the second time around. Dick Trickle used to call me the face at the race, the face of Goodyear.

> " *When Don sold his share of Competition Tire West, the man from Hoosier said thanks. He figured that business would finally come back to them."*
>
> **PAT MILLER**

A lot of people might disagree with me, but I would say that in my whole career, 20 percent of the people I've met in business are what you could call trustworthy. I'd say the next 40 percent of those people are products of the buzzword, or as people like to say now, empty suits. They say all the things you want to hear, they say they're going to do this and that for you as follow-up, and once they get your signature on the paper, they're gone. Those are the guys that burn all the bridges for all the other people who are trying to accomplish something, or build a business, or just make a living. Their reputation eventually precedes them, and people don't pay attention to them anymore. I'm pretty good at picking out phonies. I just listen to them. If every other word out of their mouth is "I" or "me," I pretty much know I've got one. They're all over the place, especially as you go farther up the scale.

There's a tendency for companies recruiting leadership personnel to focus on people with all these degrees, and the management people figure, well, they went to all these schools so they must know something. *Not.* I call them Brains in a Frame. I'd rather have someone with an imagination than one with a degree in everything. The person with the imagination is a thinker.

Another red flag that you can spot in an interview comes when you have the wrong guy asking the wrong questions. One that's easy to pick up on is, "Well, how many people am I going to have working for me?" What difference does that make? Are you going to do the job? *You* tell *me* how many people you need to work for you. People like this inevitably ask the wrong questions, the ones that are built around their self-centered attitude. When I get somebody like that in an interview, the warning buzzer goes off. "Tell me what you've done. What have you done with that fancy education up to this point? What do you want to be in this business for?"

Naturally, I hear a lot of honest answers, too, the first among them being some variation on, "I really want to work in racing." I have to help them qualify that statement by asking, "What do you want to do in racing?" If the answer is, "I don't know," the person doesn't belong in racing. The very first thing any person has to tell me is what he or she has done before. I want to know a little bit about the person. The response may be, "I had this job at the 7-Eleven, and then I got a job at Auto Zone." What did you do at Auto Zone? "I worked behind the counter." How long were you there? "Six months." Why did you leave? "Because I wanted to work in racing." Okay. That's why you're here, right? What do you want to do? "I'd like to be a mechanic." What kind of mechanical experience do you have? "Well, um, I changed the spark plugs on my sister-in-law's car." Have you gone to any schools? "No. But I always wanted to be a mechanic." Don't you think it would be a good idea to get that kind of technical training? "I really don't have time to do that." Well, I hate to be blunt, but if you don't have time to go to school, you don't have time to learn here, because we don't have time to teach you. And that's the end of that conversation.

Tex Powell and I have a similar work ethic—trust and honesty usually win out in the end. (Jim Donnelly Photo)

Another variation is when a guy comes in and says, "I want to work in racing, and I want to work for this team." Why? "Because you guys are successful." Okay, that's a pretty good answer. What do you think you can bring to the table? "Well, I work on a short-track car, and I've done it for six years." Did you ever win a race? "Yeah, we won a couple of races." What did you do then? "I got out of it because it was too much traveling." Oh. So what are you looking for now? "I changed my mind?" Well, how long has it been since you changed your mind? "What do you mean by that?" I mean, how long is it going to be before you change your mind again and decide you don't want to travel? "Well, do I have to travel?" Well, yes. "How often?" Every weekend. By this time, I begin to think the guy's never even watched a race on TV. I finally tell him that he needs to go get a job at a dealership, so he can go home every night. It's not that I'm trying to be mean to him, just honest!

Then there's the guy who comes in and says, "Look, I want to work here. I don't care if I have to start by sweeping the floor. I have a degree in engineering from the General Motors Institute"—or wherever—"and I know I can't just come in here and be an engineer, but I want to learn. The salary isn't an issue. I just need enough to live. I want to learn, and contribute, and I don't care if I have to work 10 hours a day, or 12, or seven days a week. I don't care. I want to work here."

He's got a job. We'll see how long he lasts. We'll give him 90 days to see if he likes us and we like him. At the end of 90 days, he comes

MBA (Management by Ability) **139**

in to sit down in front of me, and we see if we can go forward. Ask any of the guys I've hired and they'll tell you they did it the same way. This is what you're going to make and this is where you're going to start. If we hire you, you can start tomorrow. We want to know what you can do for us. You start, and you keep climbing that ladder, and you work your way up. That's how it happens.

The lessons here about people, and about knowing very specific things about them and their abilities, apply very strongly to racing. I don't necessarily want to name names here, but I know a really good crew chief at a top Ford team who's no engineer. He can take a spreadsheet and tell you what to do, but he can't retrieve that stuff from a computer. A team engineer does that for him, and then this car chief interprets it. You get the flip side of that from another team now, a GM team, that has all kinds of engineers and is letting them make all the decisions on race day, and that's the wrong thing to do. They'll say, "Well, according to the computer, the temperature at 9:51 A.M. is going to be such-and-such, and therefore we have to have this much air in the tires," and when they go out there, they can't hit their own asses with a baseball bat. It doesn't work that way. It's: Who was out there before? Was there an ARCA race beforehand? Were those people on Hoosier rubber? It's a world of variables. No one that's not been internally involved in the day-to-day management of a real race team has any appreciation of that. I've hired engineers, communicated with them and have total respect for them. But on a race team, you have to have some minds—real racing minds, not theoretically oriented minds—placed in charge.

> **"** *It's a challenge, more so than just money, the opportunity to make a difference. I think that's one thing Don and I have always had in common, a lot of passion. In racing, you have to believe in your driver, your fellow worker, and have a common goal. Some principles and procedures in racing, like those, have really not changed very much. It's the technology, the mechanics of it that have changed.*
>
> *I've had some dealings with a team that hired a lot of engineers and said that they wouldn't need a crew chief until the race started, that all the decisions would be made by the engineers and that the crew chief would only determine the pit stops and such. Needless to say, it didn't work. It's the mix that makes it work."*
>
> **TEX POWELL**

15
Moving South

OBVIOUSLY, ONE OF THE MOST IMPORTANT and rewarding things I've done in this sport was to form a successful Winston Cup team with Rusty Wallace and Roger Penske, which started out as Penske Racing South. But, before we can talk about Penske South, I need to tell you how Rusty Wallace came to be a Winston Cup champion. His status as a Cup star made everything else feasible.

From the standpoint of pure innate talent, Rusty was obviously ready to go in Winston Cup right from when Roger gave him those couple of runs in the Penske car, before Roger decided he was sticking with his CART operation. It took a tremendous amount of money to run Winston Cup even in 1980, and Rusty and I just didn't have it. Rusty went off into short-track racing, where he had some commitments to John Childs and others, and continued his career. It's a matter of record what happened then, including two ASA championships, plus their prestigious 400-lapper at Winchester in 1982. Rusty had also built a Winston Cup car, a Buick Regal, at the Poor Boy Chassis shop, and got a Don Kirn engine to power it. I helped him where I could but I didn't do much. Then I got him some sponsorship from Ramada Inns, through a really good friend of mine in Missouri. Chris Hebler was a real race fan and also the vice president of Ramada Inns. We headed south, trying to qualify for the 1983 Daytona 500.

We figured we had a good shot. We already knew enough small details from the Grand American races to hang the body aerodynamically, especially with the excellent skills of Jeff Thousand and Dave Wirz. Rusty time trialed pretty well. We were running in the top 10 on the backstretch in our 125-miler when we got hit from behind by Rick Wilson, who either wasn't paying attention or had misjudged the draft. Rusty got into the infield,

Rusty was the substitute driver for Johnny Rutherford in the Levi Garrett #98 whenever Johnny's Indy car schedule conflicted with NASCAR dates. (Don Miller Collection)

Rusty entered the #72 Ramada Inn Buick in the 1983 Daytona 500. Unfortunately, this car was destroyed in a savage wreck during the Daytona 125 qualifying race. (Don Miller Collection)

which was muddy from rainstorms, started to flip and rolled the car up into a ball. That was the crash where his windshield popped out and he got slammed in the face with a wall of mud that packed his helmet and goggles, and Rusty thought he'd been blinded. It really rang his bell but he was largely okay.

Rusty built another Cup car, and since I'd been introducing him around to other car owners, he managed to pick up the Chattanooga Chew-sponsored Chevy, ordinarily driven by Johnny Rutherford, when Rutherford wasn't in it. From there, right around the time that Rusty won the 1983 ASA title, we signed Gatorade as a sponsor, and Rusty hooked up with Cliff Stewart as a driver. Cliff Stewart owned a big furniture store in High Point, North Carolina, and had just fired Geoff Bodine when he signed Rusty. Cliff's son Howard owned a company that supplied hard engine parts to a lot of the Winston Cup teams.

To get Gatorade on board, we had developed a whole proposal. We put together a presentation videotape that showed Rusty's past achievements. We actually gave the presentation to a lot of different companies, including Budweiser, but we were never able to land a really big one. We persevered, however. Being in Motorsports International helped a lot, because I knew so many people, and, as I've said, it's all about relationships—if people in racing don't know you, they're not even going to talk to you. There are a lot of people who are very industrious and work their guts out, and they may have a good team and good driver, but never get to talk to the right people, the decision-makers. If you have a reputation in the industry, and you meet and talk to a lot of people—somebody mentions your name, and the person goes, "Oh yeah, I remember him. Nice guy. I should talk to him"—that's how it happens. Without that, the chances of success are hugely diminished.

Rusty was NASCAR Rookie of the Year in 1984 but the team had problems, especially engine failures, and he never won any races with Stewart. It quickly became apparent that Rusty was going to have go someplace else. I started talking to Raymond Beadle of Blue Max Racing, who owned the Pontiac that Tim Richmond had driven for Blue Max in 1984. I already knew Raymond, because he also owned Chaparral Trailers in his native Texas, and we'd been buying them at Motorsports International to make into mobile stores. I also knew him through UDRA, where he'd raced his landmark *Blue Max* fuel Funny Cars. He had a pretty good Winston Cup team, with Harold Elliott as his engine builder and Barry Dodson as his crew chief, and those guys had been eyeing Rusty for a while. At the end of 1984, Tim Richmond announced that he was leaving Raymond to go drive for Rick Hendrick. I started talking to Raymond, and ended up going down to his office in Dallas, where we made the deal for Rusty to come over. Rusty already had Pontiac sponsorship through Cliff Stewart; another sponsor we'd gotten, Alugard, agreed to follow him to Blue Max as well. The team jelled quickly, and Rusty got his first Winston Cup win at Bristol in early 1985.

    My favorite story about Don involves the influence that he's had over Rusty Wallace. Rusty was a popular driver, came out of the Midwest, was good-looking, had the gift of gab and all that stuff. All of that changed one fateful day at Charlotte, during The Winston in 1989. Rusty and Darrell Waltrip were battling each other, and they got up in the fourth turn. Who really knows what happened? Rusty got into Darrell's quarter panel when Darrell was leading, coming into the fourth turn. Darrell spun down the front, into the grass, and Rusty went on to win the race. I was in the control tower at the time. And it wasn't but a few minutes after the race was over that my assistant called me and said she had a telephone call to transfer to me. She did, and this guy on the phone said to me, 'That blank-blank is not going to leave that place.' It was a death threat. He said he was going to kill Rusty Wallace. I had learned to take those kinds of things pretty seriously.

    Rusty was obviously shaken up . . . because after the race ended, he came by the start-finish line and the people were just booing him as he came off the fourth turn. They were in an absolute uproar. Here was Darrell Waltrip, who was not the most popular guy in the world at the time, who's being applauded, and Rusty was being booed like he'd never been before.

    He kept hearing those boos when he went into the winner's circle, and it was kind of like flipping a switch with him. As was the custom in those days, after the winner's circle, all of the media were in the press box upstairs, not the media center in the infield. I waited with the security guy for Rusty to come up the elevator. I wanted to take him upstairs to the control tower first, and I cleared everybody out of the tower. I got Rusty up there and sat down with him one-on-one, and I told him, 'Rusty, I know what happened, but you've had a death threat against you.' What little blood he had left in his face just drained out. I told him I was getting him bodyguards, getting a couple of Charlotte policemen to stay outside his house that night, but right now, he had to go through this press conference. He was absolutely devastated.

I could tell his life was going to change from that point on, and I wasn't sure if it was going to be for the better. There's nothing worse for a race driver than the first time he really gets booed bad. Looking back on it now, I believe to this day that Don was the one who got him turned back around, got Rusty back on his feet again mentally. He understood that there was only one guy who could say what his real intention was going into that fourth turn, and it wasn't Darrell Waltrip. You've got two guys racing for the same spot, and only the person behind the wheel really knows. That's locked somewhere in Rusty's brain now. My interpretation is that it was racing. Contact is something that happens. We already knew that Rusty wasn't an evil, bad racer. Like I said, it was Don that got him back."

H. A. "HUMPY" WHEELER
President, The Wheeler Company
Charlotte, North Carolina

Humpy Wheeler is one of those rare individuals who understands automobile racing and really knows how to put on a show. (The Wheeler Company)

Unless you're very new to racing, you most likely know that Rusty won the Winston Cup championship with Blue Max Racing in 1989, along with 13 point races plus The Winston. It was a great, towering time for Rusty, and I was still with him during that time. I was running Motorsports International in Saint Louis, and still working some for Competition Tire West. We went up to the banquet at the Waldorf Astoria in New York and received most of our checks, but not all of them. That was because Raymond Beadle, at that point, had spent a lot of money that he didn't have. I don't know how it got to that point, and I'm never going to say he did it intentionally. I wasn't the one writing the checks. I do know that as a team, those Blue Max guys ran their hearts out, even though there were times when they didn't have enough money to buy tires, and Goodyear wouldn't extend them any more credit. That was a tough way to go in the last six or seven races of 1989, but they stuck together and won the championship.

Going into 1990, Blue Max Racing was going to lose its sponsorship from Kodiak tobacco. Rusty and I put together a deal with the

Miller Brewing Company. I did most of the work on it, because I already had relationships with Miller, through their being a Motorsports International client. They were definitely interested in sponsoring Rusty. However, when it came to the point of them doing the credit checks—which, believe me, any big sponsor is going to do before they agree to hand someone millions of dollars—they found out that Raymond was not the best credit risk. Miller's people said to me, "We're going to do this, because we signed on the dotted line. But you're going to be responsible for the money." I was going to have to ensure that the bills would be paid, and that Rusty was going to be paid. We ended up suing Raymond for the money that Rusty was due for his championship, which was a nightmare.

Rusty and I put our heads together, and before long, Rusty said, "Let's start our own team." I didn't have to tell him what a huge step that represented, but I did it anyway. It was clear that we couldn't go on as we had been, even though we settled the suit against Raymond with an agreement in October 1989 that Rusty would drive for him for the balance of 1989 and then for one more year, 1990, with the Miller colors. Earlier, I had agreed with Rusty that the time was right to go on our own, and I went to Roger and told him as much: "I'm appreciative of everything you've ever done for me. I want to stay your friend. I really want to do this team with Rusty." Roger insisted that I remain with the company to keep my profit sharing going, in case things didn't work out, since he'd been down this kind of road before. He personally assured me that if our team didn't make it, Rusty and I would always have jobs at Penske.

Tentatively, we began our moves. We'd scouted out a piece of land on Knob Hill Road in the new Lakeside Business Park just off Interstate 77 in Mooresville, which was then largely empty countryside. We bought the property from Bill Simpson, who had originally wanted to set up a Cup team for his son David, until David got hurt. We retained some lawyers for the corporation we were going to set

While driving for Stewart Racing, Rusty continued to build his own Sportsman cars. Here, Rusty races Bobby Allison for the lead. (Don Miller Collection)

up, and as a cover story, called it MR Racing. As we began putting up the first building, we went quietly to some of the guys on the Blue Max team, guys that we hoped would come to work with us. I came down to Mooresville and worked with the contractors while we hired our first couple of employees and started gathering the materials to build cars. By about August 1990, we had maybe half a dozen employees, and some of the guys were starting to leave Blue Max to come to our new team. Barry Dodson had a big-money offer to do a team with the guy who owned Dirt Devil, the vacuum cleaner company. Rusty really wanted Jimmy Makar, the Blue Max car chief, to become our crew chief and Harold Elliott to build our engines. They both agreed. We also got David Evans and a few other guys for the engine department.

Roger had been watching all this in early 1990 and knew we were serious. He called me one day just to check in, like any friend would, regardless of whether he's also been your partner and your boss. Roger asked me, "How are things going, really?" I told him they were just going along, basically. He suggested that I take on another partner, that it would help us out financially, even though I replied that we really didn't need a partner—or at least, hadn't considered one. He even said he could suggest one, and I asked him who that might be.

He simply asked, "How about me?" Roger had previously realized how big NASCAR was, saw in early 1990 how it was continuing to grow, and knew it was now prime for him from a business standpoint. But I still wasn't sure he was serious, until he told me he really wanted to get back in. And he saw that Rusty and I were working our asses off trying to get going. But I still had some reservations.

> *I talked to Junior Johnson, who wanted me to drive his car. We're thinking back and forth, and Don says, 'You know what? Penske is available, I think, to talk about going back into racing.' I wanted to try it, but Don goes, 'I don't know, he's going to expect a lot, he's a perfectionist, you're kind of a loosey-goosey-type guy.' I wanted Penske. He'd won the Indianapolis 500 all these times, everything he had was shiny and cool, and I wanted to be part of that.*
>
> *We talked to him, and by then, Miller Brewing Company wanted to sponsor me . . . Don got me hooked up with Miller. He was doing all the marketing for Miller through Motorsports International . . . I had Kodiak as a sponsor, but he kept saying, 'Let's go up and see them.' We spoke to a guy at Miller named Kevin Wolfe, and he said, we'd love to have you. That's when we went to Roger and took him up on his offer."*

RUSTY WALLACE

Roger, Rusty and I kept talking, one thing led to another, and then we went back to the attorneys. In March 1990, we created a tentative agreement under which Roger would own 52 percent of the new business, while Rusty and I would each own 24, starting with the 1991 racing season. From there, we started realigning our sponsors, even though we believed we had Miller Brewing coming aboard.

Roger has this incredible aura about him when he goes in to make a top-level presentation. He will just explain directly that to make something successful, you're going to have to up the ante. He's just laying it out to the sponsors: We're going to build a new shop, do this, do that, while I'm wondering how we're going to get it all done in time for Daytona in February 1991. But we walked out of that meeting with his commitment.

At that point, Roger just told us all, "You take it from here." He told us that he'd help us with the contracts, but told us get it done, and told Rusty to do the best job he possibly could for Raymond for the rest of 1990.

> When we decided to get back into NASCAR Cup racing it was certainly at Don's urging. He knew that Rusty, just coming off a Championship, was eager to make a change, so we had a driver, one of the best. With Don's great relations with the Miller Brewing Company and Pontiac we knew we had a solid base to start this new team. Miller was already a sponsor of our Indy car team and at our race tracks. With Don's sales ability clearly on display, they came on as primary sponsor of the new enterprise.
>
> The process went on for nearly a year before we made the team announcement at the Winston Cup banquet in 1990. Don had met with Walt, Dan, me and other key members of the organization during those months before to outline his thoughts and put the plan together. We were able to make a business case for getting back into NASCAR because its demographics appealed to our customers in the diesel engine and truck leasing businesses. It was a fit on several fronts.
>
> The unique company structure, with Don and Rusty receiving equity participation along with Penske Corporation, ensured that they were totally committed, although I never doubted that. It gave them both a chance for some upside return, which they fully realized several years later when we reorganized the motorsports operations. Over the following years, with Don's full-time attention and management, the team grew from about 15 people in a small shop in Mooresville to what we have today."

ROGER PENSKE

By mid-year 1990, we were hard at work building our new race shop for Penske Racing South. (Don Miller Collection)

"Don was working for Penske's merchandising arm, Motorsports International, in Saint Louis, along with his work with Rusty, when I first met him. I was doing the corporation's legal work for its various subsidiaries. Don had done a remarkable job of professionalizing that part of our business.

After Rusty had won the Winston Cup championship in 1989, Roger asked me to work with Rusty and Don to put this new organization in place, the team that became Penske South. The complication with forming the team was that Roger was very successful, very competitive and very professional in the way his teams had been put together over the years. You've got this very successful entrepreneur at the peak of his powers, as it were, coming together with a very successful driver as an owner. Your third partner, Don, is a very successful business guy, very ethical, in addition to being someone who'd overcome a very serious physical disability and was running the operation on a day-to-day basis. That, in and of itself, made for a very non-standard relationship."

LARRY BLUTH
General Counsel, Penske Corporation
Bloomfield Hills, Michigan

I came down to Mooresville, leaving the family in Saint Louis for the time being, and we hired 29 employees. At the same time, we began to build the first big race shop on the Knob Hill Road site—I actually used my art-school training for the first time in a while to lay out a preliminary floor plan. We hadn't been having much luck with the contractors who had been putting up the first building. They were really slow, and we didn't have the time to follow their schedule.

By mid-October of 1990, we were building cars at our little shop on Knob Hill Road for the 1991 season. (Don Miller Collection)

In stepped Danny Sullivan, who'd captured the 1985 Indy 500 for Roger in "spin and win" fashion, and whose father owned a construction company in Kentucky. Danny's father came down, brought his guys, and really started hitting it hard after I told them, "This thing has got to be done by February." They worked Saturdays and Sundays and put the building up, except it wasn't completely finished by the time we went to Daytona in early 1991. We worked out of a little 12,000-square-foot building in the rear of the property where we were building engines, welding chassis, painting cars. We got them as ready as they were going to be. We managed to get one test in at the GM wind tunnel. Jimmy Makar felt as if we were going to be okay. Harold Elliott built up some good motors.

We had a punch list of things that we were looking to finish, but there was no time left. I was concerned. I told Harold that we still had a lot of Xs that weren't crossed off. Harold answered me. "Don, I got to tell you this. It's something you've got to remember. The car is never done. It just comes time to go."

We loaded that baby in the trailer and headed for Florida. Believe it or not, we almost won the Daytona 500. If not for a late-race caution when I think that Kyle Petty and somebody else got into it, which put us out of position, I'm convinced we would have won it. We were in great shape and had enough fuel to make it to the end, while a lot of other guys didn't. It was one of those things. But by the sixth race of 1991, the Valleydale 500 at Bristol, we won our first race. That was an absolutely incredible accomplishment for a new team, and we were the most understaffed top-level Winston Cup team that was on the circuit at the time. From that point, we started to gain momentum and build on what we'd done. We realized, and so did Roger, that we had to get some engineers into our operation. Roger used his connections at GM to borrow one of their crackerjack engineers, Rex Stump, who's now chief engineer at Hendrick Motorsports. We went over to Penske Cars Ltd. in Poole, England, and came back with a designer, Andrew Scriven. Andrew had been creating the Penske Indy cars and we knew he would help Penske South, as the company was now called, with aerodynamics.

Penske South, for a while, was a microcosm or scaled-down version of the Hatfields and the McCoys. There were those on the team who wanted the engineers there, and those who wanted them gone. As it happened, their responsibilities were essentially split, with Rex on the driveline side and Andrew working on the aero package. I won't deny that it was an uphill battle, but we needed that kind of help. Rusty won again in 1991 at Pocono, even though we nearly ran out of fuel before the race was called for rain. Dale Earnhardt, in a very battered race car, pushed Rusty around for a couple of laps until NASCAR threw the red and checker. We also fell out of 10 races when the Pontiac broke.

We were frustrated. Roger sent me over to the Ilmor engine factory in England and had me sit down with Mario Illien to explain what was going on. Roger and Mario co-founded Ilmor along with the late Paul Morgan. I also met with his second-in-command, Steve Miller, who has become a really good friend and now operates the company. We all began the groundwork for a program to develop the Pontiac engine, which was an undertaking that soon had us facing many challenges.

On top of all our mechanical problems, however, we suffered a major loss. Jimmy Makar got, as they say, an offer he couldn't refuse. He left us in the middle of the year to organize Joe Gibbs' new team, joining his brother-in-law, Dale Jarrett, whom Joe hired as his lead driver. Even as a new team, with two wins, we were already going into a rebuilding mode.

Left: All prepped and ready for paint, our Daytona entry for 1991 sits in the paint booth. (Ernie Masche photo, Don Miller Collection)

Right: Our dyno room was state of the art, including computer data logging systems. (Ernie Masche photo, Don Miller Collection)

BRINGING IT ALL BACK HOME

Meanwhile, there was another, very important person I needed to pay some attention to during all this—my wife, who moved to Mooresville from Saint Louis once we had gotten the race team up and running.

I should start by saying that I have a really good family. One part of the evolution of our family is that Pat and I worked all our lives, and that we conveyed those values to our kids. We told them, "If you're going to school, you're going to get an education, not to play." We'd help them with that, give them enough money to maintain themselves in the dorm, to study, not to party. If they wanted to live in an apartment, they had to support that themselves. We paid their tuition for high school and college, but they knew they were going to have to work. At one point, our daughter Debbie was working three jobs when she was going to Michigan State. We were a family unit; we were close, but we were still scattered all over the place.

The girls knew they had to pinch pennies. When Debbie was out of money, she wouldn't come to us. She went to her sister Pam, and Pam would send her a little money. Debbie knew the rules. When you go to Saint Joseph's Academy, you'll more than likely get a scholarship to Saint Louis University, but Pam wanted to go to Missouri State in Springfield. It was a cute campus, but there was no challenge, so she decided she wanted to go to Saint Louis U. after all. She said, "Do you think they can give me my scholarship back?"

After getting her bachelor's degree, Pam went to work for a company in Saint Louis that was trying to invent artificial blood, because of AIDS. Then she worked at a camp for overweight kids in La Jolla, California, before she signed a contract to work for a year in Kauai, Hawaii. She went on to study nursing at the University of San Francisco, and that's where she met her husband Mike, who was finishing his residency in orthopedics. She's always looking for somebody to take care of her Dad, I guess.

> **"** We were parents. I had a job, he had a job, and we did it together . . . The girls come to me for frivolous things, I think. But when it comes to something serious, buying a house or a getting a job, they go to Dad. Our daughter Debbie and her husband Robert have a beautiful bungalow in Chicago, built in 1927. My friend Susan Wallace and I helped to get it set up. But it was Donald who gave them the advice about whether to buy it."
>
> **PAT MILLER**

Moving to Mooresville and helping to establish Penske South changed my life in countless ways. I want to specifically address one of those changes, because it's been extraordinarily important and meaningful to me, and to my family. I'm not going to suggest that I never would have met him otherwise, but it was here, in Mooresville, that I first met my very best friend, Ray Wallace, or as most of us call him, Razoar. We've done a lot together, both in and out of racing, since we met, not long after my wife arrived. Like a lot of people I'm tight with, Razoar is an engineer. He specialized in manufacturing design for The Timken Company, the bearing people, at their plant in Lincolnton, North Carolina.

Given some time to reflect on it, it's more accurate to say that I *needed* to meet Razoar. If you're really passionate about anything in life, you're going to focus so hard on whatever that objective is that unconsciously, without trying, you'll also build a wall around your inner being. That helps to insulate your thought processes, keep a buffer between them and outside distractions. It can produce some wonderful results, but can also alienate you from friends, relatives, teammates and even your immediate family. I found myself slipping and falling into this chasm in 1993, which wasn't that long after I'd arrived in Mooresville. Pat was with me by then, but I'd been consumed since I came south with getting Rusty extricated from the Blue Max mess, getting Penske South established, getting our shops up and running and then, running races. We were trying so hard to win the Winston Cup championship that I was working 14 or 15 hours a day, seven days a week. I only went home to sleep.

After one night like this, Pat told me, "You need to give yourself— and me—a break. I don't want to be married to a robot. I have made a dinner date for us, with my friend Susan Wallace and her husband, and YOU ARE GOING." My immediate reaction was, "Oh, great. This is going to be one of those deals where I sit all night and make idle chit-chat with someone I have nothing in common with, so we talk about what happened at the last church social."

Man, oh man, was I wrong. Susan and Pat were both volunteers at our local parish, Saint Therese Catholic Church. I don't think that at first Razoar was particularly interested in meeting me, either. But when the appointed day arrived, I decided that if I had to pick this guy up at his house, I was at least going to do it in something I liked to drive. So Pat and I headed over there in a 1939 Hudson coupe, with a Corvette engine and a GM automatic turning a nine-inch Ford rear end. Off we went to meet them at their home in Sherills Ford. I pulled up in front of their house and glanced over at the carport. No hot rods or street rods, only a Lincoln Town Car and a Ford pickup. I thought, "Oh, no. This could be a really long night. I hope this guy at least drinks beer."

We rang the bell. Susan greeted us with her usual smile and warm

"Come on in!" She moved to introduce me to her husband. Here we go, the moment of truth. Having already heard that Ray was an industrial engineer, I was expecting him to have a white shirt with seven pencils stuffed in a pocket protector. Instead, when Ray came over to me, he had to shift his can of beer from his right hand to his left to shake hands. Damn the good luck! I dared to think that maybe all my clean living was finally about to pay off. Susan explained that I worked for a race team in Mooresville, and as I recall, she then asked what I did there. I told her I swept the floor and emptied the trash cans. The joke was on Ray. He offered me a Miller Lite—yes!—anyway. The ice was officially broken.

> *We talked about at lot of things that evening but I found this guy to be very humble about what he did, and more interested in what I did and where Sue and I were from, and what our backgrounds were. He said he was in auto racing but didn't elaborate. It wasn't until several months later when we were out late after dinner, and he said he wanted to show me a rare car that his friend Vance Ferry had at the shop. Not knowing what he meant by 'the shop,' I was totally surprised when we pulled up to the gate at Penske Racing South. We went into this building filled with black #2 Miller Genuine Draft Rusty Wallace stock cars. I thought he must have been the shop foreman because he had keys to everything.*
>
> *We looked at the car, a 1950s fiberglass sports car called a Woodill Wildfire, and took it for a wild ride. When we returned, he got us a beer and said he wanted to show me some pictures. We went through the corridor of the office complex and into the main corner office. By this time, I was thinking someone was going to call the cops because this looked like the big shot's office and we shouldn't be there. Then I saw Don's name on the door. I asked what he did at Penske, and he answered that he sort of ran the place, that they called him the general manager and president. I was amazed how down to earth and likeable this guy was for a person in that position."*

RAY WALLACE

You know how some people claim that people they know have never stopped being kids? That's me and Razoar, when we're together. He's a down-to-the-bloodstream car guy and a hot rodder par excellence. How many guys do you know who have a street rod based on a 1939 Mercury hardtop coupe, and powered by a 350 Corvette engine? And right next to that in the shop, an all-original De Lorean DMC 12. Aside from being a terrific guy, Razoar knows cars, and knows engineering even more. He and Sue are originally from north-

eastern Ohio, and when they lived there, Razoar hung around the local short tracks a little bit. I got him credentials and a team shirt from Penske South and started bringing him to Winston Cup races, starting at Darlington, when I showed up at his house at 5:15 in the morning and just said, "Let's go."

His knowledge of severe-service bearing properties and design saved us, literally, from falling out of a bunch of races that we won instead. Remember when all the Winston Cup cars were constantly breaking rear ends? Razoar was the guy who traced the problem to an overloaded differential bearing and came up with a fix that's still in use. Most of the time, however, we're a lot less serious. Or try to be, anyway.

> *Although Don's really a car guy, he also has a passion for vintage wooden boats. We rebuilt a 1947 Chris-Craft that we still take out on Lake Norman. Don loves them, but things haven't always gone well, like the time I got a panic-stricken call from Pat telling me that a neighbor called and said the boat was sinking. I grabbed some materials to rescue the boat and headed to the slip. When Pat got there, I was standing on the slip and she yelled down and asked if I could see the boat. I pointed and said, 'Yes. Right down there.' It was on the bottom in about six feet of water. A thunderstorm had knocked out the electricity and the sump pumps quit, so it went under. That was only the first time it sank.*

To keep the wood swelled and watertight, you must keep a certain amount of water in the hull. Don was off racing and he told Pat to occasionally put some water in the hull. She and Sue got together and went out doing something else, and forgot about the water hose they'd put in the boat. Again, I got a panicked call. They asked me to bring some oil absorbent pads but didn't say why. When I got there the boat was on its trailer, in Don's driveway, with water and oil clear to the deck. The whole interior, including the engine, was submerged. We drained all the water and oil from the hull, drained the motor oil and water from the engine and removed the spark plugs. I got the ignition dried out and when the engine turned over, it looked like Mount Vesuvius, only spewing oily water instead of lava. The tale of Don's boat 'sinking' for the second time, in his driveway, was the talk of the race team. The wacky notes, sketches, and funny marked-up photos went around the shop all summer."

RAY WALLACE

That's me and Razoar. Best friends and each other's biggest danger now and then. What's that old line about God watching over nutcases?

16
Getting Up to Speed

AS 1991 WORE ON, our first full season of Winston Cup racing as the new Penske Racing South team, we began to assess our deficiencies, both in personnel and equipment. We all knew that, if we were going to run up front at every event, it would be necessary to increase our efficiency. When we compared our tiny machine shop to those of many of our competitors, it became obvious to us that we would need to step up our operation.

Our inventory of heavy machinery at the time consisted of two Enco mills, one lathe and a couple of manual drill presses. We knew that CNC equipment would be the way to go. CNC stands for "Computer Numerical Control" and refers to machine tools that perform very complex sequences of cutting, shaping and finishing operations based on a series of computer commands programmed into the tool. If you have a race team, or you're trying to precisely create metal parts for race cars, CNC machines are extremely helpful. When Andrew Scriven joined our team from Penske Cars in Poole, England, we had not yet acquired CNC capability. As a design engineer, Andrew knew how to create CAD (computer assisted design) drawings for anything that we needed and then program a CNC machine to make the part over and over again to the exact dimensions, weight and thickness that we required—but only if we could procure a CNC system. As he was fond of saying, with a CNC machine, even if he'd gotten something wrong, at least it would have been consistently wrong.

Andrew and I perused a number of machinery catalogs to determine the exact CNC components that our operation would require. Unfortunately, we didn't have the money to buy them outright, so we had to find a company that would partner with us. Even the most basic CNC system

Left: Our machine shop, though neat and tidy, was equipped with only manual equipment. (Ernie Masche Photo, Don Miller Collection)

Right: Our first computer-driven machinery was this Serdi valve-cutting machine. (Ernie Masche Photo, Don Miller Collection)

can easily run into hundreds of thousands of dollars. Although the systems can significantly cut the cost of machining parts correctly, with our short-run requirements it would take years to recoup the investment.

I started casting about, looking through magazines on the tool industry and noticed that Bobby Rahal had an agreement with a tool company called Mazak. I didn't know anyone there but with a little research learned that a gentleman named Brian Papke was the president of Mazak North America, located in Florence, Kentucky. I soon made an appointment with Papke and made my way to Florence to visit him and the Mazak organization. I explained that we'd just started a new highly competitive NASCAR Winston Cup-level stock car team with driver Rusty Wallace. Happily, Brian said right away that he'd heard of us.

Brian told me that Mazak's whole program of partnering with other companies was organized and approved in Japan. Mazak North America is a subsidiary of Yamazaki Mazak, the world leader in designing this type of highly automated production tools. Founded in 1919 in Niwagun, Japan, it's an enormous company, with more than 70 branches globally. Yamazaki Mazak, named for its founding family, specializes in building five-axis systems, laser cutters, "done-in-one" machines, astounding stuff. So when Brian told me a decision on partnering with our Cup team had to be made in Japan, it didn't surprise me. Brian added, though, that Mr. Yamazaki was coming to America in about three months.

I liked Brian Papke right away, and I thought we hit it off. His second-in-command was a guy from Japan named Hal Moriyaka. In my whole life, I've never met another man like Hal. He was so even-tempered, so smoothly calm. When he sat in a meeting with us, Hal listened carefully. He didn't say all that much during the meeting, but anything he had to say afterward was remarkably well thought-out and intelligent. When the meeting broke up, Brian said he'd go over with Hal what we'd all discussed, and then he'd talk to Mr. Yamazaki in Japan. I figured our business was completed, and got up and was starting to walk out when Hal Moriyaka said, "Hey, Don. Want to get something to eat in our cafeteria?"

Hal spoke perfect English. He also has an intuitive, amazingly perceptive way to get to people, to draw them out and learn about them. In the cafeteria, he asked, "So, what do you like besides stock car racing?" I answered quickly that I love world history, especially Second World War history. He was listening. Then he said, "Do you really know what Second World War history is all about?" I quickly answered, "Yes, I think so," and then remembered the way the Pacific war had ended.

After an awkward moment, he said quietly, "If you really like history, let me tell you what it was like." He went on to describe how children in Japan had been trained during the war and told that the Americans are all very bad. He talked to me about the bombings of Hiroshima and Nagasaki, and about all the people who had been terribly hurt or killed there. But at the end, he said, "When you look at it all, it was a blessing. Because millions of people on both sides would have died if America had not used the atomic bomb." We sat and we talked for what must have been two hours. I had no way of knowing at the time that Hal Moriyaka was Mr. Yamazaki's best friend.

It was only another two months before Mr. Yamazaki came to the United States; he'd moved his schedule up. Brian Papke called me and said, "I'm going to bring him down to Mooresville and show him your facility." We had just finished up our new race shop building, and it was really nice. On the appointed day, Mr. Yamazaki arrived. He was very polite; he gave me his card and I gave him mine. As I gave him a tour of our facility, we spoke through his interpreter, so I tried to speak as slowly and politely as I possibly could, being on my best behavior. Finally, I told him that was the end of our tour, and that I hoped he understood our processes a little better. To be a gracious host, I asked him if he would like something for lunch, before he had to go on to his next destination. I asked the interpreter to translate, and that was when Mr. Yamazaki looked me straight in the face, and said, "I think I'd like to have a hamburger." In perfect English.

I finally managed to ask him, "You can speak English?" I was utterly surprised, to say the least. Mr. Yamazaki replied, "Yes. I just wanted to see what kind of person you were. Now may we please get

Left: You already needed a lot of this stuff in 1991. Today, you need a lot more. We were fortunate to link up with a really good equipment partner like Mazak. (Jim Donnelly Photo, Don Miller Collection)

Right: The #2 Miller Genuine Draft Pontiac proudly displays the Mazak logo in exchange for CNC equipment, loans and technology. Today, Penske Racing cars still proudly display this logo. (Don Miller Collection)

a hamburger?" I told him about a place called Lew's, where we actually used to go drink beer but you could also get a good hamburger.

I was fortunate to be seated at a table alone with Mr. Yamazaki and his interpreter. When seated, he asked me straight away, "What do you need?" I told him and also said frankly that we couldn't afford to buy the equipment. Immediately he replied, "I don't want you to buy it. I want you to help us develop new things that are good for this sport, because I think this sport will grow." We talked more, and he told me that after the war, his best friend was Mr. Honda. *The* Mr. Honda. Together, they had scavenged old military vehicles, fixed them and sold them, and then started building motorcycles. We sat at Lew's and talked for two hours. I suppose. When we came back to the shop, Brian asked, "So, where do we stand?" Mr. Yamazaki answered immediately, "Don and I have a deal. Give him what he needs. We don't need a contract. We already shook hands. I believe that he is a man of his word."

That day, Mazak became one of the major sponsors of Penske Racing South. Mr. Yamazaki is still with us, but his son Tom now runs the company, and still honors that agreement. He's Mazak's face at the races. Today, Penske Racing has seven Mazak CNC systems in its shop, valued at hundreds of thousands of dollars each. We help Mazak do all of their beta testing, develop new equipment, and we're also a marketing partner. To this day, at Christmas time, I get a card from Mr. Yamazaki. I also get letters from time to time from Hal Moriyaka, who has returned to Japan.

In the mid-1990s, Rusty and I went to Japan when NASCAR held a Winston Cup race at Suzuka. Mr. Yamazaki invited us to his office and his factory in Nagoya, and then we were invited to his teahouse, which is a great honor for a Japanese host to bestow upon his guests. You are supposed to take your shoes off before you go in to sit down. There was a guy at the door, who looked like a Samurai warrior, to make sure we did so. Mr. Yamazaki then declared, for everyone to hear, "Everyone will honor my request, but Don is my special friend. He is not required to remove his shoes." He knew I had an artificial leg. His interpreter later advised me that, to his knowledge, I was the first guest who had ever been in the teahouse while wearing footwear.

Over the years, I have come to really appreciate the value of my relationship with Mr. Yamazaki, Mazak Corporation, and, especially, my friendship with Brian Papke.

BRAINS FROM BRITAIN

When Andrew Scriven arrived at the new Penske South shop in 1991, he was fresh from clean-sheet design and aerodynamic work at Lola on Indy cars and the IMSA GTP car. Andrew joined Rex Stump to comprise our two-man engineering team. Rex was a brilliant engineer but was only on loan to us from General Motors for our team start-up. After 18 months, Rex returned to Detroit, which left Andrew on his own.

There was culture shock, to say the least.

A good demonstration of how far apart we were, in terms of what I'd guess you'd describe as both our racing and business cultures, came after Andrew had probably been in the shop less than an hour, getting introduced to everybody. First thing he asked was, "Where are your blueprints?" After a moment, we told him that there were some basic drawings showing how a Winston Cup or Busch frame was laid out, where the roll cage tubes were supposed to be positioned, but that was it. Here's Andrew, coming from an environment where every single part of every race car, down to the smallest fastener, has a drawing, and on his first day, we've got nothing. Andrew finally ended up making a sketch of a basic motor plate, the piece of steel that helps to mount and locate the powertrain. He took it over to the machine shop, and that guy had never seen a drawing, either. I should add that "that guy" is Phil Ditmars, one of the best racing machinists in the business. He's a guy you go to and say, "Phil, I need you to make this, to fit this." You hand him the second "this," the thing you want the piece to fit to, and he makes the piece, based only on your description.

Our main objective in bringing Andrew onto the team was to recreate that long-standing principle of all Penske racing activities, gaining what other people sometimes call an "unfair advantage," which in reality is just maximizing your preparation by having the right information about the car. From the outset, we intended to develop and organize an understanding of the Pontiac and its shape, on an unprecedented level. Obviously, that meant studying its lines in the wind tunnel. We expected, and were ultimately proven correct, that Andrew's presence on the team would help a lot in developing that advantage, because of his experience as an aerodynamicist with some highly sophisticated race cars.

Andrew was, and is, extremely conversant about wings, downforce and drag. Since leaving Penske, he's gone on to design Daytona Prototypes for Crawford Cars to race in the Grand-Am Rolex series. He was also the chief designer of the wings used on NASCAR's Car of Tomorrow. Besides working at Lola, Andrew had also been a designer at both Brabham and at Tom Walkinshaw Racing, in the latter case working on the Jaguar prototypes that raced at Le Mans. So by the standards of international motorsport, it was all these megabuck NASCAR teams in Mooresville that were behind the curve.

Pretty quickly, Andrew learned that, compared to most top-level race series in Europe, NASCAR has rules that are pretty vague. He told me, "Don, I know where you want to go. I know you want to have an effective wind-tunnel model. But in order to make one, we have to know what the dimensions of the real thing are. Do the guys who build these things have any drawings?" I paused and said no. Then he asked if there were drawings in the NASCAR rule book. I showed him one and he started laughing. He calmed down long enough to ask, "Everybody builds these things from *this*?"

Almost 20 years later, by the way, NASCAR is still using the same drawing. Finally, Andrew said, "I can't do this. How do you expect me to do this?" I offered, "What if I go out and buy a chassis for you, bring it the shop and let you measure it?" That's what we did. I brought the chassis in and gave him a portion of the race shop floor and he got to work. Four hours later, he was back, telling me, "We're in serious trouble. Because there isn't a part anywhere on the left side of this chassis that matches up anywhere on the right side. Absolutely looks like some bird shit on it, instead of the tubes being welded."

There were also linguistic differences, such as when Andrew would ask for a "spanner," and nobody in the shop knew that what he wanted was a wrench. In spite of everything, with him aboard, we probably ended up being 10 years ahead of everyone else in terms of doing pure research and analysis. We also achieved an unheard-of level of uniformity in our car building. Back then, if a given part from one race car's frame, such as a piece of tubing or plating, could fit a second car, it was only by accident. Even though they were built on jigs, hardly any individual piece of any Winston Cup car's frame or cage, or body, was readily interchangeable with the same piece from another car, even another car that had been built on the same jig.

To really understand why, you would have had to go measure a NASCAR jig from those years, and if you did, you would have been either shocked into speechlessness or thrown up. As Andrew found

Andrew Scriven was our first permanent, dedicated race engineer at Penske Racing South. (Jim Donnelly Photo)

out, nothing matched up even when it was new. And of course you then had running changes, even from race to race, or as cars got crashed. The crew would cut the front clip and move it to the left, usually, sometimes by an inch or two, trying to square the chassis better. So the car comes out of the jig, gets clipped, and then it no longer fits the jig that produced it.

> *I came to Penske South from Lola in England with the original intention that I was going to get a wind tunnel program going, to get that Penske unfair advantage. Being a greenhorn, I assumed it was up to me to read between the lines of the NASCAR rule book. I didn't know enough yet to realize that in NASCAR, it doesn't matter whether the rulebook has any lines in it at all. In Europe, everything is black and white. Here, it's only gray."*

ANDREW SCRIVEN
Former aerodynamicist, Penske South
Chief Designer, Crawford Cars LLC
Denver, North Carolina

Maybe now you're beginning to understand what Andrew faced, and was trying to overcome. In the end, though, he did produce a workable model, made the wooden buck and did a body scan. It was an absolute work of art. The suspension worked. Rusty got a look at it and said, "What the hell are you going to do with that thing? Can I have it to put in my living room?"

We worked incredibly hard, and a lot of it was learning the things Andrew was trying to teach us. For example, if you're a NASCAR fan you've probably heard the term "surface-plate car." It refers to a race car whose chassis is welded together on a steel plate that's installed in the shop by engineers who assure that the plate is perfectly flat, which ensures that the basic frame is completely level to the ground. The idea is to avoid variations in construction of individual cars, and hopefully, in their handling on the race track. That doesn't make much sense if the jigs that produce the cars aren't square, or if the chassis are constantly changed without tracking the changes and being able to record their measurements.

We had one guy on the team, Dave Roberts, who would do absolutely anything you asked. Andrew would say, "Dave, we need to have a surface plate that's really level. And we need to level it with lasers." Dave had a speech impediment, and it was a real challenge when we finally took him over to England to learn more about this stuff, but when we tell him we need lasers, he goes, "Mmmm. Okay." Next, "Do you know where to get a laser, Dave?" "Mmmm. Nope. Think they're in the book?" Andrew says, "Dave, do you know how to use a laser?" "Mmmm. Nope. But I'll learn." So I say, "Okay, but we've got to get this thing within 60 thousandths of an inch." He goes, "WHUUUT?"

Andrew had some things to learn, too. We started taking him to races and I let him get up on the stand with me and help me with spotting. First, though, I had to explain to him what a spotter is and does, because spotters don't exist in European racing. Andrew has a very distinctive voice, a good thing for any spotter. We get to the Winston Cup race at Watkins Glen and I put him at the end of the straightaway to call the green flag, with Rusty in the first or second row. We all knew that the fans carried scanners to listen in to team communications, so I guess Andrew decided to give the people a little entertainment. When the green waves, instead of the normal "Go, go, go," he's radioing, "Tally ho, tally ho, tally ho." Next thing I hear is Rusty yelling over the air, "What the hell is this tally ho? Get this guy off the goddamn radio."

> As hard as we were working, we were still running around like a bunch of school kids. We still had acetylene bombs going off back in the field behind the shop. 'Five o'clock. Time for a bomb.' We'd head out back and blow something up. We were dead serious about racing to win, but not at the expense of having some fun on the way."

ANDREW SCRIVEN

This is a shot of Penske Racing's famous Pontiac Grand Prix, nicknamed "Midnight." (Jim Donnelly Photo)

History demonstrates that together at Penske South, we had a wonderful concept of what was possible to do, because we ultimately did do it. It eventually turned out that we had truly set a precedent. We were the first team to have a 40-percent-scale model for the wind tunnel. We learned a ton off that thing. Roger was behind us 110 percent, but he would not get in there and tell those guys that he wanted them to do something specific, or to do this thing that way.

We did most of our wind tunnel testing for the Pontiac program in England, at the Penske Cars facility in Poole, Dorset, or at the R.J. Mitchell wind tunnel in Southampton. That was where all the Indy cars built by Penske Cars were tested, and the tunnel was named for the engineer that designed the Supermarine Spitfire, the landmark British fighter of World War II. It was an unconventional approach, but it enjoyed full support from Pontiac. I think that by 1993, we had clearly improved our Pontiac, and Rusty understood that. He and Andrew worked together well, which was improbable, because Rusty was so intolerant of anything he didn't understand, or couldn't control, and therefore didn't really like engineers. Andrew went back to England in 1994 to work with Penske Cars, including involvement in the Ilmor-Mercedes pushrod V-8 for the Indianapolis 500 that Penske had backed, before coming back to us at Penske South in 1995.

> *It was a huge amount of learning, and we probably had more fun than we were legally allowed to have. We were just too soon in time. I'd never used UNC nuts and bolts before. I'd always used aircraft bolts, and self-locking K nuts, and I was, well, lost. Don came in with this job to do and I was butting heads with everybody. It was almost as if I could do anything I liked as long as I didn't have anything to do with the car. Our standard joke was that the biggest thing I introduced to Penske Racing in NASCAR was that I got them to stop using nails on the car. The whole race thing here was so different than anything I'd been used to in Europe. But even though it took until 1993 to get everything together, we made that Pontiac better. "*

ANDREW SCRIVEN

Andrew is one of the most intelligent guys I've ever met, brilliant. He's also a little bit nuts. We both love aircraft of all kinds and both love having fun. Onc time, Andrew and I had gone to a wind tunnel test at Southampton, and were headed back to Poole in our rental car. As I've told you, I'm really interested in the aircraft and aviation history of World War II—one of my other pastimes is building model kits of warbirds from that era, and the completed models are all around my house—and I knew, generally, that during the war, the Allies had used airfields in that part of England, on the southern coast. These were powerfully historic places, from which the Battle of Britain dogfighters and the mass bombing raids against Germany were launched. I figured they had to be around that general vicinity someplace. I managed to convince Andrew that we should go looking for one. We took the rental car down a narrow lane in the English countryside, and ended up in a field.

I was convinced that we had found a former Royal Air Force airfield, even though it was pretty muddy, since it rains all the time in England. There was a ford in the middle—the kind that goes over water—and there were signs all over the place warning, "Do not cross if the water is more than this high." We started trying to get out of the place—I think I was driving—and we're skidding around in circles. In a minute or two, the rental car was completely covered with mud. The muck on the windshield was so thick the wipers wouldn't move. Next morning, we're back at Poole and the rental car's out in front of the Penske Cars building, dripping huge gobs of still-wet mud onto the blacktop in the parking lot. Nick Goozee, the managing director of Penske Cars, was incensed. Andrew got blamed, even though he wasn't driving, because he worked there.

Andrew and I had a ton of fun, especially when I was in England.

On one occasion we were actually going to buy a real, honest RAF Lightning, a supersonic jet fighter built by English Electric during the early 1960s. He and I would go to aircraft museums and on other, less messy and more successful hunts for World War II airfields. One day we were out running around and found this scrap yard near Portsmouth that had several Lightnings sitting there for sale with their engines. They wouldn't fly, but you could still buy basically a complete Lightning fighter—the 1960s kind, not the Lockheed P-38 from World War II—for $10,000 or $12,000 and ship it home, put it together and put it on your lawn, which I almost did. The scrap yard was stuffed full of old jet and piston aircraft engines, too. We even found a complete Merlin, the iconic supercharged V-12 aircraft engine designed by Rolls-Royce, but as much as I want one for my collection, the guy wouldn't sell it to me. We had a blast.

Finally, somebody at Penske Cars told Nick that Andrew and I were conspiring to buy a used Royal Navy submarine. I'm not joking. The word got back to America real fast. Next thing I know, Roger's on the phone. "What in the hell has gone wrong with you? What do you want with a used submarine?" I just started laughing. He wouldn't tell me who had told him about it. "You guys don't need a submarine. What the hell are you going to do with a submarine?" I don't think we knew, but it seemed like a good idea at the time . . .

Despite, the fun and games with Andrew, our engineering efforts had a very serious side. Working with the aero packages of our race cars, in England and elsewhere, was part of the credo at Penske South from the outset. We were still running the Grand Prix as hard as we could, and I kept telling the guys at Pontiac that the Fords had three different front ends. Nobody believed me until we went so far as to photograph them at the race track. We made overlays of each photo, and I got Preston Miller, who was the NASCAR liaison for Ford, to agree that they were, indeed, different. No wonder the Ford teams were kicking our asses. I went into the Penske fab shop with David Munari and we cut up one of the Ford fascias. He and I made a new Ford fascia out of the pieces, and then we grafted it onto the front of our Grand Prix. Right at that moment, Rusty walked in, saw what we were doing, and went nuts. "The reason the Pontiac is so good is that little dip right behind the grille." Yeah, right. I told him we were heading to the wind tunnel, and he barked, "I don't care about what the wind tunnel says." I told him that if he felt that way, he better stop flying airplanes.

I don't remember how many pounds of downforce that nose picked up for us, but it was a lot. Rusty saw the numbers, and drove it in a test for us once we got the nose on the track, and said, "Just build me some motors that don't blow up, and we're going to win the championship." Given that we won 10 races the next year, even with Rusty flipping nine times at Talladega and breaking his wrist, we probably should have won it.

The fact was that aero testing was becoming increasingly important. In the U.S., Swift Engineering had opened its wind tunnel in San Clemente, California, for race car testing. They built a 40-percent wind tunnel that we could use our Pontiac model in, and also offered full-size testing. Ford had sponsored a test at the Lockheed wind tunnel in Marietta, Georgia. The problem with going to any of these places, however, was that GM, Ford and other manufacturers used them, too. Another issue was that we wanted to have a place to test on the road, during the race season.

> *Ford and GM had baseline numbers, but we wanted to have the opportunity to test on our own. Marietta is a full-size tunnel, but we needed to find someplace we could go where after the test, only we would know the numbers. If you went to Marietta, it wouldn't be long before everybody knew your numbers. So we began making the arrangements for running a real NASCAR car at Langley and finding out if it was viable."*

ANDREW SCRIVEN

We began a relationship with the wind tunnel in Langley, Virginia. The Langley tunnel is a hallowed place in American aerospace history. It dates back to 1931 and was built by the National Advisory Committee for Aeronautics, the predecessor of today's NASA and the organization for which the familiar NACA duct is named. It's now operated by Old Dominion University. The tunnel's so big, full scale, that it uses two fans, which meant we might be able to place two cars in the test section and simulate drafting. It's on the grounds of Langley Air Force Base in Hampton, Virginia, and thus has extremely tight security. You need a special clearance just to get on the base. To this day, every high-performance American military aircraft is modeled and tested in that tunnel, but with the end of the Cold War, they had a need for more civilian projects to justify its cost and as part of the directive to transfer technology from NASA to the public sector. So I called my buddies up at NASA, led by former Kennedy Space Center director Jay Honeycutt, who made some calls to Langley and got hold of Dr. Jim Cross. Or, as I call him, "the Aero Wizard." He was the manager of the Langley wind tunnel, and had been Dean of Engineering and Technology at Old Dominion.

We said to him, "If we help you adapt your equipment to test race cars as well as aircraft, would you be interested in developing a testing program for Old Dominion?" We hoped, at least, to learn whether

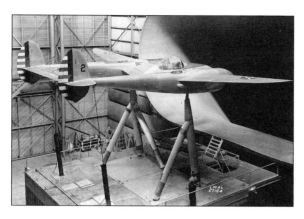

it was even viable to test a full-size NASCAR stock car in this wind tunnel. Also, whether whatever numbers we got would support, rather than contradict, what we'd learned in other tunnels, even the 40-percent ones. Dr. Cross said he would give 100-percent support to our idea but first needed to get an OK from Old Dominion and NASA. Dr. Cross and I made a joint proposal to NASA, and within about 14 months we had the go-ahead.

There was another professor of aerodynamics there, Dr. Colin Britcher, who was English, which helped because he could understand Andrew. We knew going into this that we would have to change the aero balances the tunnel used to measure and match the typical parameters of a racing automobile. At first, all we could measure was drag, but it was spectacular to watch the testing. The ground plate probably sat 12 feet off the ground. But the test numbers we started to get back with our cars essentially jibed with what we'd been getting at Lockheed and the GM tunnel.

> " It actually looks like something out of Flash Gordon when you're in there. We did a lot of standard testing, a lot of work with drag and balance, and the people at Langley were really happy with what we did. The advantage at a place like Langley is that you're freed from using a model, which is only a representation of what you think is happening, not whatever really is. You build a model, test it, then you build a real car using the data from the model and then test it to see if the data is consistent. Then you improve the models and the cycle never ends. With real cars, you'll already be taking two or three to track test before Daytona because they'll be different, so you don't have a clue why one is quicker than another. The differences are not measurable without models to consider for verification."

ANDREW SCRIVEN

Left: During World War II, every fighter aircraft produced in America was tunnel tested in the Langley wind tunnel. Here, a twin-engine P-38 fighter is subjected to the routine. (Old Dominion University Photo)

Right: The Langley full-size wind tunnel was large enough to accommodate two stock cars at once, enabling our team to do in-depth drafting tests. (Chuck Thomas Photo, Old Dominion University Collection)

Langley was so big inside, like looking in the Lincoln Tunnel bores, that we were actually able to run drafting tests with two full-size cars either front-and-aft or beside one another. No other tunnel had the architecture for that. The advantage of using an actual race car is that the 40-percent model is based on one specific car, and as we've already seen, none of the full-size cars are ever exactly the same in reality. At Langley, we could take the exact car we intended to race the following weekend and put it in the tunnel. You could change, test and correlate an individual body component.

With four types of cars—short track, intermediate track, super-speedway and road racer—there was a lot of room for this sort of real-time, full-scale evaluating. Even with the Car of Tomorrow, there are going to be differences from one car to another, and you're going to have to learn them, because the other teams will be doing just that. We even used Langley to test cars we had no intention of actually racing, like one we bodied as a Monte Carlo so we could have a control sample, a baseline. Andrew got that all worked out. It was an absolute bonus because nobody knew what we were doing—the Langley folks could keep their mouths shut—and would turn out to be especially beneficial to us down the road.

This was definitely one of those win-win propositions: Our project allowed Langley to get familiar with testing something other than aircraft, and we got to fully test real cars in secret. Normally, a day of testing at Langley would set a team back $30,000 or more. We actually managed to work a deal with them for free time in the tunnel, because Andrew had done so much work on setting up the tunnel for cars.

With all this said, we felt we were going into the 1993 season with both guns loaded.

17

Pontiac Perfection

ONSTERNATION. FRUSTRATION. Two words that speak volumes
about our shared experiences at Penske South in 1991, even though
a lot of other teams would have danced barefoot on top of thumbtacks to
have celebrated our two wins, especially as a rookie team literally just out
of the box. We weren't joyous, not with 10 DNFs, and not with losing a
really good crew chief to a potential major rival, even though Joe Gibbs
Racing was even newer than we were.

In spite of that, we were feeling pretty good about ourselves as 1992 approached, for two reasons. First, we already knew how to win as a team.
And second, we were fully confident that with guys like Rex Stump and
Andrew aboard, along with some very critical technical partners that we'd
painstakingly cultivated, we were going to redefine the modern-day
NASCAR team in terms of preparation, engineering and consistency. But
then the sport threw us yet another curve ball.

NASCAR and Goodyear had already scheduled the big switch to radial
racing tires for 1992. Before then, there were two guys who had absolutely
been the class of the field in 1991, and actually, for a couple of years prior
to that, on the existing bias-ply rubber. They were Rusty Wallace and Dale
Earnhardt. They had their own style, which included running the car sideways out of some of the corners. After the switch was made, Rusty and
Dale just did not adapt to the radials. Neither could win races, and it became blindingly obvious that the new type of tire was the problem. For the
first time in several years neither Rusty nor Dale finished in the top 10 in
points, or even won a race for that matter.

There had been some testing with the radials before Daytona but the
changeover was still really a blow. We struggled for most of the season and

had a couple of different crew chiefs. We tried to move a couple of guys from our system, Jay Smith and Eddie Dickerson, up into that position but it didn't work out. I finally told Roger that we had to find another crew chief. Roger felt that all the good guys were already taken. I told him, however, that I knew a good guy who was just coming off surgery, and who I knew was a good organizer. It was Buddy Parrott, the guy who had probably saved my life by applying a tourniquet on my leg after the accident at Talladega. After some discussion, Roger—holding true to his management style—agreed to let me proceed in the direction that I felt was best.

Buddy had been around NASCAR for years. He'd actually started out as a tirebuster back in the 1960s for Huggins Tire Company, then was crew chief or key guy on a lot of teams in the '70s, '80s and into the '90s. He'd seen and done a lot, including winning the Daytona 500 and Dover with Derrike Cope in 1990, and I thought he'd be the guy who could help us pull our team back together.

I called Buddy and we went to dinner. He was still recovering from eye surgery but he really wanted to do it, and I agreed to give him a couple of weeks to heal. When Buddy came on with us after the Watkins Glen race, it was like a breath of fresh air. Buddy was an old-school crew chief, was very direct in his management and raised a lot of hell.

Buddy told me I had to be patient. I told him that he had the rest of the season, that we were mostly building for 1993 but that we absolutely, positively had to win a race in the '92 season. He asked me to pick Rusty's two best race tracks. I named Bristol and Richmond, and Buddy said we would focus on those two races. He wasn't a guy who had all the setups burned into his mind. Instead, he was magical at getting the pit crew to do their jobs with focus, without mistakes and lapses, making sure all the nuts and bolts were tightened. He was obsessed with not losing time on pit stops. Once we picked our target races for winning in 1991, Buddy said, "We've got to get our guys in better physical shape."

I could relate to that. I was having a lot of trouble in 1991 with my legs, or more accurately, leg. I was having a great deal of phantom pain, that sharp discomfort from a limb that's no longer there. I was seeing a young physical therapist by the name of Bob Pressley—no relation to the legendary Late Model Sportsman driver of the 1960s or his son, Robert—and the guy was a fireball, really competent and enthusiastic. At a session one day, I casually asked him, "Hey Bob, would you be interested in becoming a trainer? For a pit crew?" Bob had never heard of any such thing, but did say he'd gotten his degree in sports medicine, and therefore learned how to prepare diets and exercise routines. I listened. Then I told him, not asked, "Why don't you quit this damn job? I'll pay you 50 bucks a week more to start."

I brought Bob into the shop and introduced him to Buddy, who spent about two hours explaining to him how pit stops worked. Buddy brought him to a pit practice, let him watch and then said, "All right. Now tell me how to make these guys better and faster." Bob moved into it like he'd been doing it his whole life. He put together some exercise regimens, diets, things like that. He ran with them and really watched what they ate. Our pit stops picked up immediately, and I mean significantly, not by hundredths of a second. The crew was speeding up in tenth-of-a-second increments. When people saw what was happening, and finally figured out what we were doing, they first tried to hire Bob Pressley away from us. Then they started hiring their own trainers. Our crew wasn't out of shape when Bob came along, but they weren't trim, either. They were usually a good 18-second team that was sometimes clumsy. Bob had them go from 18 seconds down to 16 seconds in nothing flat. Around this time, there was a Rusty Wallace T-shirt that his souvenir trailer sold showing the pit crew with the slogan, "Gone in 16 Seconds." That shirt wouldn't have been produced if not for Bob's success. After that, Buddy told me, "We're going to go to Richmond, and we're going to beat them all."

Ultimately, a lot of our success came down to Rusty getting seat time, getting used to the radials, and having faith in his crew chief. Buddy delivered that. Everybody was making adjustments to their chassis to adapt to the tires. NASCAR didn't want the new tire to be a failure. Goodyear certainly didn't, either, to the point that the Goodyear engineers were making recommendations on caster and camber settings and spring rates, even suggested shock valving, and were passing the information on to the teams—anything to get us on the right road. Rusty had to get used to not throwing the car around, learn to be a more precise driver and stop dirt tracking, as I called it. You couldn't do that with the radial, because unlike the bias-ply tire, there was no warning that the radial was about to go away—it would just suddenly snap loose, something Rusty had not been used to.

We had a car they had really worked on, not a new one, but one that was lightened with weight moved around to all the right spots. Rex Stump helped greatly in determining the weight placements. We went to the night race at Richmond in 1992 and won it. Rusty nicknamed the car Midnight, after the time the race ended. That car became the storied Penske race car Midnight, which Rusty used to win God knows how many races. Out of the 10 races we won in 1993, I think eight were in that car. We didn't win again in 1992, but that victory at Richmond in Midnight lit a fire under our team, and put the fire back into Rusty Wallace.

By the last race of 1992, we were running really well. I remember

Bringing Buddy Parrott aboard as crew chief set our team on fire. Joining us on victory lane at Rockingham were Roger and, far left, Walt Czarnecki. (Chobat Racing Images Photo)

that when we got to Atlanta for the final race, one of the press guys asked us how we thought we were going to do in 1993. Buddy answered him flatly: "We're going to win the championship, and probably 10 races."

 When I said that, during the media tour, Rusty turned toward me and looked at me like I was crazy. When I got there, they had a lot of different chassis and a lot of different parts, but Rusty was like me, wanted to get on the same program and stick with it.

One day, Rusty asked me to take that one car, Midnight, to the fab shop, take measurements off it, use it to make a jig, do whatever we had to do. All it was, actually, was a straight-up Ronnie Hopkins car, nothing special about it, other than that we had worked on the weight distributions and such. From then on, until I left, we'd actually buy a brand-new car from Ronnie Hopkins, bring it to the shop, put it on the jig we built off Midnight and whatever didn't fit, we made it fit. We'd cut it off and move it or whatever was required, to match the measurements we'd taken off Midnight."

BUDDY PARROTT

Well, that statement went through the press pipeline like a blowtorch, or liquid dynamite. *Everybody* was talking about what Buddy had said, how bold it was and how we'd never be able to back it up. Of course, we went into 1993 with the Pontiac that we had improved, and with Midnight in the inventory, and won 10 races. At the end of that season, we had finished second in the championship rankings to Dale Earnhardt, by about 80 points. Rusty had not only won 10 races, but he also led 28 percent of all racing laps during the entire season.

That's an astonishing expression of dominance. It also means that we should have won the championship. There are a number of reasons that we didn't, one of which is the pair of vicious, tumbling crashes that Rusty endured that year. They underscored a dangerous situation in NASCAR racing that had existed for a while, until we at Penske South did something about it.

Rusty had already been upside-down in a race car. There was the backstretch crash at Daytona in 1983 with the Ramada Inns Buick. Then in 1988, when he was still with Raymond Beadle, Rusty crashed in practice at Bristol and flipped almost all the way down the front stretch. He was unconscious when the car came to rest, and in retrospect, was very fortunate that Dr. Jerry Punch from ESPN was right there to clear his airway. So Rusty knew about crashing. We had a pretty big one right at the start of 1993, during the Daytona 500, when he tried to miss a wreck coming off turn two. Our car turned sideways, got airborne and Rusty flipped a bunch of times. Other than a cut chin, he was basically okay, but we ended up 32nd and started the year in a deep point hole.

Then came the spring race at Talladega. By then, Rusty had won four out of eight races, and we had clawed our way from 32nd all the way to the point lead. Today, that race—or at least, the last couple of seconds of it—is NASCAR folklore. Rusty had led a bunch of laps until rain brought the red out with two laps left. When the track dried, the race restarted. It was madness coming down to the flag, with 15 or more cars banging on each other at 195 mph. Rusty and Earnhardt got into each other and Rusty got airborne—again—and this time, flipped probably 10 times. It was frightening. Rusty ended up with a seriously fractured right wrist, and was fortunate the injuries were limited to that. He actually finished sixth after somersaulting across the finish line with about 10 feet of air under the car.

> *I didn't know if he had lived through it. That was the one time I called him on the radio, and couldn't get him, and it scared the heck out of me, especially after Earnhardt had gotten out of his car down there. He was shaken. Never in my wildest dreams did I think Rusty would take another ride like the one at Daytona. If I did, I would have put more roll bars in the car.*
>
> *Having said all that, this was way before the HANS device and a lot of other things. A lot of people don't know that Rusty Wallace was one of the first people who used a molded seat. When he first drove a race car for me, he brought me an old seat and wanted it in the car. Brian Butler, who came to work for me as a fabricator back when I had the Levi Garrett car, was a fabricator and went on to make the Butlerbuilt seats. But at this time, Rusty had this*

homemade seat, and I asked Brian to work on it. Rusty was delighted with it. I think that Rusty rode a Butlerbuilt seat until he quit driving. Went end over end, upside down, at both Daytona and Talladega. The other thing is, Rusty was always really in shape when he got in a race car. He had this funny-looking machine he used to keep his neck muscles strong. Rusty was ready for a crash."

BUDDY PARROTT

Rusty had surgery at Methodist Hospital in Indianapolis, where the famously expert Dr. Terry Trammell inserted a pin in his wrist. Rusty also had a special glove and brace to protect the injury, and he worked really hard with Bob Pressley on his rehabilitation. However, the next race after Talladega was on the road course at Sonoma, and we all knew, including Rusty, that he wasn't physically ready for all that gear changing. We put in a road course guy to replace Rusty during the race, which Rusty started so he could get the points. While out of the car, Rusty went to the Sears Point infield care center and had the medical staff cut away part of his cast and tape his fingers into a cup, and got back in the race car. Late in the race, he missed a shift, broke the transmission and he DNF'ed.

Rusty was back for the next date, at Charlotte, and he won six more races. The wrecks and the DNF at Sonoma really hurt us, though. It was close enough at the end that Goodyear actually made two of those gold-plated cars it traditionally gave to the new Winston Cup champ, one a #2 Pontiac and the other a #3 Chevrolet. It was heartbreaking.

Meanwhile, I was focusing on what remained of the Pontiac Rusty had destroyed at Talladega. It was tucked away at the shop on Knob Hill Road, and I kept going over to look at it, again and again. I've rarely seen a race car of any sort more thoroughly demolished. The one photo that shows the left-front corner resting on a toolbox, with the other three wheels on the shop floor, speaks volumes about the crash's power. The impact and violent rotational forces pulled the chassis into almost a diamond shape. It looked like a dishrag that somebody had twisted to wring the water out of it. It had literally been pulled apart around the roll cage. I thought, and said more than once, that if something like this happened again, we were going to kill our driver.

We all started looking increasingly closely at the wreckage. One of the first things we noticed was that while the roll-cage welds had held, the cage tubes themselves had broken—the actual tubing had failed. We had Laughlin and Hopkins race cars in 1993; there were

Rusty took a nasty flip at Talladega after contact with Dale Earnhardt in the final laps of the race. This was the wreck that inspired us to develop the roof flaps. (Jeff Robinson Photo)

several other companies producing Winston Cup cars, but they were basically all the same. I wasn't about to listen to anyone's argument that these things can happen in bad racing accidents. I decided to take samples of tubing, the standard stuff that race car builders in and around Charlotte were using, and have it analyzed by a metallurgist in Mooresville, Bill Newell.

About three days later, he called me and said, "I don't know what you've been told, but what you think you've been getting isn't what you have here." Steel tubing is imprinted with its specifications, such as hardness and tensile strength. He said that some of our tubing might have had one number stamped on it when it was first tested or analyzed, but then had another number stamped on it when we placed the order. He called the actual bunch of race car tubing I'd brought in a "hodgepodge," adding that some of it was weaker-seamed tubing whose seam had been ground down to look like it was seamless. When welded, the seamed tubing anneals itself and becomes brittle on the side of the weld. In a high-impact crash, it will break apart.

We had gone around and gotten the test tubing from five or six different sources. Our analyst said the safest thing to do was to go to the original tubing manufacturer and have a specific kind of tubing produced to order. We did just that. The manufacturer, Plymouth Tube Company, told us we'd have to buy something like 1,200 linear feet for them to make it special for us. I said, "Fine, I'll take it. I'm not going to kill my driver."

I went back to our shop and said, "Guys. You've seen these jigs that the builders use to make these cars. Make us one and get the

Left: There was very little left of our Miller Genuine Draft Pontiac after the Talladega wreck. (Don Miller Collection)

Right: Close inspection of the damage revealed that none of the welds broke from the impact, but the tubing was actually torn apart. (Don Miller Collection)

right surface plate to do it." For that, we ended up calling Pontiac Motor Division. John Erickson, who was Pontiac's director of racing at the time, before he came to work for us in the late 1990s, ultimately reached an agreement with John Middlebrook, Pontiac's general manager. Middlebrook went behind one of Pontiac's foundries and got about a 15,000-pound surface plate, which sat about 14 inches off the ground and was all scored with channels, where you could insert fittings and lock them down. Pontiac, thanks to John Middlebrook, just gave it to us. We hauled it back to North Carolina and in one weekend, dug up the fabricating shop floor and put down three feet of concrete with securing bolts sunk into it. We brought in the surface plate, secured it to the new concrete pit with special augers, and leveled it with a laser. Then we installed our fabricating fixtures on the plate and started building our own race cars.

Let me explain what a surface plate does. It's perfectly level, so that when you create a measurement, or a tubing length, it remains constant from build to build to build. You slide your fixtures into the grooves on the plate and then lock them into place with the bolts and augers. Then, the tubing drops into a notch and you weld it. Andrew Scriven was drawing the cars, so we knew where the tubing was going to be, exactly, on every car. That allowed us to find ways to make the car stronger and lighter, and still meet the NASCAR specifications. All the tolerances are much tighter, more precise. If you got the typical Banjo or Laughlin car of the time and measured it, the differences would be in eighths and quarters, and sometimes 3/8ths of an inch, from location to location. We wanted to lock it down to thousandths of an inch by building our own cars. Andrew and Rex decided to do a prototype.

In the meantime, there were cars flying off the track all the time. When they got turned around, they were going up in the air. The worst examples could have filled a Winston Cup highlight video. Not just Rusty's, either. Davey Allison had had a savage flip the year before Rusty at Pocono. Bobby Allison had come frighteningly close to going into the stands at Talladega in 1987. Ricky Rudd and Randy LaJoie had gone airborne at Daytona before that.

There needed to be a way to keep the cars down on the race track. We went through a bunch of tests in conjunction with NASCAR, which actually considered having the deck lid being somewhat unsecured, enough that if the car turned around, the lid would pop open and spoil the air. It had big tethers on it to keep the deck lid from blowing off completely and becoming a giant piece of debris. The test took place at an airport where they actually backed one of the NASCAR corporate jets up to within about 30 feet of the race car and cranked the jet engines up to full power, trying to blow the car off the ground. Eventually, everybody agreed that the testing wasn't completely successful.

I sat Bill France Jr. down and suggested to him that there might be a better way. I told him that what we needed to do was something similar to the practices used in developing early jet fighters such as the F-86 SabreJet and the MIG-15. Those planes had air brakes on the sides of their fuselages. When they wanted to stop them, or slow them down, the pilots hydraulically popped those speed brakes, as they called them. In aerial combat, they could almost bring the plane to a stop in midair, to make a tighter turn or other emergency maneuver. They'd yank back on the throttle, pull the speed brake and the plane that would be chasing them in a dogfight would overshoot them, suddenly becoming the prey itself. I thought, as I told Bill, that if roof flaps were installed in the cars, it would be the same thing as driving a pickup down the highway with a big cardboard box in the bed: Get up enough speed, and the lift will suck the box right out of the truck.

Bill asked whether I thought the air pressures would be enough to pull the flaps up on their own. I said, sure, we can put cables on them to restrict them, whatever NASCAR wanted, and he asked us to build one. We fabricated the first ones to fit above an aluminum tray inside the car that rivets underneath the roof skin. Then we took it to the GM wind tunnel.

What I'm going to say next is going to tick some people off, because the truth has never been told about this before, but I don't care. We put it in the tunnel, where the degreed plate that the car sits atop can be turned around to measure yaw. We turned the car 10 degrees at a time. Andrew had previously sat down and figured out that once you rotate the car a certain number of degrees, the negative pressure would pop the flaps. Terry Lace was the aerodynamic engineer for General Motors at the time, and when we put it through the test, it did exactly as Andrew said it would. The car's flaps would pop open, spoil the air, it would lose lift and settle back to the ground. You always want one to open first and then the other, even if the car is spinning quickly.

Terry then said that if we put a fence alongside the rear window, it would also help spoil the air as the race car began to rotate. Next, they said that if we took the flap—at this point, there was only one—and changed it to two flaps, with one mounted in the roof at an angle, the effect would be even better. We built a second car, did more testing, and took what we learned to the other teams, including Roush. After that, Roush took that whole design and made a complete prototype of it out of fiberglass, and that was what was ultimately adapted for the NASCAR package. When it came time to hand out the awards for the invention of the roof flaps, Roush got the big award because he manufactured it. I got a big plaque for participating, but today, the design for the flaps is always credited to Roush, which isn't true. The other thing that became obvious after about three years was that NASCAR had actually submitted a patent for the flap design, and that Gary Nelson had signed it as the designer. I still have the original drawing that I made for Bill France Jr. on the back of an envelope.

I don't remember exactly where it was that I discussed our proposals for the roof flaps with Bill France Jr. but it was definitely at a race. We were sitting in the NASCAR trailer, in the lounge area that's all the way in the back. If you look at the letters that Roger sent to Bill Jr., we were telling them that we'd developed a new technology to

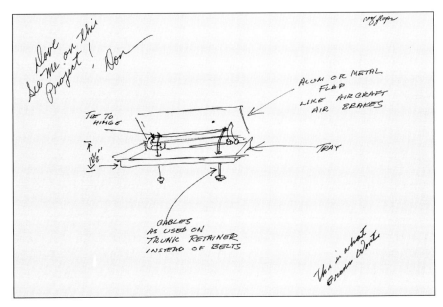

I made this rough sketch for Bill France, Jr. depicting how I thought we could solve the lift problem on the NASCAR Cup series cars. (Don Miller Collection)

PENSKE

ROGER S PENSKE
PRESIDENT

November 19, 1993

Mr. William C. France, Jr.
President
NASCAR
1801 W. International Speedway Blvd.
Daytona Beach, FL 32114

Dear Bill:

As you know, I have closely followed the progress of our Penske Racing South team's development of the NASCAR Aero Safety package.

Our team, in cooperation with Hendrick Racing and NASCAR officials, conducted a dedicated aero test at the GM aero laboratory on November 5. After personally reviewing the results of this test with our Penske Racing engineers and aerodynamicists, I am convinced that we have within our grasp a solution to the "lift-off" problem.

The Aero package as installed on our Penske Pontiacs operated as designed with excellent results. Our data shows that the lift-off speed in a 135 degree attitude was raised from approximately 132 m.p.h. to 156 m.p.h. This is a significant gain.

In addition, I have had our engineers work up a computer-generated spin diagram that indicates that the lift-off event time (the time the vehicle spends in the critical yaw angle 132-142 degrees) is only milliseconds, which accelerates the value of the flap deployment. All indications are that the air is passing over the roof flap and does not have enough time to reattach itself to the roof theory two-fold. Further analysis leads us to believe the installation of two 18" flaps in the rear spoiler will again raise the lift-off speed by six to eight miles per hour.

Bill, this is a significant breakthrough in the area of driver and spectator safety, and we are pleased to be a part of the eventual resolution of this very serious problem.

Mr. William C. France, Jr.
Page Two
November 19, 1993

As always, our team stands ready to aid your people in further verification and testing of the package. We look forward to the return of the original 1993 air-dam package, and the implementation of the flaps on our new cars.

Sincerely,

RSP/sjm

bcc: D. Miller

After our tunnel tests of the roof flaps proved positive, NASCAR remained silent but proceeded with development of their own. Roger wrote several letters encouraging development of our design but Roush got most of the credit. (Don Miller Collection)

keep the cars from flying, we were certain it would work and that we needed to get moving on it before something really bad happened. NASCAR, as events would prove, was indeed moving on it. They just weren't telling us about it.

I want to take the high road about all this. I think that in hindsight, the situation with the roof flaps is pretty black and white. Obviously, they weren't telling me that they were working quietly with Roush on the flaps, and they weren't telling either me or Roger that they were going to take credit for the design, or that they intended to file for a patent on it. Am I upset about all this? Yeah, a little bit, but I made myself a promise that I was going to move on, because it's done.

To this day, Rusty, Roger and I are disappointed that we lost the 1993 Winston Cup title after running so powerfully well. Lots of people remember that Rusty, in particular, was vocal about the fact that he didn't win the championship despite winning 10 races. By this time, nonetheless, we had some new descriptions of our shared outlook: Proud. Determined. Committed. We fully believed we would run the table with our Pontiacs in 1994. We knew we could make that

Buddy Parrott, Rusty Wallace, Walt Czarnecki and Roger Penske celebrate our second-place finish in the 1993 Winston Cup points race at the NASCAR banquet in New York. (Rusty Wallace Collection)

car even better, and that NASCAR was on the verge of allowing us another inch and a half of deck lid length, so we'd be equal to the Thunderbirds.

And then, in November 1993, Roger walked into the shop and told us he'd just been sitting down with the top management of the Ford Motor Company. He said they committed to giving us a lot more money, and that we'd be running Thunderbirds next year. It wasn't as if he came to discuss it with us. He'd already made the commitment. We were stunned, but Roger assuaged us by noting that the measurements weren't that different between the cars, that Ford was going to send us a ton of engine pieces, and that we'd been saying all along that the Thunderbird was better, which we had been. It was also apparent that General Motors had begun to move more of its factory support dollars away from Pontiac toward teams running Chevrolet.

Rusty and I both started arguing with him, but it was too late. Back to work. Switching to the Blue Oval wasn't the only change in the offing for Penske South.

18
A Ford in Our Future

WE WERE ABOUT TO BECOME a Ford team. If you consider that for a moment, then you'll probably agree that our having concentrated for several years on how to beat the Fords really hadn't been a bad thing at all. We had a very strong base of knowledge about what these cars could do. We also benefited from our ongoing emphasis on engineering, which dated to the very start of Penske South. It yielded a quantifiable and consistently positive transfer of results from one car to another, even as Roger was negotiating top-level alliances.

We started over, leaving Pontiac behind, to get ready for 1994. I went to David Evans, our chief engine builder, who'd heard the news and was already machining his first Ford block. David said, "You know, the word is that you can put together one of these out of the Ford cookbook (that's what the crews all called the internal Ford setup guidelines), and you're going to make 700 horsepower."

I managed not to laugh. We had been running, pretty much all along, since the start of Penske South, with around 650 horsepower. All the other GM teams knew what we were making. Over time, and thanks in great measure to the association we'd developed with Ilmor over in England, we'd managed to run it up to about 690 horsepower, reliably, with our best GM motor. That's about what Rusty had when he won the 10 races, I think a peak of 692 horsepower. We agreed, however, that a steady 700 would be nice if we could make it.

At the time, Goodyear was working on a new radial for 1994 and asked us to go test them at Phoenix, due in part to the fact that Rusty had struggled with the radials at first. Nobody in the world knows this until now, and I didn't want to have to do this because John Erickson was my friend and liaison at Pontiac, but I asked David if he could get a Ford engine together by the following Monday, when we'd have to be readying to leave for Arizona. He said he could if we worked around the clock. I told him to do just that, and I also told Dave Roberts, one of our best fabricators, to build some new engine mounts so we could put the Ford engine in our Pontiac and run it in the tire test. David Evans was shocked, but I explained that, hey, that was the only way to find out what we had with Ford. We had just run the Pontiac engine at Phoenix in the Cup race, now we'd find out what the same car would do with Ford power. But I added that everybody had to shut up about it, and that if anybody in the building uttered a word about it, I'd strangle them.

David got it together in time, our first Ford motor, and put it on the dyno. The first dyno pull read 708 horsepower. I told him, emphatically, "Don't tell Rusty, because Rusty will tell the whole world." It was only because I knew Rusty would get so excited by all that power that he'd want to tell somebody. Dave Roberts built the engine mounts; Billy Woodruff built a set of headers for it, and put the Ford motor into the Pontiac. We kept the hood shut, headed west, and didn't tell anybody when we got to Phoenix, starting with Goodyear. Rusty climbed in, reeled off about six laps, and came back in. "My God. This thing goes like hell. What a motor!" We were all pumped, obviously, but there were only eight weeks to go until we had to leave for Daytona. We were also supposed to have 14 Thunderbirds ready to go by then.

That was when we went to see Bill Davis. He was doing the opposite of Penske South, switching from Fords to Pontiacs for 1994. We'd already told Pontiac that we were switching to Ford, so it wasn't as if we had to keep it a secret from Bill. We agreed to swap cars with him and got Bill's Thunderbirds. We also got the shock of our lives: We put one of his Thunderbirds in the wind tunnel, and our Pontiac had 300 pounds more downforce than Bill's Ford, because of all the aero research that Andrew Scriven had done for us. We had no way of knowing that until we got it in the tunnel.

I said that since we had one of them, we should do everything we could to improve that one before tearing the bodies off all the Davis cars. We decided to take a half-dozen of the cars we'd got from Bill, look at them, strip them, bead-blast them and do the best we could to improve the aero. We saved one Pontiac to serve as a guidepost for what to do. We pieced the Fords back together and took one to the Lockheed Martin wind tunnel in Marietta, Georgia. We could only get within 200 pounds of downforce of our Pontiac. Rusty is a downforce guy. He simply told us, "Build as much downforce into it as you can for me. I want so much rear down that I blow out the rear tires."

Back in Mooresville, we were scratching our heads. Andrew finally piped up, "The only thing we can do is take one of these cars and cut the body off it. We'll move the body as far back on it as we can without getting busted by NASCAR. Then we'll start building for downforce."

We went to Daytona and kept prepping for Atlanta, the next real "downforce race." By that time, we'd gotten our Ford engines to the point where we were making 715 or 716 horsepower. That's almost 40 horsepower more than the best we'd gotten from the GM motor. Ford just had a better design, better cylinder heads, better everything. Rusty got in the car and said, "You know, we're going to get three or four races into this thing and then we're going to seriously start kicking butt."

That was exactly what happened. We had enormous horsepower, which Rusty loved, and with a lot of work, had gotten the Thunderbird aerodynamics to where they were almost as good as our Pontiacs'. Buddy Parrott was telling everyone in the pits that unless the driver ran into a wall, we were going to mop them up. Buddy was a terrific motivator, which was the other thing we had at Penske South besides all that horsepower and downforce: Chemistry. We had it back. Our guys thought they were the best, that there was no way anybody was going to beat them, and that's exactly how it turned out. They were on top of their game, our pit stops were *awesome*, our engines and our bodies started getting better and better. We just started pounding the wins out, one after another.

Somewhere in all this, we won at Richmond, with the new 12.0:1 compression ratio rule. Until then, there was no compression limit, and we had engines that routinely made 15.0:1. NASCAR tested our engine after the race, and came back and said, "Well, it's 12.0002." I said, "So what?" They started to say that we were illegal, that we were going to be disqualified. They were claiming it was 12.0002:1. No, I told them. This was a night race, with changing temperature and humidity. There was no way they were going to take that win away from us. I really got in the NASCAR people's faces. They bowed up, we bowed up, and it was getting close to turning into a fistfight. I practically yelled that we were *not* illegal. The NASCAR inspectors said they were going to keep the engine. I told them, fine, keep it, but we would be coming back with our own people.

I went to a professor of engineering I knew at the University of Central Florida, Dr. Bob Hoekstra, who taught industrial engineering and internal combustion theory. Bob had helped us in the past with header and exhaust-flow analysis, along with another professor, Dr. Joe David of North Carolina State University in Raleigh. I went down to see Bob at UCF's campus in Orlando and told him, "You've got to help me out." When I explained the situation, the first thing he asked me was whether I knew exactly, *precisely*, what instruments NASCAR was using. I assured him I would find out. I asked the NASCAR officials for everything, including the manufacturers' names and the devices' serial numbers. The officials got my drift immediately, and started in with, "Don't get mad at us."

I had already surmised that most of this had been driven by Gary Nelson, because he and I had never seen eye to eye. Bob Hoekstra at N.C. State went to the manufacturers, each of which has a tolerance built into their equipment that averages around 2 percent of the reading. The compression we supposedly tested at would have been 11.9 percent of a reading, he told me, whereas an accurate tolerance would have gone out a bunch of more decimal places. I got all this done in 48 hours and took it to NASCAR. They were beyond angry. They called Roger in. He listened attentively, as he does, and said, "I think you guys better come to some kind of a compromise. We're not going to shove it down your throat, but we will appeal it, and you'll lose."

NASCAR knew the same thing we did, that within the statistical tolerances of the testing equipment, our engine was clearly legal. The final outcome was that Bill France Jr. told Gary Nelson to make up a press release through Jim Hunter, NASCAR's director of communications, saying that after reading the fine print of the rules, we were within tolerance. They wouldn't come off their 12.0001. They said the maximum was 12.0, so, as long as it wasn't 12.1, the engine was legal. They let us have the win. We got in within their protest window before they posted the official results of the race. That compression rule had been instituted right after Daytona, and they tested people after every race. We'd won 10 races the year before, we were on our way to winning eight in 1994, and certain people didn't like that. As Bill Jr. would say, "You guys are beginning to stink up the show."

All due respect to Bill Jr., we kept right on winning, even with a new crew chief. Robin Pemberton came aboard with us in 1995 after Buddy accepted a huge offer to join the new team owned by Gary Bechtel. Chevrolet wasn't lying down, though. They were very aggressive and kept coming out with new designs: in chronological order, the trunked Monte Carlo, the aero-window Monte Carlo SS, the Lumina hardtop and then the new Monte Carlo that was spun off it.

We knew, obviously, that GM would keep coming at us. We were actively brainstorming solutions that might keep us ahead before we would have to ask for help from NASCAR, begging for a deeper front air dam or a longer deck lid, so you can get more downforce and better balance. What, we wondered among ourselves, were the best cars—or, better yet, the best traits of the other cars, the Pontiacs and Chevrolets? NASCAR had approved the five-inch-wider rear for the

We built a special research vehicle at our shop that incorporated the best of Ford, Chevrolet, and Pontiac designs for aerodynamic testing at the Langley wind tunnel. We called this our Thunder Carlo. (Don Miller Collection)

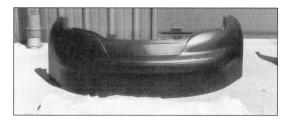

The Thunder Carlo featured a Monte Carlo nose, Thunderbird hood, and Grand Prix windshield. (Don Miller Collection)

Monte Carlo, because a stock Monte Carlo was too narrow in back to fit the spoiler. Andrew had raised a valid point: How good, or bad, did we really need to be to compete against it with the Thunderbird, or perhaps with something else? NASCAR had given us its own numbers that it got from testing the Lumina and the Monte Carlo, which were supposedly only this good or that good. Really? Everybody else, Robert Yates and all, had looked at those numbers and just walked away. Andrew, though, said, "Let's get a chassis and build a Chevy. We've got to do it."

We made a list, and I went to David Little, who ran the Penske South fabrication shop, and told him to build us a car. Not a Ford, and ultimately, not a Chevy or really anything else. Just a car that was a conglomeration of all these features of the Ford, the Pontiac and the Chevrolet, with the only ground rule being that it had to generally fit the NASCAR templates. We had another team, whose guys we knew, buy the body panels from Chevy and bring them over. David built it. It started out with Thunderbird sides and a Thunderbird windshield. We added a Monte Carlo roof, rear window and rear spoiler. We fitted a Monte Carlo rear fascia after we sharpened it up into kind of a combination of Thunderbird and Monte Carlo shapes. We added a front fascia to turn this no-brand car into a combination of Chevrolet, Ford and Pontiac. We took it to the wind tunnel, to the puzzlement of the Ford guys at Marietta, who wanted to know what it was. That was when Dave named it the Thunder Carlo. We took it to Langley after that, and then, we decided to build a full Monte Carlo, as Andrew had lobbied for, on one of our own chassis.

 We had some trouble at that time. Chevy had just replaced the Lumina coupe with the new Monte Carlo. The stock Monte Carlo body had a sort of a boat-tailed rear deck, which was narrowed and sloped downward when compared to the Thunderbird. GM had lobbied NASCAR to widen the rear end five inches over stock, and flatten the Monte Carlo, to 'allow' the attachment of the 57-inch-wide rear spoiler, to 'avoid' having the spoiler stick out about 2½ inches on each side if it had been mounted to the stock body.

This widening, in combination with the Monte Carlo's aerodynamically superior front end, resulted in superior lift and drag coefficient for it compared to the Thunderbird. Before that, the Thunderbird had kind of had its way, kicking everybody's behind. It was the combination of the Elliott brothers and a real good aerodynamic package in the Thunderbird."

DAN RIVARD
Former Director of Global Racing Operations
Ford Motor Company
Northville, Michigan

Andrew—who, I want to say right here, is the reason that Langley is what it is in NASCAR today—then said, "Think of what we've got to do, because now we've got the numbers. We have to look at the Thunderbird while thinking about what makes the Monte Carlo aerodynamically better." That's when we started cutting our Monte Carlo up and grafting the pieces, one at a time, onto our T-bird. Back at Langley, comparing numbers, we realized that the Thunder Carlo was better than the Monte Carlo, but the Monte Carlo was better than our Thunderbird. The Monte Carlo had more downforce, and it really piled it on in terms of yaw, in the corners. The shape of the C-pillars and rear window really helped the Monte Carlo in yaw. It actually picked up downforce in the corners, which is where you want it.

We looked at the numbers from our old Pontiac and found out the Pontiac was the same way, so we started really working hard on the C-pillar and backlight shapes on our T-birds. We were competitive, but we could quantify that we were still giving away a lot aerodynamically. It was an ongoing process that lasted into the introduction of the next-generation Monte Carlo and really, the Thunderbird's phasing out. The Thunder Carlo and our in-house Monte

Carlo were actually the precursor cars to a little-known race car that we developed before Ford settled on the Taurus as its NASCAR entry. That car was the Lincoln Mark VIII, or if you prefer, the Marauder.

The Marauder tale got underway when Dan Rivard, Ford's global director of racing, approached us in 1996 and told us in total confidence that Ford planned to discontinue the Thunderbird. Less than 70,000 were projected to be built during 1997. Dropping the Thunderbird, a hallowed Ford name that had been around since 1955, was a gigantic decision for Ford. That's why Dan only told Andrew and me—nobody else. Dan said Ford would stay in NASCAR but absolutely had to have a replacement ready for 1998.

I really like Dan, who is an outstanding engineer in addition to being Mister Honesty, so I said, "Well, look. This is going to cost money, first of all." Dan said, "Don't worry about it. Give me a budget and we'll fund it. But it's got to be absolutely secret. We can't let our customers know that we're not going to build a T-bird anymore." He went on to add that Ford would have to use something existing to replace the Thunderbird as a race car, by which he meant a car for which Ford already had the sheetmetal stampings, the tooling to stamp them and so forth. Presumably, nobody had seriously considered using the Taurus yet.

Here was Dan's question: Could we build a car out of the existing Thunderbird sheetmetal we had that would fit on a current chassis with the existing wheelbase limit of 110 inches for Winston Cup? Dan said Ford would build a limited production run, for the street, of whatever this car was that we created. He told us he could work it out with NASCAR. Andrew and I were the only ones who knew about this radical plan, but I told him I'd have to go to Dave Hoffert, the

A Ford in Our Future   **189**

controller of Penske South, to help us put together a budget to develop the car, and that Dave would have to keep it quiet and separate so the rest of the employees wouldn't know what we were doing.

The next thing Dan asked was, "If I gave you sheetmetal from everything Ford builds, could you make me a car?" I answered yes, but made it clear again that Dave Hoffert had to know, and so did Muttley—that's Ralph Brawley, probably the very finest metalsmith in the country. Porsche sent cars damaged in transit to the United States over to Ralph's shop in Mooresville before they were sold brand new. Ralph agreed to keep everything under cover and only work on our project on weekends, with the door locked.

Andrew looked everything over and said, "You know, aerodynamically, the Lincoln parts are pretty cool." That's how we settled on the Lincoln as our choice. The Mark VIII, the rear-drive luxury coupe, was built on a slightly longer version of the MN-12 Thunderbird chassis. We started with the Lincoln front fascia, the roof and the hood, which Ford gave us. We used a Town Car trunk lid and a rear fascia. We started calling it the Aircraft Carrier, because it was so huge. A normal Winston Cup car from that era would have had an overall length of about 200 inches, regardless of which make it was, but this Lincoln was well over 208 inches long—and still on a 110-inch wheelbase. Still, it was incredibly slick, obviously more so than the Monte Carlo with its tricked-up, considerably widened rear body that NASCAR had recently declared legal. The downside was that it was a Lincoln, which didn't at all fit Ford's racing strategy. Ford's plan, as

Every once in a while you get your hands on a project that is both productive and fun. The Marauder was both. It is still on display at the North Carolina Auto Racing Hall of Fame. (Jim Donnelly Photo)

Dan told us, was to call it the Marauder. Dan said Ford fully intended to build the required 500 street versions of the car, to be called the "Marauder by Lincoln-Mercury." But the Ford Division wanted in, too, and wanted to call it, ironically, the SuperBird, recalling the winged 1970 Superbird—lower-case "b"—raced by Plymouth during the NASCAR aero wars.

> We got a lot of things done at that time that we couldn't have done without Don. Basically, he stayed out of the NASCAR politics and was fairly apolitical. I see a lot of guys that are really good at 40,000 feet, and a lot of guys that are real good at five microns, but I see very few guys that are good at both 40,000 feet and five microns. It was very improbable to take a Mark VIII and make a race car out of it, but that set the stake in the ground. "

DAN RIVARD

As a result of all this, Andrew made up spreadsheets laying out the pluses and minuses of the Lincoln/Marauder body. It turned out to be far superior to the Thunderbird, with about 200 pounds more downforce in spite of a lot less drag. Plus, since it was so long, it had more surface area for fine-tuning the downforce when racing on shorter superspeedways, or even short tracks. It was a deadly weapon, probably too dangerous. When Muttley finished it and smoothed the whole thing out, we had to show it to Gary Nelson, along with the aerodynamic projections that Andrew had worked up. It wasn't a lengthy meeting. Nelson pretty much took one look at the Marauder, one look at the spreadsheet and said it wasn't going to happen. That was the end of Project Marauder. Today, the car we built for this initiative is on display in the North Carolina Auto Racing Hall of Fame in Mooresville.

> That son of a gun was the slickest race car you'd ever want to see. Bob Rewey, then our vice president of sales, and I showed Bill France Jr. the wind-tunnel numbers from that car, and said, 'If you force us to, this is what we're going to use.' What I said to Bill was what you've got to do is give everyone truth serum, or else forget all that and go to common templates, to avoid any more Monte Carlo-like deviations from stock bodies to gain an aero advantage. That was a long struggle, but now with the new digitized body, they've got the ultimate common template . . . . The NASCAR bodies are now digitized in three dimensions. You cannot trick that body."

DAN RIVARD

Well, almost. Dan was really excited about The Marauder, took photos to show the higher-ups in Dearborn, and we were lobbying NASCAR to let us try it in at least one race. Michael Kranefuss actually did get to try a Mark VIII body during a test session, with John Andretti driving. But it was nothing like the Marauder.

THE KRANEFUSS CONNECTION

Something else had been going on with me besides Project Marauder. Beginning around the time we were getting fully adapted to the Thunderbird in 1996, I had started to have some serious physical problems related to the injuries I'd sustained on pit road at Talladega in 1974. You'd think that after 20 years, they wouldn't have been an issue any more, or that I could put it behind me. It was clear, though, that I was getting significantly worse. The damage to my spinal cord was causing me pain, and was beginning to affect my ability to use my arms and legs.

Finally, my physicians sent me to Saint Mary's Medical Center, a hospital in San Francisco that specializes in the surgical treatment of spinal cord injuries. I got to know several of the doctors there, and they prescribed a number of treatments, including lightweight, carbon-fiber artificial limbs to take some of the pressure off my spine. Roger was very understanding, but I was still trying to do my job, like flying all night from Charlotte to San Francisco for treatment and then coming back to work in a day or two, but I was really struggling. While I was trying to get better, Roger had gone on one of those cruises that Bill France Jr. would organize for the influential people in NASCAR. They'd have these cruises after the July 4 race at Daytona among guys with yachts like the Frances, Earnhardt, Rick Hendrick and Penske. The saying in NASCAR was that if you didn't have a boat, you didn't have a vote.

On this particular cruise in July 1997, they got to talking about how Kranefuss was struggling in his position as a NASCAR team owner in partnership with Carl Haas, the CART team owner and long-time Lola importer. That team, Kranefuss-Haas Racing, was formed after Kranefuss left the Ford Motor Company, where he'd been global director of racing and previously, Ford's racing chief in Europe. It was their Mark VIII that John Andretti had run in the test at Charlotte.

Somehow, Bill Jr. talked Roger into buying out Haas and bringing Kranefuss, and his team, into Penske South. It really surprised me, although in hindsight, maybe it shouldn't have. There were sponsorship tie-ins: Kranefuss had sponsorship from Little Caesar's, the pizza chain, which had locations inside Kmart; we had an association with Kmart at that time, too, with Penske operating Kmart's automotive service centers. We really wanted to have a second team, but Rusty was one-third owner and he didn't want us running another car at that point. Even so, we'd talked to several potential drivers, including Kenny Irwin Jr., with whom we came pretty close to doing a deal. We also talked to Tony Stewart.

But Rusty really didn't want to do it, and rather than having a big battle in-house, we had stepped away from it. And then Roger put this deal together with Kranefuss, who brought along his sponsor, Mobil 1, and his driver, Jeremy Mayfield (who had replaced John Andretti since the days of the Marauder testing). Roger told us that Kranefuss would have 50-percent ownership of Penske-Kranefuss Racing, while he, Rusty and I would continue to have our existing ownership shares of Penske South. There were some heated discussions, but the deal was done.

RACING CAN BE HELL, BUT DOESN'T HAVE TO FEEL LIKE IT

And, through all of this, there was another kind of heat going on.

High-order combustion, the kind that occurs in racing engines, produces more than just horsepower. A byproduct of all that power, which became increasingly troublesome as their outputs in NASCAR continued to escalate, was intense heat. More horsepower inexorably means more heat. It reached the point where it was melting the heels of the driving shoes and in some cases, leaving the drivers with badly blistered feet, which could have left them susceptible to scarring and infections, besides being extremely painful.

Heat inside the race cars had been a major topic of conversation among the drivers, and it was clearly getting worse, not better. The guys on the team and I were talking about it, like everyone else. We, however, decided to do something about it. Through Bobby Allison, who was retired from driving by then, we had developed a very important relationship with Jay Honeycutt, a career engineer who went on to become a top officer of NASA, and who was the person who introduced us to Dr. Cross at Old Dominion.

> *I gave a tour of the space center once to Bobby Allison in the early 1990s. I showed him what we call the Back Shop here, where the thermal protection system for the space shuttle orbiter is produced. It comes in a couple of different forms, one being a consistency like Styrofoam. In another, it's woven into thread and used to make blankets, which typically goes on the back or sides of the orbiter. Bobby was very interested in the fact that it was used to keep the crew cool during re-entry.*

It's a silicon-based material developed by Lockheed Martin during the 1970s. You run it through an oven that's about 2,500 degrees Fahrenheit and when it comes out the other side, in about three feet you can put your hand on it. This material also allowed vehicles like the Stealth fighter to get rid of the thermal signature from its exhaust.

Bobby told me that one of the biggest problems in racing was the heat generated from the exhaust pipes being right under the floor, and the seats being shaped like a bowl, plus all the sweat collecting in the drivers' suits can actually start to boil. They all brake with their left foot, too, so they never really lift off the throttle.

Access to the material is controlled by the federal government, but Bobby wanted to market it through the team he was running al the time. For whatever reason, it didn't work out, so Bobby said, 'I know how we can get this done. Let's talk to Don Miller.'"

JAY HONEYCUTT
Retired Director, Kennedy Space Center
Cocoa Beach, Florida

Through Bobby and the people at Langley, Jay put us in touch with people from Rockwell, which was manufacturing the heat-resistant material, and with people on the shuttle program, and we were able to get access to the technology to apply it to racing.

" *Within the government, they have what's called a Technology Transfer Agreement. It's essentially there to ensure that if somebody gets a technology that the taxpayers paid for, they don't go running off and give it to the Chinese or somebody. We got permission for the guys at Penske South to potentially use the thermal protection system as a means to comfort the drivers.*

We actually brought Rusty's race car down here. Before that, we ran it at Daytona for three or four laps and got some measurements of the temperatures that it reached on the track. We brought the car inside our shop at the Space Center and began fitting blankets into it. That was extremely unusual: a race car in the middle of the space shuttle work area. The shuttle work crews were lined up all the way around the building to get a look at Rusty's car. We're close enough to Daytona that most of the people who work here are race fans."

JAY HONEYCUTT

We took the new NASA heat shields to the Suzuka race in Japan before they were actually approved by NASCAR. We won the race. (Don Miller Collection)

These thermal blankets are maybe an inch thick and close to weightless. We used little tie-downs to mount them in the car. In the form we used, it basically looked like quilted stainless steel. We first tried attaching it to the upper part of the exhaust system, to form a barrier between the collectors and the floorboards of the car. We moved on to wrap it around the tailpipes where they pass right beneath the driver's seat. From there, we created a blanket of insulation that would fit just beneath the seat on the floorboard, for an added thermal layer, and another that we could apply to the firewall. Also, on the firewall, we could make plugs out of the thermal shield that would fit into holes where wiring passed through. There was next to no weight penalty involved in using it.

After that, we took the car from the Cape back to Daytona and ran it again. The NASA instruments indicated that the blankets were cutting the temperature inside the race car by something like 40 percent. Ultimately, we developed a whole thermal kit for a race car, and as the NASA test had shown, it was possible to get the internal temperatures of the driver's compartment lowered by about 40 degrees once the whole kit was put together.

The next issue was getting it to market, so we went with Jay to see Bill Simpson first. He didn't want to do it, but through Bobby, we showed the kit to Butch Stevens of BSR Products, and he was all for it. We never tried to make any money from the kit but Butch has done really well with it. He actually built an addition onto his shop to produce the thermal blankets for race cars. If you look at the BSR catalog even today, there's a space shuttle on the front cover. That's why.

If you're a short track driver, even just doing 25 or 30 laps in the feature on a Saturday night, this stuff, and Jay's effort to make it widely available, can benefit you, too.

19

The Taurus Files

BEFORE YOU CAN TALK about the birth of the Ford Taurus as a NASCAR race car, you've first got to talk about the demise of the Thunderbird. No question, it had been a tremendous race car and marketing tool for the Ford Motor Company, going all the way back to the 1970s when it replaced the Torino as Ford's primary body style in NASCAR. The real glory years began with the aero-style Thunderbird that first appeared in 1983, especially as raced to all those wins by the Elliott family once they teamed up with Harry Melling.

Once the Marauder experiment was sunk, Ford latched onto the notion of somehow getting the Taurus legalized to run in Winston Cup. We would have chuckled if we'd known about it at the time. NASCAR was the home of two-door hardtops. While four-door stock cars had been run for years in Australia and in European touring car championships, the idea of racing a sedan in Winston Cup was unknown in the 1990s. Plus, the production Taurus had a V-6 and front wheel drive. Yet, here came Dan Rivard, who told us that there was to be a new director of Ford racing, Bruce Camburn. Dan wanted us to work with Bruce, along with Ford's chief engineer, John Valentine, and chief aerodynamicist, John LaFond, to take on a special project. Top management had decided that the T-bird was going away and planned to race the Taurus, even though it was a four-door. While the T-bird was expected to drop below its cutoff sales point, the Taurus was Ford's biggest-volume vehicle in North America, except for the F-series pickup.

Next, Ford provided us with a 40-percent clay model Taurus as a starting point for building a race car. Dan asked me to sit down with Bruce and John Valentine and spend whatever it took. This was February 1997, however, and there was a catch: Dan told me an approved Taurus race car had to be ready to unveil at Indianapolis, at the Brickyard 400 in August. I was speechless.

Over a weekend, I worked up a ballpark budget and a rush timeline. Just as with the Marauder, Dan made it absolutely clear that nobody could find out that we were working on the Taurus project. I assured him that I'd keep it down to an absolute minimum number of people who would know about it, and that we'd do it all with models—there was no way we could start with a full-size car. Dan, as an engineer, agreed with that plan. We had a 40-percent Monte Carlo and were happy to find out that the Taurus model would fit on the same wind-tunnel chassis. I took Andrew Scriven aside and told him that the Taurus project team would include just the two of us, and that we were going to get Max Crawford to do the scale race-car bodies. Max's shop, down the road in Denver, North Carolina, had extensive experience in composites and testing. Max had come from New Zealand and built Mazda's entry in the IMSA GTP series. As I mentioned, today Andrew is Max's chief designer, building the Rolex Grand-Am cars and the wings for NASCAR's Car of Tomorrow. The last part of the group was, once again, Muttley—Ralph Brawley, I should say—to do the actual full-scale sheetmetal fabrication.

 It was probably a step too far. I didn't have any tradition in NASCAR, but I'm thinking, this car is front drive. It has four doors. Ford gave us a 40-percent clay model of a stock Taurus. Out comes the old NASCAR rule book, and at Max Crawford's old shop, we start growing clay onto it, build an air dam on it, just guessing at where the fender heights ought to be. When we were done, the air intake for the cowl was halfway up the windshield."

ANDREW SCRIVEN

Looking through the usual vagueness in the NASCAR rule book, it was apparent that the stock body wouldn't reach the target roof and fender heights. Andrew started adding clay onto the model, pretty much sculpting the fenders and front air dam as he went along. When Andrew was done, we all stood back and tried to determine what kind of car his model most resembled, because it certainly didn't look like a Taurus, but more like a Porsche 911 GT at Le Mans. The hood seemed to be stubbed off at half the normal length. We had been trying desperately to use the Taurus production car's dimensions, but once we built the prototype it was clear that was impossible. Finally, we let Rusty's crew chief, Robin Pemberton, in on the deal. That brought the operating team to Robin, Andrew, Ralph and me.

We borrowed this 1997 Taurus from Ford and built a "1998" model using it, just for NASCAR. Ralph Brawley created rear bodywork that was way higher and flatter than any stock 1997 Taurus had. (Jim Donnelly Photo)

> " How do you keep it a secret? You manage it by keeping the circle of people very close, very tight-knit, people you can trust. The analogy here is when we developed the pushrod V-8 engine for Mercedes-Benz for the 1994 Indianapolis 500. There were only a handful of people in the Mercedes-Benz, Ilmor and Penske Racing organizations who knew what was going on."

WALTER CZARNECKI

In midst of talking, just thinking out loud, Ralph asked, "Well, how far do we have to stretch this hood out to be legal?" Collectively, we figured it was seven or eight inches. So we lengthened the hood and changed the fenders relative to the length of the passenger compartment. Then Andrew noticed that the rear deck lid was still too droopy, a characteristic of the Taurus that dated to the production car's 1996 redesign using the ovoid theme. It was way too low for a race car with a spoiler that had to take air cleanly off the back window. We told him to raise it. Andrew asked, again just thinking out loud, what we intended to do when NASCAR came over and brought a street Taurus along for comparison purposes. I thought a minute and said, "Next year, Ford's going to have a new model, redesigned Taurus, right?" Andrew said, "Yep." Ralph caught on at once and breathed, "Oh, my God."

I called Dan and got him to send us a brand-new 1997 Taurus four-door. It was a silver GL sedan with a gray cloth interior. We took it—and drove it—over to Ralph's shop. I told Ralph we had to get its whole rear end three inches higher. He said we'd have to put a whole new body on from the back vent back. That was fine; I told him to cut the whole back end off but save the deck lid. We got a broom handle and cut it off at the height we wanted, the legal height for the rear spoiler. Using the stock deck lid, Ralph made a little jig and used it as a guide to make new quarter panels, new rear fenders. He assembled the pieces and used his magic to blend it all in. Then he took the oval 1997 Taurus rear window and reshaped it to make it less round. He made a whole new rear fascia that was a lot taller than the stock one. He got it all together, painted it factory silver, and put a production Ford wing on the deck lid. Andy measured all its dimensions, and then changed the clay model to match the car Ralph had built.

We scanned a Chevy Monte Carlo and made a model of that, then took it with the 40-percent Thunderbird, plus our doctored Taurus, to the wind tunnel in Southampton, England. Andrew spent endless hours in the wind tunnel. I was over there for several days. We'd had Max build the actual models in North Carolina, rather than Penske Cars in Poole, which normally did that sort of thing. I explained to Roger that the guys in Poole weren't interested in stock cars, it would take months for me just to explain to them what I wanted, and I didn't have the time to do that and also my regular job.

At the wind tunnel in England, Andrew started messing with ride heights, which in actual, full-size testing, were more or less fixed. But when he lowered the models to where they'd really be at racing speed on the track, the Taurus just absolutely blew the other two away, with its faked-out rear deck. When Andrew found out how thoroughly the model Taurus was dusting everything in the wind tunnel, we agreed we had to get that body into a real, sheetmetal car, which NASCAR's Gary Nelson had told us we had to have before he'd approve the Taurus. (Bill France, who had known early on about Ford's intention to drop the Thunderbird, had brought Gary into the loop about Ford's desire to have the Taurus approved for NASCAR racing.)

Left: By shaving lots of clay, Andrew Scriven created this 40-percent Taurus model for the wind tunnel. (Don Miller Collection)

Right: At the Southampton wind tunnel, here is the new and improved Taurus tunnel replica, a very slick piece. (Don Miller Collection)

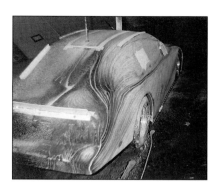

Again we went to David Little in the Penske South fab shop, and he built the car. Gary Nelson finally came into our shops, looked at it, and exploded: "What the hell are you people doing in here?" He demanded that we change the rear, even though we built it according to NASCAR's own rule book. Incredibly, he agreed to let us lengthen the hood some more, probably because he was so insistent that the deck lid had to slope downward like he'd seen on every other 1997 Taurus. Right then was when I said, "But Gary, next year's Taurus isn't going to be like that."

I told him we had a Ford final prototype of a 1998 Taurus sedan outside. Bruce Camburn, from Dan's team, had gotten us one of those blue Michigan manufacturer license plates and we'd screwed the thing onto the chopped-up Taurus Muttley had built. I convinced Gary it was all hush-hush because it was a pre-production prototype straight from Ford's design studio in Dearborn. I was making up this whole tall tale on the fly. Nelson got really interested and wanted to see it, but I said, all conspiratorially, that no photos were allowed, because the car was going to anchor the Ford marketing program for a new, redesigned Taurus. We told him that our chop job, hidden surreptitiously under a car cover, was an authentic 1998 Taurus. That new rear was done to make the trunk bigger, I solemnly told him. The prototype had to secretly go back to Dearborn in two days.

Gary swallowed it whole. Dan hung in there with us, even though he couldn't believe what we had done in faking the "1998" car. He said, "Don, if word of this gets out, you're going to get me fired." He agreed, though, that our car was the way the 1998 Taurus should have looked. I told Dan just to tell everybody that Ford couldn't get the body finished in time for 1998 and just pushed the whole thing back to 1999. Gary Nelson approved the body—Ralph's body—as legal for Winston Cup. From the time the first clay model was laid up in early February 1997 to the first public rollout of a production race car at Indianapolis at the end of that July, we had built the Taurus in just under six months.

Left: One of our initial problems, as Andrew's carbon fiber model in 40-percent scale shows, was that the oval rear window and sloping rear deck weren't very efficient. We needed a plan. (Don Miller Collection)

Right: We reached a seemingly impossible goal by unveiling the first Winston Cup-legal Ford Taurus at the 1997 Brickyard 400, despite having had to develop it in total secrecy. (Don Miller Collection)

TAURUS TIMELINE

- **December 6, 1996** Discussions begin about replacing the Thunderbird with the Ford Taurus.
- **Day 1, January 27, 1997** First Taurus concept meeting at Ford Special Vehicle Operations.
- **Day 5, January 31** Taurus launch date advanced to February 1998.
- **Day 12, February 7** First clay model of production Ford Taurus delivered to Penske South.
- **Day 15, February 10** Work begins on 40-percent clay model of race car.
- **Day 34, March 1** First 40-percent model completed using NASCAR dimensional criteria.
- **Day 48, March 15** Ford announces discontinuance of Thunderbird at end of model year 1997.
- **Day 57, March 24** First wind tunnel molds completed.
- **Day 60, March 27** First model shipped to England for wind tunnel testing.
- **Days 68-69, April 4-5** During two-day test at Southampton University, Taurus model No. 1 tested along with Thunderbird.
- **Day 108, May 14** First full-size mockup shown to Ford teams and NASCAR at Penske South.
- **Day 108, May 14** NASCAR technical director Gary Nelson requests changes to low roofline.
- **Day 109, May 15** Penske South receives go-ahead to build second 40-percent Taurus model.
- **Day 114, May 20** Second 40-percent Taurus model completed.
- **Day 124, May 30** Tests on Thunderbird, and Taurus models No. 1 and No. 2, begin at Swift Engineering wind tunnel in San Clemente, California.
- **Day 127, June 2** 40-percent clay model of Chevrolet Monte Carlo produced for comparison to Taurus.
- **Day 145, June 20** Nose and tail molds from full-size Penske Taurus sent to Roush Racing for use in building full-size race car.
- **Day 154, June 29** First test of full-size prototype at Lockheed Martin wind tunnel, Marietta, Georgia.
- **Day 164, July 9** Gary Nelson visits Penske South to evaluate Taurus modifications.
- **Day 170, July 15** Taurus model No. 2 updated for further tests at Swift tunnel.
- **Day 171, July 16** Taurus race car production begun by Ford's NASCAR Winston Cup teams.
- **Day 180, July 25** Penske South completes full-size Taurus race car for initial public display.
- **Days 182-183, July 27-28** Taurus No. 2, Thunderbird and Monte Carlo tested at Swift.
- **Day 185, July 30** Taurus race car unveiled to media and public at Indiana Convention Center, Indianapolis.

- **Day 186, July 31** Full-size Taurus shipped to Detroit for scanning to produce new 40-percent model and reference templates.
- **Day 192, August 6** Detroit meeting held to schedule final wind tunnel and initial track tests. Third wind tunnel test model approved.
- **Day 219, September 2** Rusty Wallace and Bill Elliott drive prototype in initial track test at Daytona International Speedway.
- **Days 223-225, September 6-8** Third Taurus model produces drag coefficients very close to updated Thunderbird and Monte Carlo at Swift.
- **Days 276-279, October 29-November 1** Fourth test at Swift focuses on drag reduction.
- **Day 313, December 5** Track testing begins at Homestead, Florida. Teams agree to proceed with Penske South design.
- **Days 324-326, December 16-18** Jimmy Spencer is tops at 190.723 mph during three-day Talladega Superspeedway test.
- **Day 328, December 20** Single-day test at Charlotte Motor Speedway.
- **Days 352-354, January 13-15, 1998** Kenny Irwin Jr. is tops at 190.609 in testing at Daytona.
- **Day 378, February 8** Rusty Wallace wins Bud Shootout at Daytona for Penske South in Taurus racing debut.

Ford did, obviously, introduce a 1998 Taurus. About the only changes from the production 1997 model that we'd diced up were that the rear turn signals had red lenses instead of amber ones. Of course, GM was livid at what we'd pulled off, but couldn't do anything about it—the following year, everybody was going to have to fit a new universal NASCAR template anyway, so they let it die.

We've still got that "prototype" 1998 Taurus over at the Penske racing headquarters in Mooresville. It runs, has low mileage, has insurance and current North Carolina registration. The paint's cracked in some spots were Ralph mocked up the body. This book marks the first time this story's ever been told publicly. I'll say this: Gary Nelson and I were like oil and water. It was a good thing that I had Andrew, who got along better with him, to cool Gary off after I'd set him ablaze.

Let me say a couple of things. I knew what we had to have, a racing Taurus. I also knew that NASCAR intended to go to the universal template. They needed somebody to show them the way. Did I bend NASCAR's rules? No. I intentionally misled them. But to what end? The end result was going to be the same with the new template. There just would have been a bigger fight over them if we hadn't pulled our little caper first. Plus, GM had already done a lot of really "creative" things with its own bodies, which was why NASCAR had decided to go to the universal templates in the first place. That's

In total secrecy, we created a landmark Ford race car before six months had elapsed and presented it to the public at Indy. (Ford Motor Company Photo)

where we ended up, and all the arguments went away, at least until we took the Taurus to Daytona in 1998 and right off the bat, Rusty won his qualifying race with it. I also want to say that Bill France Jr. knew well that the hardtop body style was going to disappear, and the Taurus did a lot to vindicate what he'd been saying for a long time: "One day, you're all going to be driving four-doors."

 We built the first two-door Taurus coupe. And the last."

WALTER CZARNECKI

The common longitudinal template essentially stopped everyone from whining that "my hood's not long enough," or "my rear deck's not long enough." The Taurus, though, was a big winner out of the box, blowing the GM cars away, until NASCAR went to the common spoiler and ended up taking two inches off of it for the Taurus. So, things didn't change all that much. We'd kind of anticipated, truthfully, that some such restriction or blowback from NASCAR was going to happen at some point. Remember that when we were first tunnel-testing the Taurus scale model at Southampton, Andrew—"Sir Andrew of Scrod," as I like to call him—had experimented with the model's ride height to simulate its stance on the track at speed. After we got the full-size Taurus developed, it turned out to be a much better car than the T-bird ever was.

One time, we had a four-day test at the Langley tunnel. One thing we found out was that NASCAR tested all the cars at their static ride height; blew them straight ahead and then at about a 3½ degrees of yaw. No wonder they all seemed equal. Based on what Andy had discovered, we dropped the Taurus to actual track-running height, practically dragging the ground from downforce. We had adopted the Pi Research suite of instrumentation, sensors and software so we could tell exactly where the car should ride during testing. Using that information, we took the shocks off the car and made solid links to hold the car securely at the actual race ride height.

We tested 10 hours a day at Langley and found it was significantly better than the Monte Carlo. We intentionally started to try and cripple the Taurus up and test it some more, figuring that's what NASCAR would eventually do once it became clear what a good race car it was. The car was still a bullet. In 2000, Rusty won nine poles behind the wheel of a Taurus.

COURTSHIP, PARTNERSHIP, STRIFE AND SEPARATION

In the midst of all this good news, though, an ill wind was beginning to blow.

Jeremy Mayfield, who'd come along with Kranefuss when Roger had bought a 50-percent interest in his team, had put together a fair number of top 10s in the first half of the 1998 season, with a best of second at Fontana, before getting his first win at Pocono. Rusty had won the Bud Shootout in the Taurus, had a second at Rockingham and a third in the inaugural race at Las Vegas. The finishes were probably abnormally good given the other realities at Penske-Kranefuss. We tried to improve communication, but it really wasn't there. Kranefuss ran his shop and we ran ours. And there really were two shops.

Organizationally, we had two ownership structures, and not even under one roof. Kranefuss's team was down at the end of the street on Knob Hill Road, so we were probably 300 feet apart. We had an underground cable link put in to tie our computers together. At first, it started out okay. I'd recently come back from having surgery done on my arm at Saint Mary's, because I was losing all feeling in my hand—the nerve bundles were disturbed because of the injuries to my spinal cord. It didn't take long, however, for me to notice that we had two separate camps, and that Rusty and Mayfield weren't getting along well. Part of the problem was that Michael had a chassis that he called a Kranefuss chassis, only it wasn't one. That chassis had been originally built at Bobby Allison Racing, when Bobby had his team. When Kranefuss got into business with Haas, they bought all those fixtures from Bobby and started building his chassis in their shop.

So we had two different drivers, two different teams, and we couldn't interchange any information between them because the chassis were different. We tried, though. Roger hired a Ford engineer, Glenn "Sleepy" Lyles, to try to tie the factions together. It didn't work.

Meanwhile, my body hurt. I was exhausted. The hours were getting longer and longer. And now, going into 1998, we had a new team as a close affiliate, a new driver that my longtime partner didn't want, and we were trying to produce—in total secrecy—a race car that the Ford Motor Company planned to stake its reputation upon. Roger took me aside and told me we were going to have to get some kind of help, because he knew I was physically struggling and the hours didn't change: 14 hours a day, seven days a week. We talked to a few guys, and finally settled on bringing in John Erickson. I really liked John, who had been our liaison at Pontiac, and so did Roger.

> " From Katech, I went to Pontiac, became their director of racing, then left in early 1994 to go to the National Hot Rod Association as their technical director. I want to say it was early October 1996 when I got a call from Felix Sabates, who owned SABCO, which was a Pontiac team. Kyle Petty was leaving and Felix was going from one to three cars with Robby Gordon, Joe Nemechek and Wally Dallenbach Jr. He asked me if I'd come work for him as general manager, so we moved back to Charlotte from L.A.
>
> I was with Felix through the 1998 season when I went to work for Penske. During Speedweeks, Walter Czarnecki, and later Roger, asked me if I was interested in going with them. Robin Pemberton was the crew chief at that time and I got along pretty good with him. Don had been looking to retire around that time. Penske South was a Ford team by then. Don was going to retire at the end of 1998. And he forgot."
>
> **JOHN ERICKSON**
> *Director of Special Projects for Penske Racing*
> *Troutman, North Carolina*

Roger told me to focus on being the team owner, and to let John be the on-scene, day-to-day manager, working with the guys and trying to get the teams to work together. That just increased the pressure, though. We didn't tell Kranefuss that we were beginning to develop the Taurus, which poured gasoline on the fire when he and his people finally found out. We never did fully resolve the problem of the two different chassis and the inherent preparation inconsistencies. We were accustomed to having a fantastic team in Penske South, despite changing car brands and crew chiefs, and Rusty had won a slew of poles and races since our inception. It was probably inevitable that we were accused of cheating, and even though we always—*always*—came up legal after inspection, it still stung all of us. As time went on,

The Penske-Kranefuss partnership looked shiny at first. The sheen didn't last. (Penske Corporation Photo, Don Miller Collection)

Penske-Kranefuss was solid, though not spectacular like we'd been in 1993, to name one such great year. Rusty won once in 1998 and finished fourth in the Winston Cup standings, three points ahead of Mayfield. Their results for 1999 were one win and none, respectively.

And then, pretty early in the 2000 season, there was a major flap that we eventually called Fuelgate. We got word that the #12 team, with Jeremy Mayfield as the driver, had had its fuel cans impounded after the spring Talladega race. I was in Mooresville, but Roger was in California and got the word from someone at Talladega. He was absolutely enraged. He called me immediately, demanding to know what was going on. "Roger, I have no idea. Those guys don't talk to us. They don't tell us, and we don't tell them. Unfortunately, that's the situation that's evolved here."

Roger couldn't understand it, because he had successfully run two and three CART and IRL teams under one roof. He talked to Michael, who assured him they weren't cheating. What NASCAR determined was that the 12 team had actually been running additives in their fuel that contained oxidizers, which increased the oxygen content of the engine's incoming fuel charge and thus, its horsepower. Restrictor-plate engines, which were used at Talladega, were starved for air because of the plate. An oxidizer-laced additive would mitigate that.

> That day, we were at Long Beach racing Indy cars. We didn't have a great day, and I remember that Roger had to get to the East Coast from Long Beach for a very important meeting the following morning. After the race, there was a big scramble to get out of there. Roger had his plane at the Long Beach airport and we'd staged cars outside the circuit. We were literally running through the crowd, and just as we got to the car, my cell phone rang.
>
> I can't remember if it was Don or John Erickson, but whoever it was gave me the bad news from Talladega. What this all comes down to is that if it's within the rules, or a gray area, that's one

thing. If it's blatantly against the rules, like this fuel thing was, it's another. Roger told us that we've got tens of thousands of employees—associates, he calls us—whom we try to set an example for, to be above board and ethical. That doesn't even mention your customers, the banks you do business with, lending institutions, suppliers, and on and on. Starting back in the late 1960s, we've worked to build this Penske brand, and to position Penske as the ultimate, not just in racing, but in business, too. When something like this happens, a problem like this Fuelgate, it literally wipes out all that reputation and goodwill that you've built up.

The story got worse. We finally got to the airport, with Roger beside himself over the news from Talladega, and then we had a problem with the airplane. We had to scramble to get him a commercial flight to the East Coast. He was angry enough that he probably could have flown there that night without an airplane."

DAN LUGINBUHL

NASCAR came down really, really hard. They came to Penske-Kranefuss and interviewed the people in the shop, and finally levied huge fines. Far worse, though, was that the cheating caused enormous embarrassment for the Penske Corporation, and for Penske South. When you're in a situation like that, even if you're innocent, you're tarred with the same brush. The outcome of the Talladega incident was that the 12 team's people claimed that the additive was something that their truck driver had put in the fuel and that nobody knew about it. David Poole, the late racing reporter for the *Charlotte Observer*, wrote that if you believed that story, you probably also believed in the single shooter on the grassy knoll.

Roger was not amused. He wanted to know exactly what had happened. I went back to the 12 team to find out what had taken place. We broke it all down and found out that Jeremy had a little group of guys he hung out with, and they went to the barn on his farm and came up with all these schemes. It was someone in that group who came up with the additive idea. They got together with guys in the shop, and they came up with a plan to sneak it into their gas cans at Talladega, giving them five or six additional horsepower, in a sport where any crew chief or engine builder would kill for one more horsepower. They got caught when somebody ratted them out. Kranefuss managed to get Jeremy absolved; if he'd been nailed, he'd have gotten suspended. Eventually, several crew members admitted they were part of the scheme to put the additive in the fuel. It was all after the fact and the damage was done, so we let the sleeping dog lie.

Roger was absolutely beside himself over all this. I felt so sorry for the guy. I know Roger, and I know he doesn't want to cheat. There are

too many ramifications in business for him to allow that. Whether Kranefuss knew about the plan or not, I don't know, and I don't pretend to know. I do know that he defended his guys and eventually got them off the hook. And then a few weeks later, they got busted again.

Jeremy had been docked 151 points for the Talladega violation, and the 12's crew chief was also suspended, on top of their $50,000 fine. In late April, Jeremy won the California race but then NASCAR checked the 12 car and found its roofline was too low. Mayfield kept the win, but the team got fined another $25,000. Roger came down to Mooresville from Detroit, sat down with the guys on the 12 team and insisted, "Look, I can't have this. This is over." Jeremy became obstinate and started getting really negative about Roger in the press. Everybody was reading about it. I was recovering at that point from two major surgical procedures, when Roger spoke to me and said, "I really want to have a second car. Find somebody to drive it."

Roger was hurt, personally, by this whole mess. He had extended his trust to the Kranefuss team and they burned him. What probably hurt him the most was that these guys never leveled with him. Roger took the high road, never criticizing Jeremy or otherwise saying a negative or unkind word about either him or Kranefuss. I've seen Roger really upset a few times but I don't think I've ever seen him scream or yell. He's very direct. He doesn't want to hear that you have a problem, he wants to hear that you *had* a problem, and how you solved it. In terms of Kranefuss and Mayfield, Roger solved that problem himself, one on one, with each of them. Roger ultimately bought out Kranefuss's 50-percent share of the team; Jeremy was to depart before the end of the 2001 season.

There was more, as if we hadn't had enough yet. Before the 2000 race at Sonoma, right after qualifying, NASCAR tore us down right in the open, letting the other teams see what we were doing with our engines. The other teams had gone even further, hiring professional photographers to come in and shoot all our parts while NASCAR was disassembling our engine. They were ringed all around the disassembly area. The photographers even took pictures of the scales that were weighing our pieces. I had been going for some treatment at that time, and I wasn't supposed to be at the track until Sunday. After I heard about this, I went straight there. I was absolutely livid, and I went off on the NASCAR people really bad, which I shouldn't have done. So did Rusty. But there was nothing we could do. They said they were going to disallow our qualifying time and not let us race if we didn't let them do it. It used to be that they'd tear you down, sure, but it wasn't done in public. So everybody got to see what we'd spent years, and millions of dollars, to develop. It was blatant. I'll never forget it. As it turned out, we were completely legal.

It was a real bummer, because after that all the other companies saw what we'd been doing and started developing things of their own that were similar to what we'd been using. For example, Mahle, the piston manufacturer in Germany, which had been producing pistons for the Aurora engine in the IRL, came out with pistons not unlike our Ilmor pistons. Meanwhile, NASCAR had been closing the box around engine development. They reduced the compression ratio to 12.0:1. They specified the allowable cylinder heads. They specified bore spacing. They specified weights for the crankshaft, pistons and rods. That stopped a lot of development in the engine area, and kept people from taking existing pieces and reducing them in weight to the point where they became unreliable.

After that, everybody focused on reducing friction to make horsepower. Then it went to NASCAR limiting RPM, and the only way to do that was the way they did it with Sprint cars, by limiting the cars to two or three choices of gear ratios at each track to hold everybody to 9,600 RPM. Until those rules, we at Penske South ran races where we turned our engines at 10,000 RPM all day. We'd done the work, on two continents, to make that kind of output possible. To borrow a phrase from Captain Kirk of *Star Trek*, we'd boldly gone where no Winston Cup team had gone before. And now everyone knew how to get there!

20

Hello, Newman

IN HINDSIGHT, Jeremy Mayfield was probably finished at Penske before anybody knew it, including him. By the time Roger indicated to me that the Penske-Kranefuss arrangement wasn't working, and that Jeremy was standing squarely above the trap door as Roger was reaching for the lever, I had been paying attention to the Midget racing action in the Midwest for quite a while. Keeping track of potential future talent was part of my job at Penske South. I had the USAC Midget standings sent to me from their offices in Indianapolis every week, starting around the time that Jeff Gordon came out of their ranks and set fire to everything south of the Ohio River. I was following the Big Five in the USAC Midgets, the guys who were really hot rods, which had consisted of Gordon, Tony Stewart, Kenny Irwin, Jason Leffler and Ryan Newman, with Newman the youngest of all.

To this day, I believe that the drivers who race Midgets have the best car control of any racers in America. They start out in these unruly cars and then move up into other open-wheel classes with even more power, Sprint cars, plus the Silver Crown cars that teach them to save their tires in the 100-lap races that they run. It's a fantastic farm system for top-level racing. That's why I was so shocked when J.J. Yeley—who'd won all three USAC open-wheel titles in the same year just like Tony Stewart had done previously—didn't do as well in NASCAR as everyone had expected. But I looked at that young group in USAC as being some of the very best at adapting to different tracks, tires and traffic.

I'd seen Ryan drive, at least on videotape, and knew that he had a tremendous ability to precisely control these tiny, featherweight, wildly overpowered race cars. He'd grown up in South Bend, Indiana, and had lived in USAC heartland country all his life. He was 21 years old in 1999,

and I knew he was an undergraduate mechanical engineering student in the prestigious program at Purdue University in Indiana. I really liked that—you know how it is with me and engineers. Greg Newman, Ryan's father, told me he was both shocked and flattered when I called, but said he didn't want Ryan to lose focus on graduation while he was finishing his final year at Purdue. He agreed graciously to let us conduct a test in a stock car for Ryan but asked us to hold off on trying to hire his son, again citing Ryan's education. I respected this, and so I agreed.

This was in November 1999. I talked a little more with Ben Dillon, Ryan's manager. Then in 2000, Roger, John Erickson and I gathered some of the Penske South team together to discuss the preliminary talks I'd been having with Ryan Newman's people and what I knew about Ryan. Everybody was okay with it, but Rusty had reservations. He protested that we already had other concerns, beginning with the question of even having the second team with Kranefuss and Jeremy Mayfield. He felt that bringing in someone else was only going to make everything worse.

In a sense, Rusty was right. There was too much going on at the time that wasn't productive. I agreed with him, not for the same reasons, but rather because we were trying to move ahead. I told Rusty to calm down, that we were going to be progressive about filling the other seat without turning the whole operation upside down. I made it clear to Roger that, in my opinion, Ryan could deliver the results that we needed, and we agreed to set up a couple of tests for him when the time was right and see how things went.

Before we go any further, let me tell you a few more things about Ryan, and what made him attractive to us. Remember, I'm a car guy from Chicago, and a racing guy, even though my early background was primarily at the drag strips. I knew a little bit about the Midgets long before I actually started to watch them with an idea of recruiting their drivers. The Chicago area has a rich, powerful history in the annals of Midget racing. The Midgets used to race at Soldier Field, the shrine of the Chicago Bears, and not a few of those drivers went all the way to Indianapolis. My buddy and onetime racing partner Ed Rachanski had run with these guys in his early days. Gary Bettenhausen, who was driving our Matador in Winston Cup when I got hurt at Talladega, was a tremendous racer with a great background in both Sprint cars and Midgets. If you won in a Midget, you knew how to race. Greg Newman had given Ryan the means to start out, and win big, in Quarter Midgets right from childhood. Ryan became a state Midget champion in Michigan when he was just 15.

Ryan's father owned a small auto-repair shop right on the Indiana-Michigan border. The Newman family has made a lot of sacrifices so that Ryan could be where he is today, and to this day, Ryan is deeply appreciative of that. Ryan progressed from driving his father's Midget to driving for Mel and Don Kenyon of Lebanon, Indiana. The Kenyons run the most storied team in Midget racing, in addition to being two very classy individuals. Mel has over 100 wins in Midgets, despite having nearly had his hand burned off in a crash, and he went on to race the Indianapolis 500 repeatedly. Having a guy like Mel Kenyon as a mentor says a lot about the person being mentored. Ryan wasn't completely unfamiliar with other types of race cars, either. He'd had a 1997 start in a second Bill Venturini ARCA car, and after some thought, turned down an offer to do IRL testing for Andretti Green Racing. So Penske South wasn't the first non-USAC operation to pick Ryan up on its radar.

> *We had run an asphalt Late Model in Indiana in a couple of races, and he did a test up in Michigan for Hans Nicholas, whom Bob Senneker had driven for, up at Johnny Benson's track, Berlin Raceway. Ryan really impressed the guy and we had a couple of Late Model races up there with him. He had also tested the #59 car in Busch, the Kingsford Charcoal car.*
>
> *I really didn't even know of Don Miller until the first time we were at Daytona, and somebody in the garage area came up to us*

and said that Don wanted to meet with us at the Penske trailer. I really didn't know who he was at all.

He showed us around the garage area, got us something to eat, and wanted to talk to us about Ryan. He had talked to Buddy Baker, who'd gotten to know us a little because he had been a commentator for some of the telecasts of the USAC races on TV. We had had some conversations with Felix Sabates and a couple of other people in NASCAR, but Don was the only one who really wanted to talk to us. Some guys at the Penske South shop were really into open wheel, too, and they'd been bragging to Don about Ryan."

GREG NEWMAN
South Bend, Indiana

When Roger asked what my plans were for Ryan, I told him my game plan was to take three or four guys out of the shop, and one or two cars out of our system, and put them all over in a corner. That would be the nucleus of the test for Ryan, and from there we could decide how, or if, to move forward. I found two of our oldest cars and claimed them. I went over to Matt Borland, who, in my opinion, was light years ahead of the curve in NASCAR when it came to engineering. Matt was a young guy, a graduate engineer from Michigan, who had written the Pi system with Rex Stump when Pi Research in Indianapolis first tried to apply the system to testing in stock cars. Andrew Scriven was getting ready to leave us to go work with the Cal Wells team out on the West Coast, where he'd wanted to live, which was when Matt joined us as a testing and simulations engineer.

For some reason, Matt and Kranefuss didn't see eye to eye, which as far as I was concerned constituted another nail in the Kranefuss coffin. I asked Matt to work with Ryan on this test—I was trying to create a test team for our young new driver from Indiana while also still working to keep the Ford Taurus evolving as a race car. I convened a face-to-face meeting in the garage area with Ryan, Greg, and Roger just before the 2000 Daytona 500. That's the one now legendary because Ryan and his Dad used fake credentials made out of art paper to get inside the garage area for the meeting.

❝ *I went up into Rusty's trailer, the #2 trailer, and I said, 'Is Don Miller there?' And I asked the guy I had spotted there, 'Are you Don Miller?' It turned out to be John Erickson, who was vice president of Penske South at the time. He said, 'No, but he'll be back here in five minutes. In fact, RP will be here in five minutes as well.' So here, in 2000, at Daytona, I actually got to meet Don and Roger at the same time.*

My Dad and I were supposed to be down in Daytona for Thursday through Sunday, and after Thursday, we figured out what color credential we needed to have to be there through Sunday. We went to the local convenience store, bought some construction paper, and did a little bit of fancy stencil-type work so I had my own credentials to sneak into the garage. It was a little easier to fake it if you also had a lanyard, but lanyards were pretty hard to come by at the time."

RYAN NEWMAN
Driver, Penske Racing, 2000-2008
Winner, 2008 Daytona 500
Driver, Stewart-Haas Racing
Troutman, North Carolina

Pain and numbness from my old injuries had been an increasing issue during this period and I had been trying to cut back on my travel. That meant that I was going to have trouble going to the tests myself. Plus, I knew that Ryan would need a driving coach. I called my old friend Buddy Baker. There is no better teacher and evaluator of young driving talent in NASCAR, anywhere, than Buddy. He's a tremendous fount of driving knowledge and a terrific guy, beyond the obvious fact that he's also a living NASCAR legend. I asked Buddy to

Even a prodigy needs a professor. We picked the best out there, Buddy Baker. (Steven Rose Photo, Don Miller Collection)

do me a favor and work with Ryan, and he agreed. I'd known Buddy probably as long as I'd been involved with NASCAR.

I'd actually asked Buddy years earlier to help Rusty develop his superspeedway talents, and he had obviously done an excellent job. He had just the right amount of tact with Rusty. We took two race cars to the track, and Buddy showed Rusty how to get around in the right line, drafting past him once to underscore the danger of the line he'd been running by himself. Buddy has a manner when it comes to schooling people on the race track: Not dominant, but more a case of, "Try this. See what you think." I call it the soft sell. As Buddy himself says, "I've made all the mistakes you can make, and you can learn from that." To hear Buddy get so excited about Ryan was the final stamp of approval for me.

I set aside an older trailer and stocked it with parts. I assigned Gordon Miller, Matt McSwain, one or two other guys and Matt Borland to be the test team. Buddy met them for the test at Gateway International Raceway outside Saint Louis, where Ryan had once won a USAC feature. The test wasn't completely flawless, but it was more than enough for Buddy. They came back and Buddy told me, pretty excitedly, "You've got a hot rod here. This kid's really good. You've got to get him some more seat time."

> We went to test at Gateway International Raceway, outside Saint Louis. Ryan's out there in the race car, putting around, putting around, putting around. It's getting time for me to call Don and give him a progress report. I was getting about to my limits with Ryan. I was pretty sharp with him. I didn't give him roses when he was doing poorly. When he came in, I just walked up and said, 'Boy, are you giving us 100 percent?' And he said, 'Well, no.' I asked him why and he said, 'I didn't want to mess up.' I said back, 'My grandmother wouldn't mess up, the way you're running.'
>
> With that, he jerked that thing into low gear and went back out, and drove that thing down to where you see Elvis. I told the guys, 'My God, I might have killed him. But if he makes that corner, I think we've got a driver.'
>
> The next lap was faster than the track record. Then I did call Don, and said, 'This guy's the real deal. Give him a little bit of time, don't push him too quick, and you'll have a franchise driver.'"

BUDDY BAKER
NASCAR legend
Winner, 1980 Daytona 500
Sherrills Ford, North Carolina

We were still in a pressure cooker, what with the problems concerning Kranefuss, who didn't want to work with Ryan, and then Mayfield, who did everything he could to run Ryan and Roger down, including some nasty interviews with the media that are now public record.

It didn't matter, because we started Ryan out in ARCA and it was an explosive coming-out: Ryan won three of the five ARCA races that he entered. Roger and I had started Ryan in what was then a radical concept, the A-B-C program, to get him seat time at the necessary tracks in ARCA, Busch and Winston Cup events before turning him loose on a full rookie Winston Cup campaign. All teams now use a version of the A-B-C concept to train rookie drivers.

We secured sponsorship for Ryan from Alltel, which persuaded us to take Ryan to Phoenix in late 2000 for his inaugural Winston Cup start. To put it less than politely, we stepped on our crank there, even though Ryan had raced at Phoenix and actually held the Midget lap record there. In the race, he went laps down because the car wouldn't handle, couldn't get out of its own way. We ended up behind the pit wall tearing the car completely apart. The press was having a field day, saying that none of us knew what we were doing. Ryan was upset but I told him to take it easy.

Despite everyone's disappointment at the team's terrible finish of 41st, Robin Pemberton and Matt Borland put their heads together on the flight home, trying to figure out what had gone wrong. Once back in Mooresville, Robin and Matt completely disassembled the car and went through it closely. They discovered that the length of a brake pushrod in the master cylinder was slightly too short. After Ryan had hit the brakes hard several times, it popped out of its little cup next to the brake cylinder and hung up there, so the brakes were on all the time. That threw the car's handling completely out of whack. The bad finish made more sense.

There's another element to this story that we might as well discuss right here. It's a matter of historic record that there was friction between Rusty, Ryan and me, from the time when we first brought Ryan aboard. That said, not all the speculation about it that got into the media was correct. It's a fact that Rusty was getting near the end of his Cup career, and no, there wasn't a perfect bonding between him and Ryan. Yes, they talked, but they sometimes didn't communicate. The difference between the two is that with communication, the parties are absorbing something. When it's talk, you just have words flying back and forth. Ryan and Rusty's conversations usually never had any substance. If Ryan said something was blue, Rusty might insist it was orange.

> *Don's and my relationship would have been even stronger if we hadn't started a second team. It's well documented that Newman and I never got along, and after Don decided that he wanted to retire, he did, and hired John Erickson to run the team. When they decided they wanted to do a second team, he decided to come out of retirement and start helping Ryan Newman the way he did with me. And that really put a strain on the relationship. It's something I wish hadn't have happened, but it's water under the bridge now."*

RUSTY WALLACE

I get interviewed from time to time, too, just like the drivers do. Sometimes, an interviewer will ask me to compare drivers who have raced for Roger Penske at various junctures. Most often, they ask me to compare Rusty to Mark Donohue. I can't do it. Rusty and Mark were both ferocious racers, at the top of their game when they were at their peak, but beyond that, they had nothing whatsoever in common. By definition, by DNA, the fact that both were racers, exceptional racers, meant they both had egos, which I define here as having absolute, unshakable confidence in their own abilities and sound judgment. The same is true for Ryan. I think that part of the problem was that when Ryan first arrived, he was getting a lot of ink as an obviously exceptional talent, and that may have upset Rusty even more.

Both Roger and I sat Ryan and Rusty down together countless times. When you have two guys who are stallions, they really don't want to hear what you have to tell them. Racers, at least real racers, are like fighter pilots. You can lecture them all you want in the ready room, but once they take off on that mission, they're completely alone and in total control of the outcome. I'm not going to deny that it was tough. I'm not interested in burning either Rusty or Ryan. I worked very hard not to do that when we were all there. And during most of the time when this was going on, we ran quite well. We all knew that in this business, you're only as good as your last move. In our philosophy of life, we worked. This was Thursday, and whatever happened Tuesday isn't important anymore. Sunday is important.

Meanwhile, Roger had finally reached his breaking point with Jeremy Mayfield. Having bought out Kranefuss, he sent Mayfield down the road after 28 races and put Mike Wallace in the car for the rest of the 2001 season. The Penske-Kranefuss team was then merged fully into Penske South.

When we made the deal with Ryan, I told Greg Newman that he could go to the races with us in an official capacity if he was interested. We had another guy spotting for us at the time, but Greg asked if he could try it, and turned out to be pretty good at it. He stayed as Ryan's spotter and we just went down the road from there. I'm pretty sure he's still spotting for Ryan now at Stewart-Haas. With all our stock car operations now integrated as a single team, we had put together an A-B-C plan in 2001 consisting of four ARCA starts for Ryan, a dozen in the Busch series and seven in Cup, to keep Ryan's rookie status intact for 2002. We scheduled a whole bunch of tracks, giving Ryan the opportunity to race and learn, not chase points. He rewarded all of us immediately by winning the ARCA 200 at Daytona, with Buddy then spotting for him. In the Busch series, Ryan won two poles, along with the Michigan race.

It was good, but not perfect: Ryan and I got called into the NASCAR trailer a couple of times when he got into scrapes with Tim Fedewa and Elton Sawyer. In only his third Cup start ever, he won the pole for the Coca-Cola 600, beating Jeff Gordon, but crashed while leading after just 10 laps. We also cut the ARCA program short after Ryan wiped out a car at their Kansas event after a tire blew. We examined the ARCA-mandated Hoosier tires and weren't happy with them, so we decided to have Ryan concentrate on NASCAR for the rest of 2001.

There was some more difficulty after Ryan, who was already on probation over a post-race altercation with Fedewa at Darlington, accidentally ran over Mike McLaughlin's lapped car at Chicago while he was chasing Jimmie Johnson down for the lead. The contact with McLaughlin's car tore up the left front corner of Ryan's car so badly that the left front tire blew and locked up the wheel. The sparks started flying immediately, and it took about half a lap before NASCAR gave Ryan the black flag. We were only about three or four laps before the end of the race and Ryan did not want to come into the pits as directed. He continued to run down Jimmie Johnson, on three wheels, and actually finished the race on three wheels in second place, but he and I were told to report to the NASCAR trailer immediately after the race ended. Or as they put it, IMMEDIATELY. I knew this was not going to be good.

I met Ryan at the car as he was getting out, and said, "Our presence has been requested in the NASCAR trailer by Mister Darby and Mister Helton. You know that you're on double-secret probation already. What do you think they are going to do to you this time?" Ryan looked at me sheepishly and asked quietly, "Do you think they're going to be upset?"

When we reached the trailer, Mike Helton was standing in the doorway of John Darby's office, and the first words out of his mouth were, "Newman, what the hell do you think you were doing out there?

One of the smartest things we ever did at Penske South was promote Matt Borland to crew chief and team him up with Ryan. (Don Miller Collection)

We shocked the world when Ryan outgunned Dale Jr. to take the Winston as a Cup rookie. (Steven Rose Photo, Don Miller Collection)

I'm sure you know what the black flag means." NASCAR sat Ryan and me down on the hot seats, plural, in the trailer and gave us both a serious dressing down. Darby advised us that if we had come in when the black flag was flown, we would have lost two laps. Therefore, he was going to go back through the finishing order and determine where we would have finished had we obeyed the flag. The final outcome was that Ryan was docked those two laps and officially placed 26th. Mike Helton left the meeting to take care of other business, leaving Ryan and me alone with John Darby. John shook his head and looked Ryan straight in the eye and said, "These are the rules, and I have to enforce them. But, I have to tell you, that was one of the most outstanding driving performances I have seen in a long time. You were actually running 160 mph on the backstretch on three wheels and gaining on the leader!" Then he added, "Of course, I didn't tell you that." As we were leaving the trailer, John told me, "Damn it, Don, you have got to get that kid under control or you're going to have a permanent seat in this trailer."

After these episodes, we had to convince Roger that Ryan really was our future. But Ryan, once he found his footing in the Cup series, richly repaid the confidence we showed in him. First, though, we had to get him a car number for 2002. When Ryan first moved up to Winston Cup, even on the part-time 2001 schedule, his official number was 02. Alltel had based all of its advertising with Ryan driving the #02 car. The slogan was something like "the #02 in '02." Everybody was ready to go with it until Roger decided otherwise. He wanted that team to stay the #12, the Penske Racing number previously used by Jeremy Mayfield. Despite this bit of confusion, Ryan had an incredible rookie year.

> *I really didn't know Ryan at the time, other than when I was in Indy cars. Somebody had mentioned him as a young guy who was good in open-wheel cars. I think our success was due to the group that Don put together. He had a direction in mind for us. Ryan, Don, and I formed as close a group as you can imagine. We also had Mike Nelson, the race engineer for us right from the start, who also became Ryan's crew chief in 2007 and 2008. We had a real team together."*
>
> **MATT BORLAND**
> *Crew chief, Stewart-Haas Racing*
> *Cornelius, North Carolina*

For all of us, in fact, 2001 had been a hell of a year. Ryan won races in ARCA and the Busch Grand National series, and also posted some significant numbers in the Cup series. The whole process vindicated our decision to create the A-B-C program, and despite all the confusion at the end of 2001, Ryan went on to post an incredible 2002. We top-fived them to death all year long. Ryan banked a small fortune by winning The Winston over Dale Earnhardt Jr., not only as a Cup rookie, but after having to race his way into the starting lineup by winning the preliminary Winston Open. The tour made its way to New Hampshire for the second time that season in late 2002, where Ryan got his first full-point Cup victory over Kurt Busch. Rain cut it short by close to 100 miles, but it was a race of races, with Ryan and Kurt side by side for something like 30 laps and never touching each other. Even for a rain-shortened race, the fans more than got their money's worth that day. We were all thrilled, but Greg Newman was positively ecstatic, and I was too. We were locked in a battle for Rookie of the Year with Jimmie Johnson. Even though Jimmie won two point races in 2002, the point system throws out a driver's 16 worst finishes. On the basis of average finish in the remaining races, Ryan won the award.

I've never had a son, but Ryan comes pretty close. I love him. (Don Miller Collection)

> **"** *If it wasn't for Don's influence around here, Ryan might still be in open-wheel racing. He had been considered by four or five other teams before he got the chance to work with Don and myself at Penske. They sent him packing, but Don saw something in him. There's people who have the ability to see beyond what you get in a first test, or a second. Ryan, when he goes to bed at night, ought to say a little prayer of thanks for meeting Don Miller."*

BUDDY BAKER

Ryan and I share a love for vintage cars, and we had previously decided to spend time before the New Hampshire race at AutoFair, partly a gigantic show for old cars and partly a swap meet, held at Charlotte Motor Speedway. The plan was to go early on Thursday and just root for parts and check out some of the hundreds of collectible cars for sale. As it turned out, Ryan had to leave Wednesday night to fulfill some sponsor obligations in New Hampshire. I wasn't scheduled to leave until Saturday with the race day crew. While I was walking around, window shopping the old cars on the infield, I spied a 1953 Plymouth Cranbrook two-door sedan that was exactly like the one Ryan had driven to high school and college in Indiana. Ryan still had the old Plymouth, but there wasn't much left of it, although he always said that someday he hoped to restore it.

I eyed the Plymouth closely. It was in strong condition and the price was right, so I made a deal with the owner on the spot. I gave him a check and had Razoar, my friend Ray Wallace, follow me back to Mooresville. We didn't say a word to anyone, just dropped the Plymouth off in Ryan's driveway and left the keys in the ashtray. After the race in New Hampshire, I told Ryan's wife Krissie to expect a surprise when they got home. Krissie told me afterwards that when they pulled in their driveway at almost midnight, Ryan remarked, "Someone's in our driveway!" He looked at the Plymouth, thought for a moment, and simply said, "Millerman."

Ryan's an old-car guy. He drove a 1953 Plymouth Cranbrook in college, so I decided to buy him this one. (Don Miller Collection)

" Don's done a lot for me, on and off the race track. Even just simple things, like helping me get around here when I came down to North Carolina. Don put me up in a motel, so I would have a place to stay while I was spending time at the shop with the guys. Gave me a car to drive. Helped me out with my souvenir things to get them started for the first time. He's old enough so that he's been there, seen it and done it. Then learned from it, and did it again, a better way. Don's just done it all, and when you have somebody in your corner who wants to help you, and to grow your future, and who's been successful, you listen. You don't try to talk."

RYAN NEWMAN

21

Changing Horses

W E FELT STRONG AND READY. The 2002 season was ending, and the relevant numbers told the story: As a team, our performance was steadily improving. Ryan had posted his first victory in the Winston Cup Series, won The Winston, won Rookie of the Year and was a solid sixth in the points chase. Despite no wins, Rusty still finished seventh in points and was running strong every weekend. In mid-October, Dan Davis, who was now in charge of Ford Racing globally after Dan Rivard's retirement, came to our shop and made a proposal to me to renew our manufacturer's contract for three more years.

Dan was open and vocal about his desire to keep Penske Racing in Fords, to the extent that Ford might have even considered pulling back on its involvement in Winston Cup to three teams: Penske Racing, Roush and Yates. He felt a consolidation limited to those three operations would make the Ford effort stronger in the long run. He also talked about Ford's desire to toughen itself up and maximize its racing resources in anticipation of Toyota's looming arrival in Cup. Rusty and I went over Ford's proposal together, made some small changes and sent it back to Dan for consideration, copying Roger for his comments. The following day, I got a call from Roger. He told me not to sign anything because he was talking to Dodge about a pretty big deal.

I had no idea the manufacturer change was even being contemplated. Roger, who, as I've said many times, is his own best salesman, had been talking to the people who counted at Chrysler. I've also said that Roger is a people person, only at a very different level from most. Deals like this one are an example. He is a hugely influential person in the global automotive industry. People at the pinnacle of the industry listen to Roger Penske.

They want to do business with him because they realize his success
will rub off on them. Like any truly successful business leader, Roger
has the gift of foresight, and arguably, a lot more of it than most people in racing, or anything else. As 2003 loomed, he saw the ground
shifting at the peak of motorsports before most others did, including
the rest of us at Penske South.

When I told Rusty about Roger's call, he simply cratered. "We just
got the Taurus figured out," Rusty moaned. "And he wants to change
again?"

Roger, as things turned out, put a meeting together. Besides himself, the attendees were Dieter Zetsche, president and general manager
of Chrysler Group during its ownership by Daimler-Benz, Rusty, Walt
Czarnecki and me at Chrysler headquarters in Auburn Hills, Michigan. Dieter immediately took control of the meeting and began
speaking about our team as if we'd already agreed to change manufacturers. I quickly got the impression that Roger's prior discussions
with Chrysler, whenever they'd occurred, had been a lot deeper than
he'd let on to Rusty and me. The meeting continued and eventually
came to a break. Dieter then invited us to take a tour of the engineering, research, and development departments at the Dodge division of Daimler Chrysler. When the meeting concluded, Dieter shook
our hands and welcomed us to the fold. Rusty and I looked at each
other as if to say, "What have we missed here?"

"There were a lot of things that I think influenced Penske's decision. First, Roger already had a relationship with Mercedes-Benz and Dieter Zetsche because of his European diesel business and his other businesses that kind of interfaced with Mercedes. So Roger saw some synergies from the business side. He also knew that Dodge was very interested in coming back to NASCAR and being successful.

The Mercedes-Benz pushrod engine that Penske used to win Indianapolis in 1994 didn't enter into it, actually. The Ilmor relationships with their customers were always very confidential, and Dodge Motorsports was not an Ilmor customer, but Penske was. So most of the information we got about their programs came from Penske himself and from Don Miller.

Don has a lot of attributes. One of them is his rapport with everybody, from Roger Penske to the guy who cleans the toilets. It's just amazing. He knows most of the people, the families, their histories. We were very comfortable with him. He could ask for things, therefore, that a simple business relationship might not be able to get. He is extremely loyal. I think he feels, correctly, that's he's a good judge of people. He's very good at picking out the phonies."

JOHN WEHRLY
Retired engineering manager
Dodge Motorsports and Mopar Performance Parts
Madison Heights, Michigan

By the time we got race cars on the track and started winning, we were all smiling. (Steven Rose Photo)

On the way home, Rusty and I discussed what the ramifications of a change like this would be. Our conclusions weren't very promising, but we agreed to sleep on it and talk to Roger further.

A couple of days later, Rusty, Roger, and I spoke on the telephone and talked openly—maybe the right word is "frankly"—about the potential changeover to Dodge. At the same time, Dan Davis was continuing to press for the renewal with Ford. Finally, Roger said, "Look, you guys, I am a businessman. I have a great relationship with Daimler Chrysler related to my dealerships, and they have agreed to match—or better—any deal that we have with Ford related to our race team. Switching to Dodges is my decision, and I really want to do it."

Obviously, this decision wasn't the end of the world, but, according to Rusty, "You could see it from here."

Switching manufacturers in big-time racing is huge. The very next morning, I called Scott Courier and Larry Wallace at Penske-Jasper Engines and told them what I thought was about to happen. I told Larry, "This is going to be another one of those deals. It's time to make chicken salad out of chicken shit." Larry responded, "Just get me some basic parts, like the block, heads and the rest of the castings, and we'll see what we can put together for an engine."

Fortunately for us, the engine program that served Penske South had been expanded significantly during the relatively recent past. In 1997, Penske Racing South had purchased Power Tech, in Concord, North Carolina, an engine-development builder and research company. Three years later, we bought Jasper Motorsports in Indiana from its owner, Doug Bawel, incorporating it into the same unit with the former Power Tech as Penske-Jasper Engines, with Doug as a part owner. Doug is a very good guy, a good friend. We'd been aware of each other since the early years at National Engines and Parts, but I hadn't gotten to really know him until we both found our way to NASCAR. Doug would become an even more critical person in our teams' development in a very short while.

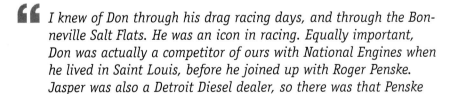

I knew of Don through his drag racing days, and through the Bonneville Salt Flats. He was an icon in racing. Equally important, Don was actually a competitor of ours with National Engines when he lived in Saint Louis, before he joined up with Roger Penske. Jasper was also a Detroit Diesel dealer, so there was that Penske connection as well."

DOUG BAWEL
President and CEO
Jasper Engines and Transmissions
Jasper, Indiana

Because of the brand switch, I suggested that we contact Joey Arrington, who was then the Dodge engine development program leader in Martinsville, Virginia. Joey and his father, Buddy Arrington, had been friends of mine for a very long time, and lifelong Mopar racing stalwarts. Joey offered to give us everything he had on the Dodge engine, including parts, dyno-testing information and additional specifications wherever necessary. This is a prime example of what I've been talking about all through this book when I describe how absolutely essential having trust with people in your industry is, because at this point, we still hadn't signed a contract with Daimler Chrysler.

It was about this time that I had a meeting with John Wehrly, program manager for the racing division of Daimler Chrysler, and his assistant, Ted Flack, whose responsibility was the Winston Cup Series. John was very open with his assessment, saying, "I know this is difficult, but believe me, I will make all of the technical information available to you electronically." My doubts were assuaged, remarkably so, by the fact that I'd known of John for some time from our days around the race track, especially after Dodge had re-entered Winston Cup.

> I can't honestly remember whether I was the motorsports engineering manager at Dodge when I first met Don Miller. It may have been when I was in charge of the NASCAR truck program, before I was placed in charge of all our motorsports. When they were beginning to get involved with Dodge in late 2002, our engine manager, Ted Flack, had a good rapport with Don, and I think that I met Don through Ted. We were almost the same age and had very similar backgrounds in drag racing, Don coming from Chicago and me from Detroit, although I'm originally from right near Winchester, Indiana. Remarkably, I hadn't known him during those years. We had a lot of mutual friends, but had never met each other.
>
> When I met him, he was actually the president and general manager of Penske South, and he had a special interest in the engineering side, especially the engines, because they were going to be switching from Fords to Dodges. Penske was very successful with what it had done with the Ford engines, plus it had a lot of background with European help, such as Ilmor. They had already made the decision to switch and were very concerned that they be competitive with our engines, which was how I got involved. I think the actual case was that Roger had made the decision and the other guys had found out, and were a little uncomfortable. But they realized that they had straight shooters they could talk to, and that's how the friendship between Don and me started.

The first thing Don did, I would say, was try to build on the re-lationship he had with Ted Flack. Don was kind of trying to build confidence and really verify that this thing with Dodge was the real thing. He was kind of feeling out the people here, trying to see that they were going to be straight with him, give him the same answers, seeing if he could build a relationship with them. That sort of thing. The specifics about the engine program, even discussions about drivers and technology projects, would come later. The Penske organization was more able, in some cases, to fund research programs such as aero work than Chrysler was. Don really spearheaded some of these things for which we just didn't have the money."

JOHN WEHRLY

By early November, I knew for sure that we were going to be a Dodge team, not a Ford team anymore. I asked Roger if I could be the one to break the news to Dan Davis, and he agreed. I called Dan and explained the situation. He took the news like a real professional. Even though I expect he had a good idea what the outcome was going to be—based, in part, on our slow follow-up to the Ford proposals and some speculation to that effect in the media that covers NASCAR—Dan was disappointed but nonetheless understanding. The last words he spoke on the topic were something like, "Don, if you guys change your minds about this, we will be here. Please give me a call." Oddly, within moments of my phone call to Dan, Ford issued a news release announcing that Penske Racing would not be re-newing its contract for 2003. The disclosure didn't make the PR people at Dodge very happy.

Fortunately, the concerns we'd had about changing manufactur-ers proved to be mislaid. If anything, the Dodge engines were better than Ford's; however, our Penske engine shop couldn't build them fast enough. When we ended 2002, we had 70 or so Ford race en-gines in our inventory. After the switch to Dodge, we had only nine new engines with which to start the season. The actual car inventory was a little bit better, because NASCAR had tightened the template rules to the point that the actual differences between a Dodge and a Ford were limited to the front and rear fascias (both fiberglass) and the new quarter windows, which were simply replaced. Matt Borland told our fabricators, "Don't get too up in arms over this change. We're just giving the old girl a new dress."

The 2003 NASCAR Winston Cup season started off with a bang, or should I say, a crunch—no, make that a lot of crunches in very quick succession. During the Daytona 500, Ryan cut down a tire and crashed in spectacular fashion, right in front of the monstrous crowd. The Alltel Dodge turned sideways, slid into the infield and started flipping, almost Rusty-style but this time, at the other end of the track.

As a team, we quickly recovered from that wild spill and marched onward to win eight races during 2003. Nevertheless, that whole first year with Dodge was a story of monumental internal struggles—that's right, it happened once again—between those who believed in engineering and those who didn't. It was quite a battle for a while. We had Matt and the other engineers on one side, and the old-school guys on the other, butting their heads so hard you could practically hear them cracking.

Roger's trust in Ryan had begun to grow, and our overall faith in the combination of Matt Borland and Ryan Newman had been justified. Even Rusty conceded that Ryan had been a good choice. Matt and Ryan had begun to develop a solid engineering foundation for their assault on the 2003 Winston Cup season. Evidently, things were going well enough that outside observers even started to notice a change in my own demeanor. Godwin Kelly, writing in his column for the *Daytona Beach News-Journal*, suggested that if Ryan hadn't come along when he did, I might have been clipping coupons out of the newspaper or playing bingo someplace instead of still working with Penske South. I'm not saying he was wrong.

As a new Dodge team, we still racked up wins. This one was at Kansas. (Kim Watson Photo)

Eyes and ears open, always. In this case, I'm spotting for Ryan at Michigan. (Don Miller Collection)

> "In the beginning, Roger had actually wanted to move Ryan along faster than he did. It was Buddy and Don who said, 'No. We're not going to do that to that kid. We're going to give him the time he needs to develop.' Buddy was adamant about that, and Don agreed. He ended up exceeding expectations."

GREG NEWMAN

Ryan scored victories in 2003 at Chicagoland, Pocono, Richmond, Michigan and Kansas, along with a sweep of both Dover races and an incredible 11 poles that season. The 12 team's members had convinced everyone that they were here to stay. I had already made the decision that I was going to keep Ryan and Matt together for 2004, that they were an indestructible, unbreakable link in the chain that wrapped Penske South into a tight organization. They were sixth in 2003 points. Rusty had a much more difficult season, as he marked his 48th birthday, with no wins or poles at all and a ranking of 14th in the point standings.

> "Don has always been an innovator and clever thinker. I think it is a result of his drag racing background where you had to be creative to win. He was in the forefront of the change to a more engineering orientation in NASCAR racing and his hiring of good technical people early on is evidence of that. Don has the ability to develop people into skilled professionals and that has paid us some big dividends. I am still glad about the day I introduced him to Ryan Newman and for the contributions Ryan made to the team under Don's guidance. His helping Rusty Wallace grow into one of NASCAR's greats is another illustration. Don, like all good racers, is always looking for the edge."

ROGER PENSKE

Meanwhile, in the background we were anticipating that at some point there would again be a third Penske team in NASCAR, and Roger decided that we'd take that step for the 2004 season. He knew that the leading owners in the future were going to have three or four cars, and he was right. The simplest way for us to go forward without disrupting our whole current system—there was no way we would be able to build enough race cars to support a third team in the time we had left before 2004 started—was to make a deal with my friend Doug Bawel, who owned the Jasper Racing team. That team's race shop, coincidentally, was located right between Penske South and the ex-Kranefuss shop in the Lakeside Business Park. Doug was excited to join us and was a tremendous contributor to the expansion of the

team, business-wise. He was unfailingly a positive guy who moved us forward, and had an incredible number of contacts in the sport.

> *We started out the engine partnership about two years before we combined our team with Penske South. Roger and I put together the whole deal at his dealership in Phoenix the night before the Phoenix race. We had a close affiliation through the engine partnership, but when the movement really got traction was when Roger got the Kodak sponsorship late in the season. You can't really start a whole team from scratch, and we were a single-car team that had finished 19th in points in 2003.*
>
> *A lot of people asked why in the world anyone would want to buy a 19th-in-points team, but the fact was that the big boys were operating off $18 million budgets, while we were operating off $11 million. I think both Don and Roger were impressed by the fact that we could stretch a dollar and that it would go toward performance, not bells and whistles. Most importantly, we brought in people with the expertise of making Tier 1 auto parts, people like Federal Mogul and Fel-Pro, who would be able to make the parts we needed when we needed them. I'm most proud that we brought five people from our engine shop over to the new company, of which three are still there today, two in managerial positions."*

DOUG BAWEL

Roger decided he wanted Brendan Gaughan, who had been a hot shot driver in the truck series, to drive the third car. I really didn't want to see it happen. When we were in New York for the 2002 banquet, I had told him, "You know, it's one thing to drive a truck and do

Left: Ryan soaked me in champagne—not orange juice—when we won the Tropicana 400 at Chicago. (Kim Watson Photo)

Right: My daughter Tricia loves racing. Especially at times like this. (Don Miller Collection)

We started our third Cup team with Brendan Gaughan in the seat. It didn't last. (Penske Corporation Photo)

it fairly well, but the level of competition between trucks and the Cup series is like being in another galaxy."

To be perfectly honest, I was hoping we could keep the guy who'd been driving for Doug, Dave Blaney, the former World of Outlaws champion. I really didn't believe that Brendan was ready for Cup racing. But Roger and John Erickson were set on Brendan, who was out of Las Vegas, where his father owned the Orleans casino. Roger listened to my concerns and said we'd get Brendan's current truck crew chief to join the team. He'd get John to really concentrate on the new #77 team while I worked with Rusty and Ryan. We made the deal with Doug to take over the #77, which would take the form of a buyout over several years, and began rebuilding Doug's cars, which were Fords at that point.

We brought in Brendan and his crew chief, Shane Wilson. Brendan had a degree of talent. We ran him in the #77 for one race before the 2003 season ended and made plans to go all out with him the following year.

22

Three to Get Ready, Four to Go

IT WAS DAYTONA TIME ONCE AGAIN, February 2004, and this time, Penske Racing had a full-fledged three-car Nextel Cup team. Rusty Wallace was back aboard the #2 Miller Lite Dodge, Ryan Newman was in the #12 Alltel Dodge, and now Brendan Gaughan was behind the wheel of the #77 Eastman Kodak/Jasper Dodge. The #77 car was entered in the Daytona 500 by Penske-Jasper Racing. This preserved the owner-points position that the #77 had earned in 2003, giving Gaughan a guaranteed starting position in each of the first five races in the 2004 season despite his rookie status. Doug Bawel, who was the owner of record at Jasper Racing in 2003, maintained an ownership position in the #77 team for 2004, hence its new name, Penske-Jasper Racing. Both Doug and I went back quite a ways at this level of racing, so the tie-up was more than just good business. He was a partner with us right through 2008, when Roger bought out Doug's share of both the team and the engine business.

Pre-season testing went fairly well, despite the fact that we were consistently short of everything you could name: spare parts to backup cars and, of course, race-ready engines. But when it came time for us to leave for Speedweeks at Daytona, the bell rang and we hit the beach running.

Bud Shootout, pole qualifying, twin 125s, practice, and then it was time for the 2004 Daytona 500. Despite all the positive projections on the media's part, both the #2 and #12 experienced problems, finishing 29th and 31st, respectively. Brendan did a little better in his maiden Daytona Cup start, bringing the Kodak/Jasper Dodge home in 19th, one lap down. Though the final Daytona tally was far less chest-swelling than we'd hoped for, there was indeed an upside. Collectively, we were able to pull through the tunnel and arrive at NASCAR's biggest event for the first time as a

In 2004, Rusty announced that his driving career was ending. (Penske Corporation Photo)

three-car operation, and leave when the show ended with some fairly reasonable results.

After the first five or six races, things began to smooth out a little on the performance side. The three teams were working fairly well together, with the drivers and crew chiefs actually communicating better than expected.

Unfortunately, for me personally, things began to hit a downward slide in terms of my health. It was a few very grim months, let me tell you. The injuries that I sustained in 1974 were once again taking their toll, and this time with a vengeance. I had had several surgeries in the early and late 1990s, which had in each case relieved the pain somewhat, given me a respite and allowed me to keep going with building the teams, first with Rusty and then Ryan. But by the spring of 2004 I was dealing with continuous pain and frightening symptoms.

Just prior to the Talladega race that May, the issues with my leg had reached a point where they were almost intolerable. My travel schedule required me to sit on planes or in cars for hours at a time, but with the problems that I was having with my leg and my back, immobility for that length of time was out of the question. On top of that, I was beginning to have problems with my hands, too. I had been receiving therapy over the years that had helped some, but I had put off previously recommended major surgery because of the pressures of my job. Now, not willing to let myself deteriorate any further, I decided to skip the Talladega race. Instead, I flew out to Seattle to see the specialists at the Puget Sound Spine Institute in Tacoma, Washington, where my son-in-law, Dr. Mike Martin, is a spinal surgeon.

What they had to tell me was disturbing: Surgery would be necessary, and very quickly, if I didn't want to totally lose the use of my hands within the next four to five weeks. According to the test results, my spinal cord was being gradually, irreversibly crushed by compression of the vertebrae, with surgery or complete disability being my only realistic options.

> " *I met Pam, Don's middle daughter, during my fellowship at Saint Mary's Hospital in San Francisco in 1992. For the first six months or year after I met him, I didn't know that Don even had a prosthetic limb, because he does such a good job of not letting on that he has one. Still, as time went on, it became obvious that he was having residual issues lingering from the horrific injuries that he'd suffered in 1974. The state of medical care at that time for traumatic injuries was in the dark ages compared to today. The mortality rate from a multi-trauma injury such as Don's in the mid-1970s was probably close to 25 percent. It's what we'd call an Open Grade 3 fracture of his tibia and fibula, plus a pelvis fracture, soft-tissue injuries and he'd lost a ton of blood. I'm not even sure about the crush injuries to his chest.*
>
> *It takes so much more energy, and it's so much harder to execute, walking after an amputation like that. The reality is the Don had a less-than-ideal stump, plus a fracture of his femur and hip, which left him with some mechanical problems as to how his leg worked. They'd been thrown off for him, which made it increasingly problematic for him to be on his feet for a long time, walk around or work for long periods.*
>
> *I ultimately referred him to a friend of mine, Dr. Don Johnson, down in Charleston, South Carolina, to perform the surgical procedure he needed.*"

MIKE MARTIN, M.D.
Don's son-in-law, Orthopedic spinal surgeon
Federal Way, Washington

I was referred to the Cooper Spine Center in Charleston, South Carolina, where Mike's friend performed the surgery—a surgical slice through the front of my neck to remove discs and bone spurs—and that finally relieved some of the pressure on my upper spine. My recovery took place at Doug Bawel's retreat on Isle of Palms in South Carolina. Although it only took about six weeks, the whole dragging interruption seemed to me like six years away from the track. Even though the beauty and serenity of Doug's hideaway near the sea was so tempting, I was still willing to trade it for the smell of racing fuel and scorched rubber. My doctors, including Mike, had cautioned me about gently pacing my recovery, but I still returned to work as soon as they allowed, eager to resume my familiar routine. Roger, Rusty, Ryan, and John were all very understanding and supportive of my somewhat limited capabilities once I did return. They agreed in telling me to take things slowly, and even to consider reducing my workload.

When I reported back to duty at the race shop, it didn't take very long before I came to some harsh realizations. The first, and most obvious, was that physically, I was going to have to adjust my pace noticeably. Secondly, however, it was equally clear to me that the Penske team was very strong in its own right, without requiring my presence on a daily basis. While I was recovering, Ryan scooped up a victory at Michigan, following up on Rusty's Martinsville win in April 2004. I felt for the first time that I might finally be able to step back a little bit from the front lines, and refocus some of my energy on trying to make a full recovery from the injuries I'd sustained a full 30 years previously.

> *People should realize that this is a business, one with extremely long hours and very hard work. People will jump into it and be enthused at first, and like the travel and glamour, et cetera. That wears off. You find out it's about long hours and detail and performance at a very, very intense level. Some people just mentally and physically can't take that grind. There are rare people that can enjoy what they're doing in the kind of environment that racing is. Don is one of them."*

H.A. "HUMPY" WHEELER

One thing I'll always gratefully remember about my first days back is my assistant, Karen McGee, and how she reassured me that daily tasks associated with the race team had been handled in my absence and that I wouldn't be facing a crushing, overwhelming amount of catching up. Next, Karen walked me over to the mailroom, where she'd been organizing the correspondence that had arrived for me while I was out. When she opened the door, I was stunned by the pile of mail she meant, literally piled to the ceiling—and this was after she'd tossed the usual junk mail that lands in everyone's mailbox. I was moved and humbled by the number of cards and well wishes sent

Ryan brought the #12 car home seventh in the 2004 points. (Penske Corporation Photo)

by countless people I'd met over the years, and I've been trying to get caught up on replying them ever since, which, at the time of this writing, is nearly five years. If you're reading this book and haven't received a reply from me to a card or message that you sent, please understand that I have only about two more feet of mail to go through before I'm done!

 Don was gone for several months. I came in when he came back and helped him get himself together, dealing with all this mail he had gotten and stuff. It started out being a couple of hours a week, and ended up being a full-time position. I had been a part-time Penske South employee previously, as a receptionist. Don saw me there and said he needed some help. When I got there, there were several big black trash bags, and big boxes, on the floor that were full of mail. I went through it for hours and hours and hours.

I became Don's executive secretary. I enjoyed that the most of anything I did at Penske. It was so much fun. His door was always open and everyone would stop and talk. Not just about business or racing, but about things like old cars."

KAREN McGEE
Don's former Executive Secretary
Cornelius, North Carolina

On another front, while I had been recuperating from the surgery, Rusty had been thinking hard about his career and his future. I knew that Dale Earnhardt's death in 2001 had rocked Rusty to his core. Those two were extremely close friends, much more so than rival superstars in a top racing series usually become. Rusty was now nearly the same age that Earnhardt was when he was killed. In late August 2004, Rusty gathered the media and announced that he intended to quit driving, but would stay with the team through the end of 2005 on a farewell tour. His goal was to win a Daytona 500 before he stepped out of the car for good.

For me, things improved somewhat over time, physically, and I slowly got back into the swing of the team, but I could nevertheless feel the stress of the season's critical time beginning to creep up on me. It was time for me to start planning my own retirement.

By summer's end, things were decidedly anxious and hostile on the performance front. Brendan continually gave vent to his displeasure with the supposed poor quality of the equipment he was receiving from the team and had a lot of negative things to say. At first he was down on the engines, then it was the cars, and finally, he said he was unhappy with his crew chief. I finally had a sit-down discussion with Brendan at the track, during which he again repeated his previous complaints about his supposedly inferior equipment. I reminded him—gently, I thought—that he was driving the very same race cars, with the same engines, that his teammates were using to win races. I could say that authoritatively because I knew what all the guys on the team were doing with the equipment we had.

My reminder to Brendan seemed to be the straw that broke the camel's back. When I finished my little refresher course for him on Penske cars and engines, Brendan remarked that what I probably needed to do was find another driver to "drive this junk," as he put it. With what I still consider to have been a great deal of restraint, I calmly told Brendan that I thought he was right, and that we would begin to explore some options for the following season.

The next day, I filled in Roger, Rusty, and Doug about my conversation with Brendan, and they concurred with my assessment that we, as a team, should move on. While we began the driver search, Ryan picked up another win at Dover in September. Looking back, I have no ill feelings towards Brendan. In fact, I rather like the guy. At the time, however, it was simply time for Gaughan to be gone.

We weren't very far into our search before the name of Travis Kvapil came up, suggested to us as a driver who'd likely be a good fit for the Penske organization. Travis was, at the time, the reigning Craftsman Truck Series champion, having won it in the final race of 2003 over Brendan, no less, and Ted Musgrave. He had a reputation for

Despite a lot of promise, our partnership with Brendan ended abruptly. (Penske Corporation Photo)

possessing a very strong knowledge of the mechanical aspects of a race car. Travis is also a Wisconsin native, and came out of the extremely tough Late Model wars in the Midwest that I knew from the years of Competition Tire West and the Goodyear track tire that we'd made for those guys. This time, I suggested that we try to work something out with his truck owner, Bang! Racing, so we could test with him using our equipment. Our objective was the chance of running a couple of Nextel Cup events with Travis before the end of 2004. This, of course, would mean that we would have to field a fourth car at those events, since Brendan was still finishing out his contract with Penske-Jasper Racing.

Making that deal, we tested with Travis and assigned Roy Mc-Cauley, our chief engineer, to be his temporary crew chief. I went to NASCAR and obtained the use of #06 on a temporary basis, listing myself as the car owner. We decided to enter Travis in the October 2004 Martinsville race, where he qualified a very respectable fifth and finished 21st. Ironically, Brendan Gaughan, in the Kodak/Jasper car, had a miserable day and ended up 34th, 76 laps down. With Ryan's third-place finish at Martinsville and Rusty's 10th, everyone was thrilled about the team's performance. Their enthusiasm, very sadly, was dampened by what had happened on race morning. Ten people associated with Hendrick Motorsports, including Rick's brother John, his son Ricky, and chief engine builder Randy Dorton, were killed when their team plane crashed in fog while en route to Martinsville. Jimmie Johnson didn't learn about the tragedy until after he'd won the race for Hendrick.

On the Monday morning after Martinsville, Roger called and suggested that we move immediately to sign Travis to a contract for 2005. I said that I thought Travis would be a good future candidate, but I'd prefer to see him complete more of an A-B-C-type season, to use the phase we'd coined, before throwing him directly into the war for the Nextel Cup. Roger listened, and countered with a suggestion that instead, we enter Travis in several more races during 2004. Because of our sponsor obligations, this meant that Travis would have to compete for rookie of the year in 2005.

Travis went on to run at Atlanta and Homestead before the end of 2004, with less than stellar results. Rusty finished the season 16th in points, while Ryan placed seventh. Brendan ended up a mediocre 28th in the final Nextel Cup standings, but we were able to carry his car's points over to the 2005 season to help Travis get off to a less intimidating, in-the-hole start.

23

Circling the Wagons

BACK IN 2003, while we were considering Brendan for a third Nextel Cup team car, Roger was already looking ahead and thinking about facilities. He knew that having Penske Racing's teams spread out among three different buildings over the area of a square block didn't lend itself particularly well to the free exchange of information or teamwork. As a result, we started looking at the possibility of getting all our people under one roof, in reality as well as figuratively. We knew we were going to need a lot of room, and as it turned out, more than we originally realized: At this point, Porsche was developing its new RS Spyder race car for the LMP2 class of the American Le Mans Series run by Don Panoz. Roger ended up running their factory team—his return to world-class road racing, and won three straight LMP2 titles beginning in 2005. That team ultimately ended up in the same facility as our NASCAR teams.

We didn't know about that part yet but in early 2004, we kept coming back to the facility issue. I was talking one day to John Erickson and mentioned to him, "There's that Panasonic electronics building here in Mooresville. I wonder if they've done anything with that yet?"

"That" was a massive industrial building located in another part of Mooresville, opened around 1990 as an assembly plant by Panasonic, or more accurately, the Matsushita Industrial Electric Company, as it was then called. The plant was located in the South Iredell Industrial Park off Mazeppa Road and State Highway 801, north of Mooresville proper and about five miles away from where Penske Racing was then occupying a trio of buildings. I'm telling you, the Panasonic building was gigantic. It had been opened to produce Matsushita-branded rotary compressors, but closed in about 2001 once Panasonic decided it could build those things

more cheaply outside the United States. It had been vacant for about a year and a half when John and I decided to take a ride over there. The doors were open when we got there, with workers taking equipment out of the building for shipment to, I guess, China.

Panasonic built the plant on a 110-acre site with 404,000 square feet under one roof. It was a majestic thing, because the Japanese corporation had taken extremely good care of the property. Everything outside was beautifully manicured, but because it was a construction area, the inside of it was a disaster. When Panasonic decided they were going to leave the United States and move operations to China, they just took all the equipment out and left everything else dangling, with holes in the floor. It was quite a sight. However, the building itself was structurally sound, with a solid roof on it, and all the driveway and approaches were really good, too. We found out who was handling the sale and contacted the real estate firm.

The realty people told us that in 1989, it had cost them $21 million to build it, in addition to all the things they added to it, a whole list. They'd depreciated it over time but the realty folks said that Panasonic had to get $14 million for it. We said there was no way we could afford that and kind of let it slide, while noting that if the selling price could be adjusted, we'd be interested. I broached the subject with Roger, who agreed with me that the price was too high.

Months went by, and we'd looked at a lot of different facilities. We'd moved some things around in our existing shops at Lakeside. We put all the chassis-building and body-hanging equipment into the old Kranefuss shop. We had the chassis dyno in the #77 shop, and the final-preparation area was centered in the original Penske South shop. We were trying to get everybody to communicate better. Then one day, the real estate group called me and said there was a developer from Florida who was interested in buying the Panasonic plant, and who said that he knew me.

The developer offered to buy the property and give us a long-term lease agreement for the factory, which would become a race shop. For whatever reason, that deal didn't get done and the developer lost his option on the property. I informed the realtor that based on our conversations with the developer, we understood the number for the property had gotten down to about $10 million, which apparently was news to him. I added, without much subtlety, that we might be interested at about $7 million to $7.5 million, which he replied was out of the question.

So another two months or so went by before he called back, asking, "Would you be interested in making a real offer?" I talked to Roger and Rusty, and we did make an offer. After conferring with the Panasonic people in Japan, they indicated that there was a good chance our offer would be accepted. Then we had to really scramble to unload our other properties and generate the cash for Panasonic. Of course, during much of this period I was recuperating in South Carolina from my surgery. However, I stayed in touch by phone, and Dave Hoffert brought large packets of real estate information and documents out to Isle of Palms for me to review, so I never missed a beat.

We owned Penske South outright, and had a lot of equity in the former Kranefuss building, while we were leasing the #77 team's building from Doug Bawel. Doug just said, "Hey, I'll sublease it to somebody else." In the end, Roush Racing took over the #77 building's lease. We sold the Kranefuss building to Braun Racing, not even using a realtor to do it, and sold the original Penske South building to Team Red Bull. It was a wild time because we had to complete all these transactions within a short time. We sold all the stuff we could sell and came up with enough money to buy the Panasonic building at the end of July 2004.

> " We had looked at that building early on, and dismissed it, considered whether we should build a new building, and came back to it, in part because the economics were good. The former owner, Matsushita, had kept the property in excellent condition. It represented a major investment, but Don, working with the general contractor, and with some of our own internal people, had to put the whole plan together, the floor plan, where everybody was going to go, etc. That was his responsibility . . . a hell of a job to do in less than four months."

WALTER CZARNECKI

I figured we'd invest another $2 million or $3 million into upgrading and improving it. I was also really thinking about retiring, Rusty was thinking about it, too, but Roger wanted to keep going.

When you get Roger Penske involved in rebuilding something, just hang on, because it's going to be first class all the way. Roger put twice as much as we'd anticipated into the new shops. For example, there's one million pieces of Italian tile in there. You cannot imagine what that all that looks like stacked up on pallets at once. Where did we get it? From Italy, of course. The neat thing about these tiles is that if one gets broken, or otherwise damaged, you just take it out and put in a new one. The floor looks exactly the same, whereas if it's a more conventional coated floor, with the usual gray finish, you get a big notch in it and it never looks the same again, no matter what you do. Roger's actually gone on to use the same sort of Italian tile on the floor of the service departments in a lot of his dealerships because it's so durable.

Hours and hours were spent on developing the shop, finessing little details like that, and making sure everything was done on time so the move would go smoothly. The chassis shop was the first thing we moved into the new building, in December 2004, and we were all moved in by January 2005 and fully ready to start the new season. The street it's on is now named Penske Way, and it's the home for all three Cup teams, our Nationwide team, our ARCA team with Parker Kligerman as its driver, the Indy Racing League teams, and also the team that competed in the Grand-Am Rolex Series. John Erickson, by the way, is in charge of that sports car side of the operation.

Ever since we established Penske South, Roger had said, however casually, that having *all* of his racing operations under one roof would be the most ideal situation. I don't know, however, that it would have ultimately happened in the manner that it did had it not been for the huge flood that hit the Reading, Pennsylvania, area over the summer of 2006. The flood destroyed everything in the Indy car shop, which was right along the Schuylkill River. At that point, Roger said he wasn't going to rebuild in Reading but instead go forward with the consolidation of all the racing operations in Mooresville. The NASCAR and Porsche teams were already in place when the IRL team moved in.

By late 2006, there were 303 people on the NASCAR side, around 60 with the IRL operation—which is the only one based in North Carolina, let me add—maybe 40 with the Porsche team and about 50 in the engine department. That's a big team, in a big shop, which would have never been occupied by Penske Racing but for a really big effort on the part of many, many people.

Our varied history is writ large in the expansive wall murals. (Jim Donnelly Photo)

TRYING HARD TO HIT A TRIPLE

By the time Travis Kvapil started out for the team, driving the Kodak car, we were already into the new shop. We started moving into the facility on Penske Way in the latter part of 2004. We went to some tests on short tracks in Florida so we could get the car more developed and give Travis more seat time, before we moved into 2005 for a full season of running three cars.

I thought that as a group, we were moving in the right direction. Ryan was running well. Rusty was running well. Travis had the makings of being good, too, but I think the problem was that he simply didn't have enough experience in this kind of race car, despite having come out of the truck series. The key factor was that as the season went along, the seat time he was getting was not enough. His crew chief was Brendan's old crew chief, Shane Wilson. Travis had to adjust to a new series, a new car and a new crew chief, so he was triple-whammied on the whole deal. He ran OK, his attitude was great, but we really just weren't hitting on it, even though he didn't miss any races—he was locked in for the first five—and Travis was a pretty good qualifier.

While our other two teams continued to pick up, we were constantly trying to finish the building, refine it, get all the new people we had into their places. We actually completed it all by the end of February 2005, even our first gift shop. We were reconstructing our departments within this building—the ultimate race shop, in my estimation, a monumental undertaking.

Through all these wonderful things, however, there were still some unsettling undercurrents. The most critical one was that Eastman Kodak was suffering financial difficulties. When digital photography started becoming really popular, people didn't need as much film anymore, which meant that Kodak's core business had very quickly gone completely off kilter. At that point, Kodak was in the second year of a three-year contract with us. They came and talked to us after Daytona, said they might have to pull back, and wanted to discuss the possibility of redoing the contract.

Roger, being the astute businessman that he is, put together a reduced program for Kodak, which didn't take effect until June even though everybody in management knew it was coming. We carried on for the rest of the season, but bits and pieces of the Kodak troubles started to show up in the news media about how the company was going to have to pull out of racing and so forth. That's very disruptive to a race team. We were already having to brace ourselves internally to absorb that blow and we didn't need the media chasing us.

Halfway through the 2005 season, Roger told John Erickson and me to sit down and really figure out where we were going to go from the point of Kodak's pullback. He told us, going in, that without the sponsorship to support a real effort from a third Penske team, we were probably going to have to cut back to two. In Kodak's defense, this was a completely unforeseen situation, given business conditions when the sponsorship contract was first signed. We had a moral obligation to work with Kodak and help them step back from it. Could we have gotten the money out them? Yeah, we could have, but that wasn't the idea. Some day they might be able to come back to racing as a sponsor. We hope they'd like to come back with us.

By late 2005, we had a plan in place. We knew that we were going to have to cut back to two teams and cut our staffing significantly. Just before the end of the season, we talked to some of the key people on the Kodak team and told them it wasn't likely that we would be carrying on. We also told them that we'd make every effort to meet our own obligations, contractual and moral, but that if they thought they had other opportunities, to go ahead and pursue them.

As it came closer to the end of 2005, Roger said he wanted to meet in Detroit with me, John Erickson and Tim Cindric, who headed the Reading, Pennsylvania-based IRL teams for Penske. The crux of the meeting was that we'd already made all the personnel adjustments necessary to adjust to the Kodak situation and the realignment of the people who remained, plus the ongoing movement to Mooresville of the ALMS and IRL operations. Roger said that this was the logical point for Penske Racing to make the further changes it needed to continue after my retirement and Rusty's, given that Rusty had already announced his own plans to step out of the cockpit following the 2005 Cup season. Earlier in 2005, Roger had asked us to really think about what we, Rusty and I, wanted to do. He wanted to invest a lot more money in the racing end of his business empire, make it more directly into an arm of his corporation. He wanted to do what was needed to make that happen after we left.

I had already talked to Rusty about this, a conversation that, essentially, came down to, "What do you wanna do?" Rusty had said, "Well, you know, let's just sell our shares to Roger." The meeting continued, which was when Roger disclosed that he was going to move John over to run the sports car side of Penske Racing, the ALMS teams. He was also going to have Tim Cindric, who would be moving to North Carolina from Reading, work with me and learn the NASCAR side of our racing. We then proceeded to agree upon the price with Roger and closed the deal. Roger asked me to stay on for an interim period and help Tim get his footing in Mooresville after Rusty left, and of course, I agreed.

The time was right: I simply didn't have the physical strength to do what I'd been doing for so many years. I'd talked about retirement earlier and talked myself out of it. Then John came in and took part of the load off me. That was a godsend for me, because then we could share the work, and we both wouldn't have had to go to all the Cup races. With Roger's personnel changes, though, I would have had to go to them all again, because Tim would have had to be at all the IRL

Ryan Newman was one of the best decisions I've ever made in racing. He's phenomenal. (Don Miller Collection)

races, while at the same time trying to get his arms around the stock car side of Penske Racing.

Ironically, 2005 was a great year for our team. Ryan decided that he wanted some extra seat time on race weekends, so we put together a Busch Grand National team for him, with Alltel and Mobil sponsorship. Mobil wanted to be more deeply involved, but it was an interim deal because Mobil was in the process of being sold to Exxon, so we did this to keep Mobil involved until that merger was completed.

We took our chief engineer, Roy McCauley, and made him crew chief on that Busch team, under Penske ownership. They had a phenomenal run, winning six times in nine starts, including four in a row. Ryan actually started out the season seeming a bit distracted and struggling a little, but the Busch team cleared his head. Besides winning, it helped him understand the performance of the new tires and how they related to the chassis setups. Meanwhile he and Matt worked to transfer his new knowledge over to the Cup side.

The next year, 2006, was a year of transition. I knew I was going to retire the following year, but Roger and I had agreed that it wasn't in the best interests of the team to announce that. Unfortunately, all the changes seemed to affect Matt more than I had anticipated when I told him quietly that I would be leaving. He knew, of course, that I would retire at some point, but he wasn't completely happy with what was going to happen next. Matt talked to Roger, and said he wanted to step back a little bit because he and his wife had just had another child. He hoped to share leadership with Mike Nelson, who had been

team engineer on the #12 car. Rather than cause a lot of disruption, Matt finally stepped away completely, moving to Michael Waltrip Racing for the 2007 season. Mike Nelson then stepped up to become Ryan's crew chief. Larry Carter had gone through Rusty's last season as his crew chief, and then went to Roush. Roush is where we found Pat Tryson, who took over the #2 car after Larry left. Jack got one from us and we got one from him, plus Kurt Busch, who took over as driver of the #2 car following Rusty's retirement at the end of 2005.

As for Rusty, I think that he has already firmly established his legacy in this sport. He's been voted one of the top 50 drivers, ever, in NASCAR history. In my estimation, he's closer to being one of the top 15 drivers in NASCAR, ever. Fifty-five wins and a Winston Cup title, the most short-track wins in Cup history, along with 36 poles. Even if Rusty had never been a Cup superstar, had never come South, he'd still be one of the greatest short-track Late Model drivers who ever raced, with a triple-digit listing of major victories. He's created his own life after retirement, his TV career with ABC Sports and ESPN, plus his own race team with his son Steven and Brendan Gaughan

Two of the best. It's heartbreaking that they both didn't make it to retirement as drivers. (Larry McTighe Photo)

driving his cars in the Nationwide Series. That's some irony, because Rusty and Brendan were never that close when Brendan was driving for us. Racing makes some strange bedfellows, too. Rusty's still flying, still upgrading his jet license, and now has his helicopter rating. He's an excellent pilot. He's a really successful, accomplished guy, not just a retired race driver. He's a person all unto himself. He's matured immensely in the past four years, because he has a lot more responsibility, making the judgment calls himself. He's the hand, not just one of the fingers on it.

I was glad to see him retire. He's my friend. I didn't want to see him come to a bad end like Dale did. I was afraid for Rusty there for awhile. It really bothered him when Dale was killed, and it should have, because they were so close. It relieved me to see him step back. I don't think he should ever get back into a race car again, and the people who keep saying that he will one day are living in a fantasy world. He takes his life into his own hands every time he gets in the cockpit of his airplane and flies across the country. Why put yourself in a situation with more risk? As you get on, life should be about less risk and more reward. He's worked very hard. When we started out, neither one of us had anything, but we established a direction for our lives, and then lived it. We did it one step, one day, at a time. Not these long, drawn-out empty-suit projections. In this business, you become an opportunist, which means that you have opportunities presented to you every day, and it's your job to pick the best one. If you pick wrong, you're not going to be around very long.

I wasn't sure how long I was going to be around myself, no matter what the doctors had pulled off in the operating room. However long it was, I sure as hell wasn't going to waste it. I had a family, and a lot of unresolved personal business. It was time to get busy, starting with a trip out West to see my grandsons. And on the way, I just might stop off at the Bonneville Salt Flats to see what was happening out there.

Bonneville has always held a very special place in my heart. Just thinking about a possible trip there brought back wonderful memories of some earlier adventures I'd had at that magical spot—the end of the Earth as we know it.

24

Assaulting the Salt

THERE IS A PLACE ON EARTH, which six and a half billion people call home, where you can go that no living creature is visible. A place where on a clear day, you can clearly see the curvature of the Earth, and for 300 days each year, the stillness is so complete that you can almost hear your heart beating. This place is foreboding, yet fascinating. Not a blade of grass grows anywhere, and when you walk on its surface, the crust of its ground crunches beneath your feet as if to warn you that it's unstable and that trespassers must beware. This is Bonneville, known to most as the Great Salt Lake. Nestled between two mountain ranges 100 miles from Salt Lake City, it is one of the most desolate places on Earth, until August and September arrive each year. Then, like a chameleon, it transforms itself into a Mecca of pure, naked speed, a cathedral of horsepower in which knights in colorful metallic chariots wheel themselves onto an altar of hardened salt to do battle with time itself. Speed is the Holy Grail.

To racers, this world of dazzling whiteness at the reaches of the briny lake is known as the Bonneville Salt Flats. Yes, I have loved this place, deeply, since the first time that I laid eyes on it personally during the mid-Sixties. I promised myself that I would race there someday, and follow that long, black line that marks its speed course all the way to the end. Of course, like any kid of my age who read the car magazines growing up, I knew about Bonneville. It was a holy place. To countless people, including me, the ultimate test of a traditional hot rod is maximizing its speed through a measured mile on the salt flats.

Though I'd been to Bonneville several times, it wasn't until 1989 that I finally built a dedicated vehicle to compete for a class record there. At that

I went to Bonneville the old-fashioned way, with a street rod, which I converted to a race car. (Don Miller Collection)

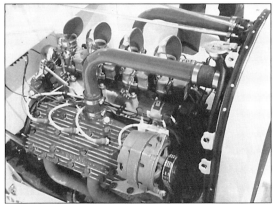

Left: Our first outing in the unblown flathead '29 Ford wasn't everything we hoped for. But hey, after having dreamed about it since childhood, I was a land speed racer at Bonneville. (Don Miller Collection)

Right: Four pots on a flathead. Very traditional, but too slow for a class record. (Don Miller Collection)

point in my life, I was working the usual hectic and intense schedule, helping guide Rusty's Cup career, constantly on the road for Motorsports International and handling a number of other projects for Roger. But I still managed to carve out a little bit of time for myself and that early love, the challenge of the Salt. The experience was both wonderful and absolutely essential for me, personally. I was tired, my body was wracked by pain almost constantly, and for both reasons, I started giving some serious consideration to the number of years I had left to achieve a few lifelong dreams. Bonneville was one of them. I had to do it.

At the time, I had put together a 1929 Model A roadster for the street, powered by a small-block Chevy engine and transmission. It was nearing completion when one day, I had a conversation with Tom Hutchinson, a friend of mine from California. Now Tom was a long way from being your ordinary senior citizen, even though he was in his mid-70s. Tom was a great mechanic, and a world-recognized expert on flathead Ford V-8 engines. He was a veteran of the early speed contests at Muroc Dry Lake, in the Mojave Desert northeast of Los

Angeles, and a seasoned competitor at Bonneville. Tom and I traded both old car parts and racing stories for years, and he always told me how much he wanted me to get back to Bonneville to run a "proper race car," as he termed it, which in his context meant an early Ford roadster with a flathead. I'd heard him say that before, but for some reason, this time I said, "Yes, Tom. You know, you are right. I'll meet you there next August." The following day, I pulled the Chevy engine out of the street roadster and started disassembling the car.

My deadline to get to Bonneville for Speed Week was August 1990. It's not as if that was the only thing I was doing, because Motorsports International was still running wide open. Thankfully, I had Jeff Thousand and Dave Wirz from my team at M.I. to help me with my car, or I never would have made it. As it was, we barely completed it in time to make the blurry dash from Saint Louis to Wendover, Utah, just in time for the start of time trials in 1990. We had done a complete buildup according to the rule book to compete in the category for Unblown Street Roadsters. In the parlance of the Southern California Timing Association, which has sanctioned record runs at Bonneville since just after World War II, the class is XF/STR or, as it's expressed verbally, XF Street Roadster.

> That car was originally mine, and then Don wanted a roadster, so I gave it to him. Then, NHRA was going to go back to the C/Street Roadsters at the drags, which is flatheads and inline sixes. I had run a B/Street Roadster forever, and he knew that I liked racing roadsters with flatheads, so he gave it back to me. I put a roll cage on it and started building a race flathead, and then NHRA changed their mind. So I put a Chevy in the roadster and gave it back to Don again.
>
> That's when somebody talked him into going to Bonneville. So

Left: They say you can tell real racers by their eyes. I'm definitely in the zone, strapping in for a flat-out run on the salt flats. (Don Miller Collection)

Right: This is more like it. More cubic inches, and a big B&M blower to boost the flattie. (Don Miller Collection)

he takes the Chevy out, puts a flathead back in, and I drive down to Saint Louis from here in my Suburban, with all my tools and stuff. And just as we're about to leave, we're in his office when Roger calls, and says, 'You've got to get up to Detroit, to the wind tunnel.' It was for testing, back when Penske South was preparing to run Pontiacs. I think it was something like $30,000 to rent the tunnel, a horrendous amount of money, and Roger wanted Don up there for the test. And Don says, 'Roger, you know that I'm going to Bonneville. There will be more tests this year but only one Speed Week.'

I guess Roger got a little snippy with him, and made some remarks about this shitbox, or something like that, junk or whatever—Roger's into Indy cars and all the whiz-bang stuff. I've never seen Don so angry. The look on his face was frightening. He slammed the phone down. I'm not going to tell you what he said next. I looked at him and said, 'Don, I'll tell you what. We're going to Bonneville.'"

VANCE FERRY

We submitted the roadster for tech inspection on Thursday at the old airport in Wendover, the little town that straddles the state line between Nevada and Utah. This was a doubly special day for me, because the Wendover airport was originally an Army Air Forces base. It's the base from which Colonel Paul Tibbets and the crew of the 509th Composite Group trained with the Boeing B-29 bombers *Enola Gay* and *Bockscar* before heading out to Tinian Island in the Pacific Ocean. Because of their efforts, we all enjoy the freedom that we have today. We passed tech inspection, and the next day, put the roadster in line to make an official driver's licensing run. A licensing run requires the driver to make a part-throttle pass under the scrutinizing eyes of an SCTA official. The officials want to make sure you're qualified and able to control your race car before they turn you loose on an all-out run.

The '29 drew quite a crowd, as it gleamed resplendent in Pennzoil yellow. It was a totally finished, purpose-built racer that looked like a cover car from a 1950 edition of *Hot Rod* magazine. Our roadster was completely traditional in appearance, with a tonneau cover, open front wheels, bobbed rear fenders, big Moon discs and the required vestigial headlights.

In my Nomex firesuit, I pulled on my helmet, squeezed inside the roll cage, strapped in and tried to get comfortable. Off we went. Everything went fine as far as the SCTA requirements were concerned, and everyone on our volunteer crew was pleased, except me. We ran a little over 100 mph, which was exactly what the SCTA re-

Bonneville is challenging, exhilarating, breathtaking and sometimes heart-breaking, especially when it rains before you can really put the hammer down. (Don Miller Collection)

quired for the licensing pass, but the engine was flat and listless. Old Tom assured me that we could tune her up and make some real speed when they turned us loose for an actual flying-mile run. I didn't think so. The flathead just felt soft, way too soft. We made two more runs over the next two days and picked up 10 mph, but then blew a head gasket. We repaired the engine Friday night, and were ready to go again on Saturday, but, mercifully, it rained and the salt flats once again became part of the Great Salt Lake before we could go out and run too slow again. The balance of Bonneville Speed Week for 1990 was canceled. It was a long ride back to St. Louis, because, in my heart, I knew we had failed. It was going to be a long winter.

I realized fully that we hadn't come close to running at the Ford's potential, or even remotely approaching it. The normal rush of events pushed that ache backwards in my consciousness. Rusty Wallace and I had decided to consummate our long relationship in racing by establishing a Winston Cup team together. I resigned from Motorsports International and relocated to North Carolina. On a trailer behind me came the roadster. While we assembled the new race team, which became Penske Racing South after Roger agreed to become involved with it, I still had some time left over to think about what we were going to do at Bonneville in 1991.

Some of the guys at Penske South became fascinated with my Bonneville obsession. We heavily refined the roadster, greatly dropping its ride height, fabricating some slicker body panels—sheet metal guys who work for NASCAR teams are exceptional at doing that—and most importantly, doing a major upgrade on our engine package. It

Left: In the old days, land speed cars ran in drag races, too. So did mine. We won Street Eliminator at the Mid-America Nostalgia Nationals in Wentzville, Missouri, in 1990. (Don Miller Collection)

Right: We also ran the roadster, in full land-speed trim, at the ECTA meet in North Carolina, on an abandoned World War II airstrip. (Don Miller Collection)

was still a 276 cubic-inch flathead V-8, like we'd had in 1990, but I removed the four Stromberg carburetors and instead installed a B&M-made, Rootes-type pulley-driven supercharger topped by a Holley 850 CFM four-barrel carburetor. Like everyone else at Bonneville, I wanted more speed and some relief from constantly trying to keep four carburetors in proper tune. Though still running on gas, the Ford thus moved up a class into Blown Street Roadster, or as it's lettered on the car, XF/BSTR. In 1991, the record for that class over the measured mile at Bonneville was around 140 mph.

We were loaded up in Mooresville, with two blown flatheads and a ton of spare parts, besides the roadster. We were late hitting the road, and drove to Wendover nonstop from North Carolina. My old drag racing pal from Chicago, Vance Ferry, and David Munari were along, as were Larry Penn and Steve Triplett from Penske South. We ran like our butts were on fire to get to Utah on time. The balance sheet for the three days that followed was two blown engines, a blown transmission, and a single complete pass of 129 mph. And of course, another long, glum ride back, only this time, a longer one.

Despite these disappointments, we all still wanted a record. For 1992, we decided that we needed yet more underneath the hood. We concentrated on building a single power plant this time, a very big flathead displacing 296 cubic inches. Steve Triplett and Bird Schaufner—Bird is one of Penske South's engine builders and a drag racer of very long standing himself—put a great many hours into building it up. We made our own aluminum rods, made our own lifters, and cut down Chevrolet titanium valves to fit the flathead's guide lengths. I spent four straight nights on the mill cutting down and refinishing the crankshaft. Meanwhile, Dave Roberts, a fantastic fabricator at Penske South, lowered the roadster's ride height by another inch. He also installed boxes directly above the rear axle, which we filled with 250 pounds of lead to prevent wheelspin while I was going through the traps at maximum power.

Lots of people get into my roadster. One of them is my pal Kim Watson, whom I've known since she was born. Her father is my old Chicago drag racing buddy Larry Nowak. (Matt Litwin Photo, Don Miller Collection)

We were really ready by the time we again towed all the way from Mooresville to Wendover. I clocked a warm-up pass at more than 143 mph, running right on the class record. We then laid down two successive passes at 150-plus, setting the official record in XF/BSTR, even though we were still spinning the rear wheels through the measured mile. It was beyond description. I chased the black line at top speed and outran it. But then, once again, before we could celebrate, it rained. That sent us back east once more. More than 15 years later, it's still hard for me to verbalize the pride and accomplishment we felt at becoming part of Bonneville's recorded history. We didn't make it back until 1994, when it rained continuously. The roadster never turned a wheel during all of Speed Week.

I haven't been back since. I doubt if I ever will be in my full previous capacity, which is to say as an owner-driver. I simply don't think that my body will tolerate it any longer. If you look at photos or video taken during various Speed Weeks, the car is so far off in the distance on the measured mile that it looks as if it's gliding across a sheet of glass. The truth is precisely the opposite. Even though the annual rains smooth out the crust somewhat, it's still very uneven, and the faster you go, the sharper the bumps get. At the speeds I'd have been

You can be a land speed racer on the East Coast, too. Speed runs are conducted several times a year on the former military airfield at Maxton, North Carolina. You better have a parachute if you run there. (Don Miller Collection)

realistically traveling to keep the class record, the pounding on my lower spine, strapped into a racing seat with very little padding, would be simply too much. My gait from using an artificial leg had damaged that part of my back over the passage of more than 20 years. It got to the point where my son-in-law, Dr. Mike Martin, had to do some reconstructive work on my lower back. Part of it was building a structure around my back and neck to protect my spinal cord. So, it wasn't just an issue of pain; I was concerned that if I damaged my spine any more, even from just the rough ride of a Bonneville record car, I might lose my ability to walk. If I go back to Bonneville, most likely, somebody else is going to be driving the roadster.

 Don's always got some skunk works project going, he always did. The one thing I did tell him, at some point, was, 'Please, Don, don't go back to the salt flats. Just keep doing what you're doing.'

WALTER CZARNECKI

Nowadays, none of us has the time to tow to Utah at the height of the late-summer racing season. Since 1994, we've run the Ford a couple of times in events sanctioned by the East Coast Timing Association. It conducts LSR-type trials on former airfields, initially at Moultrie, Georgia, and more recently at Maxton, North Carolina, about halfway to the Outer Banks from Charlotte. The runs are on concrete, and we got the roadster up to 156 mph at one point. It was fun, but it wasn't the same as Bonneville, running flat out across that shimmering ribbon of gleaming white salt.

As age closes in on me now, I know it is too late for me, but that little yellow 1929 Ford sits patiently in the North Carolina Auto Racing Hall of Fame, on display, waiting for one more chance to split the wind and travel down the long black line.

25
Following Dad's Lesson

IT'S BEEN A LONG TIME SINCE I had a conversation with my Dad, other than the sort that's silent, going on inside my head. He was troubled by heart disease and died very young, closing in on 50 years ago. I haven't seen my Mom in quite a while, either. She was young, too, when I lost her, just 70 years old when she passed on in 1983. I know they'd both be pleased that I try every day to make sure that the values they held so closely, believed in and passed on to me and my sisters, still matter for something today.

Neither one of them made it as far from Chicago as I did. Mooresville is home to Pat and me, and has been for a long time. It's a cool town, very conscious of its history, located near the southern end of Iredell County, North Carolina. I'm proud and happy that this is my hometown, and now the hometown of Penske Racing, as well. Despite a huge spurt in both residential and commercial growth since I first got here in the early 1990s, Iredell County, and Mooresville in particular, still has a small-town ambiance that you can feel. The people are great. They welcome new residents, and I've always tried hard to be a good neighbor to them.

My parents made sure that my sisters Pat and Mary Alice and I lived in a supportive home that valued decency, education and a healthy upbringing. To an increasing degree, and for reasons too complicated for this book, that's less true today. Even in an outwardly idyllic place like Iredell County, full of churches and parks, a lot of youngsters struggle every day for basic survival. Too frequently, they're also harmed, either physically or verbally, with parents who simply don't have the skills or intellect to have been parents in the first place. A lot of their parents abuse drugs or alcohol, or can't afford to make ends meet.

261

I wanted to do something about that. I love children. I always have. There's no specific reason I can give you that explains why, and maybe, it's beyond explanation. It's a passion of mine, to use an over-used word. Some of the reason, however, probably is that I missed a lot with my own kids, because I was working so hard and gone so often and so long. I lost a lot of time with them. If it hadn't been for Pat, I don't know how they would have turned out, because I wasn't around enough to provide anything but guidance. I thought about that a lot over the years, and finally came to the realization that I was lucky enough to have good parents who taught me the right things, and that I had enough brains to understand what they were trying to teach me.

My goal, then, was to share some of that knowledge, that gift from my parents, with others. I did some more thinking, and some research into what constituted the most needy areas in our community. I already knew that if you don't start with a good foundation, the house is going to fall down. I came to the conclusion that if I was going to give back, I should start with the children.

For most of the time before Penske South was formed, I didn't really have the time to do much, again, because I was always on the road. But in 1989, when Rusty and I first came down to North Carolina, we had a breakfast meeting with a gentleman named Pete Melities, who was one of the active members in the Mooresville-South Iredell Chamber of Commerce. Pete mentioned his shock at how bad the child abuse situation was both in Iredell County and the surrounding counties, which really surprised me, too. Pete said that he'd been to a meeting a few days earlier with a new area organization that was just getting started called SCAN, which stands for Stop Child Abuse Now. He'd learned that the neglect of children was probably as big a problem as actual abuse.

Rusty and I told Pete we'd like to do something to help with this problem. Pete suggested that we find a way to use our popularity to help the kids out, perhaps through a fundraising event. We suggested that we could get some of the racers together to participate in a race car show and have the drivers come in and sign autographs. Pete really liked the idea and thought he could help us get the armory in Mooresville to use as a venue.

Rusty was away most of the time because he was driving for Raymond Beadle at that point, and I was tied up getting the shop built for what became Penske South. I got together with another guy from the Chamber, whose name was Wallace, too, and who later became its president. We enlisted the help of Mooresville then-mayor, Joe Knox. The National Guard enthusiastically pitched in as well.

We were utterly shocked on the day that first car show finally took

place. It was cold, the weather was miserable, but the event was a booming success. I still don't know how many people actually showed up, but it was in the thousands, easily. Even more amazingly, they came from everywhere, all over the Carolinas, everywhere. We took all the money and the toys that we collected that day and presented them to the group that Pete Melities had mentoned, SCAN. It's part of a national network of groups that provide educational and in-home intervention services to protect children. That first car show has since evolved into the annual Stocks for Tots fundraising gala in Mooresville, which brings NASCAR, NHRA and other motorsports stars together with their fans each year to raise funds and toys for kids who really need them.

Left: Tony Stewart, a great benefactor of charitable causes, is a big star at Stocks for Tots. (Don Miller Collection)

Right: Dale Earnhardt Jr. and Martin Truex have also given their time to aid abused kids. (Don Miller Collection)

> We had 34 children last year in the state of North Carolina who died at the hands of a parent or caregiver. More than 1,800 were reported abused or neglected in the same year. And those are just the cases that were reported. So the problem is definitely there.
>
> I first met Don at one of the very first Stocks for Tots fundraisers in Mooresville. He and Rusty Wallace and Pete Melities have worked really hard to raise funds for our center, by getting together some of the race car drivers to sign autographs, have an auction and the toy donation. Our website is www.iredellscan.org.
>
> Don has been a staunch supporter throughout those years, and perhaps more importantly, getting awareness of our name and our mission out in front of the public. For example, Women's Auxiliary Motorsports and Speedway Children's Charities have both given to

SCAN because they learned about us from Stocks for Tots. Don's work has been the catalyst for that. He's expressed to me that his interest is in making sure children are safe. His wife is right behind him in this, too.

I understand that right now, Don is working on refurbishing a doll house that he originally built for his daughters for our visitation room at SCAN. Don is always a behind-the-scenes guy. He does not do things to bring glory on himself."

AMY EISELE
Director, Iredell County SCAN
Olin, North Carolina

I'm proud to say that the 2008 edition of Stocks for Tots was our 20th. We've raised hundreds of thousands of dollars for SCAN in that time, probably going on $1 million by now, and collected somewhere in excess of 50,000 toys, which we give away to both abused kids and children undergoing treatment at area hospitals. We had an auction in 2008 with 55 pieces of actual race cars that were donated, including a JR Motorsports deck lid autographed by Mark Martin and Dale Earnhardt Jr., and an IRL wing that Sam Hornish Jr. signed. There are drivers and personalities galore, dozens of race cars and all kinds of fun.

We've long since outgrown the armory. Stocks for Tots' home is now the Charles Mack Citizen Center in downtown Mooresville. We've expanded to include a couple of motorcycle and street rod events. One result of Stocks for Tots has been the creation of two parenting centers that provide local people year-round with the skills they need to raise kids. I'm happy with what we're doing, even though the problem is still serious and made worse by the increasing population and poor economy.

A couple of years after we started the Stocks for Tots program, maybe in 1991, I was talking to a friend of mine, Bob Ebert, whose daughter was the manager of Lakeside Business Park, where we built the first Penske South shops. Bob said, "I can't believe you're so involved in the community, in bringing the teams down here, doing this and that. What I'd like to start around here is a museum, a hall of fame. There's no museum down here for stock car racing."

Bob, who passed away in 2007, was absolutely right. I was amazed when I thought for a few seconds about what he'd just told me. There were sports halls of fame in North Carolina, but nothing that recognized racing, stock cars or otherwise. In 1994, the Charlotte metro area was already the home of top-tier stock car racing, and an ever-growing number of teams had followed Penske to Mooresville. There's a museum at Darlington, South Carolina, and had been for years, but it's a long way from Charlotte.

We started checking around for a possible location well before we even had a firm idea of what, or who, would be in the hall. Then Bob told me that the steel tubing company in Lakeside, right across the street from Penske South on Knob Hill Road, was moving to a bigger location. He noted that the building was in good shape, even though it would require some upgrades inside, and that we could probably get hold of it for a reasonable price.

Bob and I each put in funding. We hired a manager. Razoar and a couple of friends helped us gut the inside of the place and build an office. We opened the North Carolina Auto Racing Hall of Fame in 1994, and it was an immediate success. I told the other guys that we'd be able to pay our bills and certainly be able to donate to charity whatever we made beyond that. By 1996, the Hall of Fame was really rolling and we were already averaging 100,000 visitors per year. I told Bob that I really didn't want my investment back and that we ought to turn the Hall into a foundation, with its proceeds all earmarked toward helping abused children. Bob agreed, and after obtaining the needed charter to make the Hall a non-profit entity, we created the North Carolina Auto Racing Hall of Fame Foundation. We put a little away to save up for any future expansion, and all the rest has gone, like Stocks for Tots, to SCAN. The Hall has continued growing in popularity every year. It's become a destination address for race fans.

 I've been here since 1998, but Don actually started the museum and Hall in 1994. Don has helped a great deal with raising the money, and with restoring the cars and the other displays here that tell the story of racing in the Carolinas. We have several chari-

Donna DeNardo moved down here from upstate New York, and runs the Hall of Fame on a daily basis. She's really good at it. (Don Miller Collection)

ties that we work with at the Hall of Fame, but the main one is to help the abused kids. That's what he wanted.

When they first come in, I don't think that most of the people who visit here are aware of our connection to those children, but we stress it to them and made sure they're aware of it when they leave."

DONNA DeNARDO
Manager, North Carolina Auto Racing Hall of Fame
Mooresville, North Carolina

Over the years, we've raised hundreds of thousands of dollars for SCAN through the Hall. It's organized as a 501(c)(3), and we have our own board of directors, which includes Rusty and Ryan, Bobby Allison, Buddy Baker, the NHRA Top Fuel champ Darrell Gwynn, John Dodson from the NASCAR Technical Institute, and myself, among others. Bob Ebert's daughter Cecile is also on our board.

The Hall of Fame wouldn't be very useful if nobody was in it. We inducted our first Hall of Famer in 1997, the icon himself, Richard Petty. One inductee a year has gone in since, ranging from Dale Earnhardt to Tim Flock to Benny Parsons, all honored for making racing history in North Carolina. We created a parallel class of honorees beginning in 2000, the Golden Wrench Award, supported by Snap-on Tools and intended for mechanical geniuses of the sport. The first so recognized was Richard's longtime crew chief Dale Inman. Leonard Wood, Buddy Parrott, Waddell Wilson and the irreplaceable Harry Hyde have since joined them.

We've also dedicated a Hollywood-inspired Walk of Fame on Main Street in downtown Mooresville, in front of the Mack Center, which memorializes the Hall's current inductees. The Museum has a ton of historic race cars, including both Rusty's original Penske Chevrolet

I'm really happy with the way that the North Carolina Auto Racing Walk of Fame came together in Mooresville. Richard Petty's shadow can be seen in this photo from the Walk of Fame's opening day. (Jim Kenney Photo)

Ray Evernham and A.J. Foyt were honored in 2009 by the North Carolina Auto Racing Hall of Fame as its 14th inductee and recipient of the Snap-on Golden Wrench Award, respectively. (Tim Vogel Photo)

and the prototype Winston Cup Marauder that we built at Penske South. Being a North Carolina museum, there's an authentic display on moonshine put together by the marketing and broadcasting veteran Johnny Hayes, who's also on our board.

The Hall shares one of the attributes that made Mooresville attractive to so many top race teams, in that it's located right off Interstate 77 at Exit 36. We are a full partner in the Race City USA strategy that defines Mooresville as a hub of the American motorsports industry. We also have other charitable fundraising activities in the area that we're deeply involved in promoting, such as the annual Penske Hot Rod Picnic, and the art show that Cotton Ketchie, a native of Mooresville, has been presenting since 2004.

I'm proud to be from Chicago, and always will be, but Mooresville is my home. I love the place. I probably love it even more than I did when I first arrived down here in 1989 with Rusty. A lot of people give me credit for attracting a bunch of racing-related businesses to locate here after Penske South did, but really, Mooresville sells itself better than I ever could. Its own success proves what a lovely town it is. I have tried constantly to help the people who live in this area, especially the young ones who are the most vulnerable, simply because they deserve it, and I owe them for making Mooresville a pleasant, welcoming hometown. From the time I first moved here, a guy from the Midwest who had little experience in the South outside of racing, people made me feel like a native. Over the years, I've talked up

Mooresville, its people and its enthusiasm for new arrivals to anyone who would listen. When it came to Mooresville, the message got across.

> **"** *I'm one of the few people you'll come across in Mooresville now who was actually born here. It was a textile town, although our largest mill, Burlington, went to Mexico, so we had a lot of people here who needed to be retrained and find new jobs. Had it not been for Don Miller happening upon Mooresville, I don't know where we would be. We were destined to be a ghost town.*
>
> *When Don showed up, that was the beginning of what we are now. Penske became the anchor. Since then, the population of Mooresville has probably tripled. I still live on the dairy farm where I grew up, only it's not a dairy farm anymore.*
>
> *Don has been instrumental in our community, especially SCAN. He brought more to Mooresville than just a race team."*
>
> **KAREN RAY**
> *North Carolina State House of Representatives, 2002-2008*
> *Former Iredell County Commissioner*
> *Mooresville, North Carolina*

It's not as if I was the only person promoting Mooresville, either, but a lot of people involved in the sport of professional racing figured out, like I did, that it was a good place to both live and do business. Penske South was not the first race team or business in town. Bill Simpson was there before we were, allowing us to buy his shop. Mooresville has some excellent attributes that appeal to a race team operator, one of the most important being accessibility. Interstates 40 and 77 cross Iredell County and Interstate 85, which feeds almost directly into Charlotte Motor Speedway, is maybe a half-hour from our shops. You can load up your haulers and easily send them anywhere in the United States. It's tax- and business-friendly, and there was room to build. It didn't take very long for the word to get around. Dale Earnhardt chose Mooresville as the headquarters for DEI. Chip Ganassi had his operations in Mooresville before he merged with Felix Sabates. Jack Roush still has a location in Mooresville. The Red Bull Racing team, where my pal Tex Powell is a consultant, has their shops right across the street from the Hall of Fame.

The NASCAR Technical Institute is also located in Mooresville. A lot of the Cup drivers who field short track or Nationwide Series cars on their own, such as Greg Biffle, Kasey Kahne and Kurt Busch, also have their own shops in Mooresville, about 70 teams in all. The team infrastructure has attracted about 100 associated businesses that serve the racing industry, selling everything from fuel systems to HANS devices. You name it, you can get it here. Mooresville is probably home to more racing-related businesses than anywhere on the planet and also to some whose links to racing are indirect: Lowe's Home Improvement Centers recently opened a gigantic corporate headquarters here, and expansions are scheduled at major facilities at NGK Ceramics and Ingersoll-Rand. I didn't bring them here. Mooresville, and its citizens, did it. But it was cool to be part of Mooresville's growth, even if it was only peripherally.

> " Mooresville probably had about 8,000 people during the 1980s. Today, it's close to 30,000. And if you make a one-mile sweep beyond its borders, that population probably goes to 50,000 or 55,000. Very few of the people who work in Mooresville, in the racing industry, commute here. They live here because they like the community. Our team total includes Cup, Nationwide, Truck, ARCA and Hooters Cup. Plus, you have people like Kasey Kahne, who has a shop here for his dirt track cars. CR Radiators, Simpson and those people are here, too, even people who wrap the cars instead of putting stickers on them. To me, it's because one man, Don Miller, decided to come here and set up a race team."

AL JONES
Mayor and Town Councilman, 1993-2005
Mooresville, North Carolina

Obviously, as Mooresville has grown, so has Stocks for Tots, and the amount of donations it has been able to generate for SCAN. I fully intended to stay active with SCAN, Stocks for Tots and the Hall of Fame as I contemplated my retirement from full-time involvement with racing, which was announced during NASCAR Champions Week 2007 in New York City. I never expected what happened next, however. In conjunction with the NASCAR banquet, I was named the inaugural recipient of NASCAR's Humanitarian of the Year Award, which was created to recognize an individual who's given back to his community in a meaningful way. I was selected for helping to raise money for SCAN, but there were two other worthy candidates: Spencer Leuders, who started the 24 Hours of Booty cycling marathon to raise money for cancer research, and Kyle Petty, whose Victory Junction camps have made life more pleasant for countless ill and disabled children. In 2008, Richard Childress won the award for establishing a pediatric trauma unit at Wake Forest Baptist Medical Center in Winston-Salem.

Besides a lovely crystal presentation, the Humanitarian of the Year award also included $100,000, which I gave to SCAN. That donation is co-sponsored by The Home Depot and KaBOOM!, a non-profit

I've always loved people and tried hard to treat them right. That's why this award means so much to me. (©CIA Stock Photo, Inc.)

Penske Racing, Ryan and I are all grateful to Mooresville. We built this playground at a local school with help from KaBOOM! and The Home Depot. (©CIA Stock Photo, Inc.)

group based in Washington, D.C., whose aim is to build a playground within walking distance of every child in the United States. They allowed me to build a playground at the school of my choice, and I selected Pine Lake Preparatory here in Mooresville. We got it built in one day. I'm humbled by being selected for that award, but happy that I was able to make a difference in people's lives around here.

Dad, you see, was right all along. I'm happy to think that along the way, I've tried to give more than I've taken.

26

I'm Retired

A S THE 2007 SEASON drew to a close and the time arrived to actually lock my office door for the last time, I found myself with mixed feelings. The overriding emotion was that of sadness that this part of my adult life was finally over. There would be no more celebrations in Victory Lane—but then there would be no more 5:00 A.M. wake-up calls or all-night airplane rides either. Mixed emotions to say the very least.

After so many years in the auto racing business, you develop a routine and your system adjusts to short nights and long days, endless hours of hard work usually culminating in disappointment late Sunday afternoon. Then on Monday morning the cycle starts all over again. From early February to late November, this routine never changed. I would often ask myself what was so alluring about this job. Now that it's all over, it's crystal clear: It's simply the challenge presented by the competition, that continual urge to make more horsepower, go faster, raise the bar for your competition. It's all about winning. For me, it's never been about the money. It's about the trophies.

When I finally came to understand this single fact, it was easier to close that chapter of my life and open the next. After all, I was able to take with me the most valuable trophies of all: the friendships and relationships I had made over the years and the memories of all the good times, which I will treasure for the rest of my life.

When people ask me what made me decide to retire when I had everything going my way, I simply tell them this story. One day, late in the fall of 2006 while I was visiting my grandsons in Washington, I was having lunch with my grandson Jack, who was eight or nine years old at the time. I was planning to leave the next day to go back to Mooresville and then travel with the team to the next race. Jack asked me what I was going to do when I got home. "Well, Jack, I am going to get on an airplane and fly to Dover, Delaware, because Thursday is our travel day. Then Friday, we will practice and qualify for the race, because Friday is qualifying day. Then Saturday we practice and Sunday is race day." Jack looked me straight in the eye and asked, "Grandpa, when is there going to be a Jack day?"

It stopped me cold. I answered as honestly as I could. "Soon, Jack, there will be a lot of Jack days."

On the flight back to North Carolina, I thought about that conversation a lot. My body had been telling me for years that it was ready to retire. My family was telling me it was time to slow down; the doctors were warning me that I was "bumping the rev limiter;" but now Jack had hit me right between the eyes with a sledge hammer. What if I did keep up this pace, something awful happened, and there couldn't be any more "Jack days?" It wouldn't be fair to my grandsons or, for that matter, to the rest of my family. God knows they have all waited a very long time to do some very simple things, like taking a vacation together that did not include a day or two at the track. I decided then and there that it was time to retire before it was too late.

Since my retirement, there's been a lot more time for Pat and me to be with our family, including spending time at the small vacation home we built near Seattle, and just hanging out with our daughter Pamela, Mike, and the grandsons. We go out there frequently over the holidays.

You've already met my youngest daughter, Tricia, the ardent historical preservationist. Tricia has always been her own person and has spent most of her life studying various types and techniques of historic restoration processes. She specializes in analyzing stone work, but more recently she's gotten into other types of materials, including the models to assess them. She first studied at the Art Institute of Chicago, and then received a master's degree from Columbia University, but she's studied around the world, including a year in Scotland. Tricia was initially very interested in art, but I don't think she really got a footing in it until she was at the Art Institute and discovered just how fascinated she was with the artifacts of history. That, in turn, led her to study intensely everything from metal casting to repairs on stone to building monuments.

She has gained a lot of respect from colleagues in her field. Not long ago, she was called over to Bath, England, to work at some archaeological digs. She's been to the ancient city of Carthage (in today's Tunisia in North Africa), which was founded by the Phoenicians and destroyed by the Romans during the Punic Wars. She's probably best known, however, for her work with the remains of the

My daughter Tricia, who can identify pieces from a sunken ship and run a drill press with the best of them. (Jim Donnelly Photo)

Titanic. She has a really good mechanical background, maybe from all those years hanging out in our garages. When the team was trying to make recoveries from the *Titanic* debris fields, they had located some of its portholes. The metal was badly twisted because the ship had broken in half, but Tricia was insistent that those portholes could be made to open. She sat down with some of the engineers at Penske Racing, and working together, they developed hinges that could be fitted into the twisted porthole frames, whose glass is an inch and a half thick, so they could be displayed in the open position. The biggest piece they recovered for display is probably 20 feet tall and 60 feet long, a pretty sizable chunk.

I'm amazed at how Tricia can retain and process all of this information. Right now, she's involved in some projects in New York, working with statuary at a Frank Lloyd Wright structure. She's still interested in cars. She can work a lathe and shape metal. She still drives her Nash Metropolitan. She's a brilliant lady and we're very proud of her.

" *Restoring cars and architectural conservation both involve the same sort of tactile appreciation for physical things. With Dad, it's all things mechanical. With me, it's art or industrial artifacts be-*

tween the industrial and architectural worlds, whether they're from a Saturn V rocket to the RMS Carpathia, the liner that rescued the survivors from the Titanic. We share an appreciation for history. And if it's man-made, it interests us.

I was brought up around garages and tools and equipment. I went into sculpture on the fine arts side and then into conservation. I knew very early that you had to use the right tools to get what you wanted, starting when I was assisting Dad while he was under a car."

TRICIA MILLER

My third daughter, Debra, is an actress in Illinois, whose specialty is portraying Mary Todd Lincoln in a two-actor production with Michael Krebs, who plays Abraham Lincoln during his presidency. They've performed as the Lincolns at countless historical events, and had an exceptionally busy year planned in 2009, the bicentennial of Lincoln's birth. It started out with a 200th birthday commemoration in Springfield, the capital of Illinois, attended by both President Barack Obama and Governor Pat Quinn. I hope to see a lot more of Debra now, too.

I get to see a little more of my daughters now. This is Debra, an actress in Chicago. (Aria Management Photo, Don Miller Collection)

Except for cars, old wooden boats are some of my favorite things, especially once you get them out on Lake Norman. (Don Miller Collection)

There's a lot more time for play. I've got a boat, an old wooden Chris-Craft speedboat, powered by a 400-cubic-inch Chevy. Are you surprised that I named it *Miller Time*? Early wooden boats are another one of my passions. The planking used to make up their hulls is usually cut, shaped and varnished by hand. They're incredibly, exquisitely detailed, as much a work of exotica as the most sophisticated race car or military aircraft. Only boats are purely built to be enjoyed. My best buddy Razoar and I have spent many an hour skimming across the surface of gorgeous Lake Norman, which is pretty close to both our homes and just seems to go on endlessly. One of my favorite pieces of trivia to throw out during a cocktail party is the lake's sheer size, which you can't fully appreciate until you're on its water—more than 520 miles of shoreline. With all the NASCAR drivers and other prominent people who live along Lake Norman now in fabulous homes, it's staggering to think that when Duke Energy first created the lake in the late 1950s by building a hydroelectric dam, nobody was really interested in buying the lakefront properties at first. Believe me, it's not that way anymore.

The nice thing about retirement is having time to appreciate cars, not just work on them, although that's fun, too. One of the best things about cars, bar none, is car people, the ones you meet who enjoy the same thing you do. It cuts across all strata of life: Car people come in both genders, all kinds of income and educational levels, and every age. Sometimes, they'll fool you. My daughter Tricia knows her way around a machine shop and toolbox pretty well. Matt Borland, a really young guy, has a wonderfully restored early 1960s Corvette, a nasty and very quick car. In the shop behind his house, Ryan Newman's got a gorgeous collection of stuff built way before he was born, including a 1950 Buick convertible—it's the actual car from the movie *Rain Man*, which his wife Krissie bought for him. He also has a stick-shift 1961 Ford, nothing fancy, that he drives around during the day. It didn't take long after I moved to Mooresville to realize how many cool and beautiful cars there are around here, some owned by race people, some not.

Happily, I had some experience at setting up a race shop before Razoar and I built "The Halfway House," where we work on the cars we are building or restoring. It's got all the equipment you'd need for fabricating unique pieces, including a computerized milling machine, lathe and band saw. What we don't have or can't find, we'll make. I've got a lot to keep me company mechanically, including a wedge-powered 1960 DeSoto Adventurer, a very rare 1957 Ford Ranch Wagon with a factory E-code engine, and a Fordillac, which is a 1939 Ford coupe stuffed with a 390-cubic-inch Cadillac V-8 with triple carburetors, just the kind of thing that was once used in these parts for hauling moonshine. Razoar's got a wonderful hot rod, too, a 1940 Mercury hardtop, one of the first American two-doors that really was a hardtop. We both own supercharged Studebaker Avantis that we keep there—I still love performance Studebaker V-8s. Revell, the long-time producer of model kits, just stopped by to measure my E-code Ford. There's going to be a model made of it.

There's a few more that I keep at the house, including a 1956 Ford Sunliner convertible, fully restored, the same kind of car Pat used to have when we first met. It's her collector car. Like I said, car "guys" can be girls, too. I've got a more extreme hot rod, too, a 1934 Ford roadster with a supercharged flathead. Very traditional. It's great to rumble around town with it, and on that point, I *drive* my cars, not just look at them or run a dust wand over the paint. On a slow night, I love to take that E-code wagon over to the eighth-mile strip at Mooresville Dragway—another good thing about living in this town—and show the bracket guys that an old Ford wagon on skinny rubber with a column shift is quick, even if it doesn't look it. I fool those kids a lot.

I am now in the second year of retirement and I still haven't established any kind of formal schedule. But I am never at a loss for something to do. With our house in Washington near Pam, Mike and our grandchildren, there are now plenty of "Jack days." The house

Don't think Pat doesn't love old cars. This is her 1956 Ford Sunliner convertible. (Don Miller Collection)

has a garage where I keep an old Chrysler "letter car" to drive for fun. The big project at the moment is to build Jack and Tom a hot rod. Tom prefers to call it a "rat rod," which is the current rage on the Left Coast. The cool thing is that we get to do it together. We have 18 months before Tom gets his driver's license.

When I am in North Carolina, I spend most of my time working on restoring some of the classic and muscle cars Razoar and I have accumulated. Razoar retired last year as well, so we are always working on some project together. Our shop has become a kind of gathering place for all the "car nuts" in the Mooresville area, and you never know who might come walking in there. Buddy Baker, Bobby Allison, Ted Musgrave, Kurt Busch, Sam Hornish and a lot of the guys from

Left: My daughter Pam attended as many of the West Coast races as she could while living in San Francisco and Seattle. (Don Miller Collection)

Right: Ryan pays it forward. He coached my grandkids in this Quarter Midget, built by my friend Vance Ferry. (Don Miller Collection)

I love my grandsons and want them to grow up right. So I'm building them a hot rod. (Allison Green Photo, Don Miller Collection)

the race team are regulars. Last week my old friend Rick Mears, who's got a place near Mooresville now that he's a consultant and driver coach for Penske Racing's IRL team, stopped by to show me his 1933 Ford. Of course Ryan Newman is there whenever he has a spare moment. Sometimes the bench racing gets pretty serious.

I visit the Penske shop about once a week to do my mail and visit with the guys. I don't miss the racing half as much as I miss the people. They're terrific, all of them, and it's a privilege to associate with them, starting with the founder. Roger and I still talk pretty frequently. We'll call each other, just to see how each other's doing. That's because he has always been more than just a business partner, a lot more. Roger and Kathy Penske are family to me, and to Pat and the girls. Roger calls me, and then Kathy gets on the phone to see how I'm doing at my old age. We all talk to each other whether we

Here's how I like to play. This, folks, is a 1933 Ford hot rod, all steel, with a blown flathead in it. (Don Miller Collection)

agree with each other or not, because we are a family, and even if we don't immediately agree, we still come back together. Roger and I have had a very long business relationship, but we have much more than that.

Rusty, I'm happy to say, is still Rusty and he's doing fine. I see him more now than I did when we both worked for Roger. We do things together, charity events, and I help him with some of his TV stuff. We're getting closer and closer, a lot more than when we had to deal with each other every day. We've grown back together. That's good for both of us. Obviously, I really like the guy. He travels a lot, but I'll still stop over to the Rusty Wallace Racing shop, which is next door to the Hall of Fame, and see how he's doing. We joke about things that we couldn't joke about before, because it was business. The other day, I told him, "I bet you're not cutting off any fenders now just because they don't look right. Now, it costs you money."

I've maintained my passion for the North Carolina Auto Racing Hall of Fame and museum, remaining active as Chairman of the Board and giving as much time as I can to the museum and the charities it supports, such as SCAN and the annual Stocks for Tots fundraiser. December 2010 will be that event's 22nd anniversary. And as I've told you, I love living in Mooresville and working with the town on a variety of community projects.

So have I adjusted to retirement? Pat says she thinks so because she doesn't see much more of me now than she did when I was racing, but at least I sleep in my own bed every night. I doubt that I will ever be one of those guys who sits on the porch swing and drinks lemonade all day. I have no idea what the future will bring, but whatever it is, I will try to make the best of it.

Until then I'll just pour another cup of coffee, take that wrench out of my back pocket, and see if I can get this old Ford to start!

Acknowledgements

I AM DEEPLY GRATEFUL for the patience and support of my family and many friends throughout this long project. This book would not have been written without the encouragement and contributions of friends like Dan Luginbuhl, Dick Berggren, Allison Green, and Kim Watson. I am also indebted to my relentless editor, Cary Stratton, and her staff at Coastal 181 Publishing for their vigilant scrutiny of the manuscript.

My thanks also go out to the many photographers and colleagues who donated their photos or provided photographic assistance to this project and the worthy cause its proceeds will serve. In particular, my appreciation goes to Steve Rose, Kenny Kane, and Janet Erwin.

Of course, this story could not have been told without the talent and dedication of my co-author and friend, Jim Donnelly, whose grasp of the written word and storytelling attributes are without challenge.

Jim credits much of the development of his automotive writing skills to Dan Eisenhuth and Nick Nagurny, two editors from his New Jersey newspaper days, who encouraged him to add cars and racing to his writing portfolio. Also to Dick Berggren, for giving him access to a wider audience through *Stock Car Racing* and *Open Wheel* magazines. Whatever the source of his talents, he is in my view an excellent writer and accomplished journalist, as well as—very important to me—a car guy. Jim would also certainly send special thanks to his wife Jacquie, his number one fan.

Last, but certainly not least, my fervent wish is that you, the reader, find this story not only to be interesting but also entertaining, and that through the proceeds of this book, many abused and neglected children will receive aid and relief in their time of need.

Index